LEGAL NORMATIVITY IN THE RESOLUTION OF
INTERNAL ARMED CONFLICT

With an estimated 95 per cent of the world's armed conflicts occurring within individual states, resolution and prevention of internal conflicts represent a main driver of global peace. Peace negotiations stand outside the traditional formalism of lawmaking and represent a uniquely privileged moment to observe the rise or adjustment of the legal framework of a given state. Based in a socio-legal and pluralistic understanding of law, this book explores the normative dynamics of peace negotiations. It argues that the role of law in the peaceful resolution of internal armed conflicts has been greatly underestimated and that legal theory can and should contribute to a better comprehension of these processes.

Including thematic case studies from Darfur, North–South Sudan, Uganda, Côte d'Ivoire, Colombia, Sri Lanka, Sierra Leone, Mozambique, Bosnia and Israel–Palestine, this volume will be of use to scholars, students and affiliates of international organizations and non-governmental organizations.

Philipp Kastner is an assistant professor at the University of Western Australia. His main teaching and research interests are the resolution of armed conflicts, international criminal law, public international law and legal theory. He is the author of *International Criminal Justice* in bello?: *The ICC between Law and Politics in Darfur and Northern Uganda* (2012).

Legal Normativity in the Resolution of Internal Armed Conflict

PHILIPP KASTNER

University of Western Australia

CAMBRIDGE
UNIVERSITY PRESS

CAMBRIDGE
UNIVERSITY PRESS

University Printing House, Cambridge CB2 8BS, United Kingdom

One Liberty Plaza, 20th Floor, New York, NY 10006, USA

477 Williamstown Road, Port Melbourne, VIC 3207, Australia

4843/24, 2nd Floor, Ansari Road, Daryaganj, Delhi - 110002, India

79 Anson Road, #06-04/06, Singapore 079906

Cambridge University Press is part of the University of Cambridge.

It furthers the University's mission by disseminating knowledge in the pursuit of education, learning and research at the highest international levels of excellence.

www.cambridge.org
Information on this title: www.cambridge.org/9781107514874

© Philipp Kastner 2015

First published 2015
First paperback edition 2017

A catalogue record for this publication is available from the British Library

Library of Congress Cataloging in Publication data
Kastner, Philipp, author.
Legal normativity in the resolution of internal armed conflict / Philipp Kastner, University of Western Australia.
  pages cm
Includes bibliographical references and index.
ISBN 978-1-107-10756-4 (hardback)
1. War (International law) 2. Civil war. 3. Peace-building – Law and legislation.
4. Postwar reconstruction – Law and legislation. I. Title.
KZ6745.K37 2015
341.6′6–dc23   2015007706

ISBN 978-1-107-10756-4 Hardback
ISBN 978-1-107-51487-4 Paperback

Contents

Preface

This book is based on my Doctor of Civil Law thesis that I completed at McGill University in 2013. The constructive feedback of my main supervisor, René Provost – who always refrained, however, from pushing me in a particular direction – was invaluable. Merci beaucoup! I have also benefited from discussions with and comments from, among others, Frédéric Mégret and François Crépeau, the members of my doctoral advisory committee, and Peer Zumbansen, Jaye Ellis, Thomas McMorrow, and the two anonymous reviewers solicited by Cambridge University Press. My special thanks go to Elisabeth Roy Trudel for the numerous discussions we have had about my research and for her support throughout this project. Finally, Rod Macdonald, who sadly passed away in 2014, was a constant source of inspiration.

Marc Andre Robinson, the creator of "Right of Return", has kindly agreed to the use of a photograph of his art installation as cover image for this book. While law is typically focused on and expressed in words, images are evocative and convey important messages. In other words, the visual discourse behind – or before – the text is significant. "Right of Return" expresses both more and less than a stereotypical image of a common, Western-type setting of negotiations, such as a round table. The circle of chairs is, at least to me, reminiscent of a set of chairs around a negotiating table, but it allows and calls for imagining new ways of negotiating both peace and law. I chose this image instead of a peace pipe, a non-Western but easily recognizable and already existing symbol, which could have drawn the viewer's attention to the fact that peace has various meanings and can be made in different ways. In addition to expressing this meaning, and without running the risk of abusing a symbol created and cherished by Indigenous peoples, "Right of Return" encourages the viewer – very much in line with my pluralistic and interactional understanding of law – to imagine meaning. And, as I believe, both well-entrenched and new forms of conflict in our world are in dire need of creative approaches.

List of Acronyms

CEDAW	Convention on the Elimination of All Forms of Discrimination against Women
FARC	Fuerzas Armadas Revolucionarias de Colombia (Revolutionary Armed Forced of Colombia)
FRELIMO	Front for the Liberation of Mozambique
ICC	International Criminal Court
ICCPR	International Covenant on Civil and Political Rights
ICESCR	International Covenant on Economic, Social and Cultural Rights
ICRC	International Committee of the Red Cross
ICTY	International Criminal Tribunal for the Former Yugoslavia
IRCSL	Inter-Religious Council of Sierra Leone
LRA	Lord's Resistance Army
LTTE	Liberation Tigers of Tamil Eelam
R2P	Responsibility to Protect
RUF	Revolutionary United Front
SPLA	Sudan People's Liberation Army
TRC	Truth and Reconciliation Commission
UN	United Nations
URNG	UNIDAD Revolucionaria Nacional Guatemalteca

1

Introduction

Il Est Plus Facile De Faire La Guerre Que La Paix
Georges Clemenceau

This book deals with the creation and role of legal norms in the context of the peaceful resolution of internal armed conflicts. Peace negotiations aiming to resolve internal armed conflicts are a complex and multifaceted enterprise. They are also of great consequence, since their outcome – ideally the conclusion of a workable and widely accepted peace agreement – determines whether violence will resume or whether durable, positive peace is given a real chance. The negotiations leading to the conclusion of such legal documents are still poorly understood, especially from a legal perspective. They have been mainly considered and analysed as political processes to solve political problems, with law offering only a utopian *ought* perspective and playing a subordinate role because of the crushing grip of political necessity. Peace negotiations are, however, not detached from the realm of law but take place within a legal-normative framework. Legal norms and legal obligations are omnipresent. Failing to recognize the existence and importance of this normative framework and its use and continuous development would misconceive the reality of peace negotiations and would miss the central contribution that law can – and ought to – make to the resolution of internal armed conflicts.

The actors involved in negotiating peace frequently rely on international legal norms that are recognized to a universal or near-universal extent and that are, in some cases, codified in human rights treaties. In addition to realizing the value of such a relatively formal and clear legal framework anchored in international law, this book argues that orthodox legal theory cannot fully account for the normative dynamics of peace negotiations. Instead, a socio-legal and pluralistic understanding of law with a focus on human interaction[1] is better suited to analyse peace negotiations and the conduct and role of peace negotiators and mediators. Such a process-oriented approach allows us to recognize the norm creative capacity of the actors involved and to appreciate, more generally, the normative dynamics of peace negotiations. An understanding of the context in which legal norms arise, change, facilitate and restrict human behaviour is, indeed, more revealing about legal normativity and the ways in which the various actors participate in norm generation processes than a precise description of a particular, presumably enforceable norm in a given space and moment in time. Consequently, considering peace negotiations from a legal perspective cannot solely consist in describing specific legal norms. This endeavour of locating legal normativity in peace negotiations is, moreover, not overly concerned with clearly delineating legal norms by exposing their distinctively legal nature from other norms. In the words of Lon Fuller, "Both rules of law and legal systems can and do half exist. This condition results when the purposive effort necessary to bring them into full being has been, as it were, only half successful".[2] Some commitments that are shared by the negotiating parties or by peace mediators might give rise to norms that the relevant actors would explicitly assess as "legally binding"; others might be influential despite their implicit character; other commitments, in turn, might not materialize into a norm but remain significant as a proposition and hence as a possible source for the future normative framework of peace negotiations. The identification of what will be called "emerging legal obligations" should therefore be understood merely as an illustration of the normative dynamics of peace negotiations and the kind of norms to which they may give rise. These norms and associated obligations are not static and may not (yet) form a strong basis for consistent action; they are rooted in the social interaction between the actors involved and are constantly reassessed and renegotiated.[3]

---

[1] This understanding of law relies heavily on Lon L. Fuller and Roderick A. Macdonald. See e.g. Lon L. Fuller, *The Morality of Law*, rev. ed. (New Haven, CT: Yale University Press, 1969), e.g. at 192–193 [henceforth Fuller, *The Morality of Law*]; Roderick A. Macdonald, "Here, There ... and Everywhere: Theorizing Legal Pluralism; Theorizing Jacques Vanderlinden," in Nicholas Kasirer, ed., *Étudier et enseigner le droit: hier, aujourd'hui et demain – études offertes à Jacques Vanderlinden* (Montreal: Éditions Yvon Blais, 2006), 381, 406 [henceforth Macdonald, "Here, There ... and Everywhere"].

[2] Fuller, *The Morality of Law*, *supra* note 1 at 122.

[3] It should be noted that the creation of such norms, and also conduct in accordance with obligations they have given rise to, are not necessarily informed by conscious consideration. As Fuller has argued, "Our conduct toward others, and our interpretations of their behaviour toward us, are ... constantly shaped by standards that do not enter consciously into our thought processes". See Lon L. Fuller, "Human Interaction and the Law" (1969) 14 *Am J Jurisp* 1

They are, in other words, purposive and aspirational in character.[4] Based on such an understanding of law, it is possible to appreciate some emerging normative trends. It will be argued that the role of peace mediators is normative and normatized and that obligations are emerging with regard to an increased involvement of civil society actors and to the inclusion of transitional justice issues in peace negotiations.

By exploring the normative dynamics of peace negotiations, this book aims to contribute to a better understanding of how legal norms are created and what role they play in this context. It also attempts to clarify the more general question of how to conceive peace negotiations from a legal perspective. A related objective, based on the hypothetical usefulness of a socio-legal and pluralistic understanding of law, consists in strengthening this theoretical approach through the analysis of peace negotiations as remarkable norm-generating processes.

The focus on the negotiated resolution of internal armed conflicts is not only driven by the fact that this kind of conflict has become more frequent in comparison to interstate conflicts and that this form of conflict termination has become more popular over the past decades (as discussed in more detail later in this chapter). Peace negotiations also have an important potential to end conflicts earlier and also more durably, with fewer costs both in the loss of human lives and destruction of property.[5] Whereas the main goal of state-to-state negotiations aiming to end traditional wars is to negotiate a truce and resolve an underlying, rather easily identifiable problem,[6] intrastate negotiations must address numerous issues and involve a wider range of actors, whose relationships are characterized by a higher degree of interdependence. They are, therefore, more complex endeavours dealing with polycentric problems.

Peace negotiations may bring about a new legal structure, sometimes for a whole state, and try to provide a lasting framework to prevent future violence and to establish a more peaceful society. In this sense, peace negotiations may be not only a means to end an armed conflict but also an opportunity to embark on an endeavour akin to a constitution-building process. It is, in fact, the very

---

at 9 [henceforth Fuller, "Human Interaction and the Law"]. This means that the rise to consciousness of emerging norms and obligations in the context of peace negotiations is not an all-decisive factor determining their existence.

4   Fuller, *The Morality of Law, supra* note 1 at 11–12, 145–151.
5   For a similar approach based on these arguments, see Caroline A Hartzell & Matthew Hoddie, *Crafting Peace: Power-Sharing Institutions and the Negotiated Settlement of Civil Wars* (University Park: Pennsylvania State University Press, 2007), 8–9.
6   This is not to say that interstate negotiations may not be complex or do not carry heavy weight. However, compared with intrastate negotiations, it is typically clearer which issues would be put on a possible negotiation agenda.

experience of conflict as a feeling of relative weakness that may permit transformation.[7] Many substantial peace agreements are, indeed, constitution-like, or at least transitional constitution-like, documents that aspire to bring about more just and legitimate governance. It is striking that an analysis of the role of legal norms in the negotiated resolution of internal armed conflicts is missing; the literature in the field of conflict and peace studies is hardly concerned with "law", "rules", or "norms".[8] As we will see, this practice is largely due to a still prevalent orthodox, prescriptive and coercion-based understanding of law. While it would be naive to assume that peace can be made through law, the role that law plays in the peaceful resolution of internal armed conflicts has been greatly underestimated. Hence, legal theory can and should contribute to a better comprehension and conception of these processes, which are not only governed by certain norms and embedded in a certain normative structure but are also significant norm-creation processes.

1.1. THE SHIFTING SPHERE OF PEACE NEGOTIATIONS

The focus in this book on internal armed conflicts can be explained by several factors. First of all, internal armed conflicts have by far outnumbered interstate conflicts: in the 2000s, approximately 95 per cent of all armed conflicts took place at the intrastate level.[9] Their resolution and prevention has therefore become a major, if not the main, driver of peace and human security at the global level. In addition to their frequency, with military victory having become an increasingly less frequent type of conflict termination,[10] and peace agreements often being the only available option to achieve peace,[11] the amplified complexity of the negotiated resolution of internal armed

---

[7]　Robert A. Baruch Bush & Joseph P. Folger, *The Promise of Mediation: Responding to Conflict through Empowerment and Recognition* (San Francisco: Jossey-Brass, 1994), 191. In their chapter on transformative mediation, Bush and Folger argue that "conflict is an opportunity to transform human consciousness and conduct to the highest level of compassionate strength" (249).

[8]　By way of example, skimming over the titles of the publications of Uppsala University's Department of Peace and Conflict Research reveals that none of these titles includes the word "law", "legal", "rule", "norm" or "obligation". See <http://www.pcr.uu.se/research/ucdp/publications/>.

[9]　Human Security Center, *Human Security Report 2005: War and Peace in the 21st Century* (New York: Oxford University Press, 2005), 23. As an update of the report reveals, all armed conflicts in 2009 took place at the intrastate level, although nearly a quarter of them were internationalized. Human Security Report Project, *Human Security Report 2012: Sexual Violence, Education and War: Beyond the Mainstream Narrative* (Vancouver: Human Security Press, 2012), 158 [henceforth Human Security Report Project, *Human Security Report 2012*].

[10]　Human Security Report Project, *Human Security Report 2012, supra* note 9 at 173–176.

[11]　Ibid., 184.

conflicts, as compared with interstate negotiations, warrants greater attention. This complexity is linked to the fact that today's peace negotiations are rarely conducted between two equal sovereigns, but rather bring together a variety of actors: members of a government representing the state and representatives of one or several armed opposition groups typically constitute the primary negotiating parties. Often, a few individuals, such as the leaders of armed opposition groups, are considered key players, without whom it would be rather futile to embark on the endeavour of negotiations. The frequent asymmetry between these actors regarding political and military power as well as negotiation capacities – some parties may, for instance, be able to include experienced political and legal advisers in their delegation – is one reason why additional actors routinely get involved in the negotiations. As we will see, a variety of external players may assume the role of intermediary,[12] and since an internal armed conflict and its resolution do not only concern the belligerents, various civil society actors may be engaged.[13] The involvement of such actors in addition to the primary negotiating parties may take different forms and may be dependent on whether the negotiations are conducted openly or, as it is still sometimes the case, secretly. As we will also see, it is the involvement of external actors that has contributed to the development of an additional layer of normativity in the context of peace negotiations and to their increasing normatization.

Over the past centuries, the great majority of peace treaties have been concluded between formally equal entities. With the emergence of the sovereign state in Europe, the modern system of international law, based on the principle of state sovereignty, started to develop.[14] Up to the seventeenth century, the lack of an autonomous treaty law meant that peace treaties took a similar form to private contracts.[15] The distinction between international and internal treaty practice had also been murky,[16] and treaties concluded in the fifteenth and sixteenth centuries show that the rulers of the European powers did not necessarily have a monopoly over the decision to enter peace treaties.[17] By the middle of the seventeenth century, the treaty-making capacity

---

[12] See Chapter 3.
[13] See Chapter 4.
[14] Randall Lesaffer, "Peace Treaties from Lodi to Westphalia," in Randall Lesaffer, ed., *Peace Treaties and International Law in European History: From the Middle Ages to World War One* (Cambridge: Cambridge University Press, 2004), 9, 43.
[15] Lesaffer, *supra* note 14 at 17.
[16] Karl-Heinz Ziegler, "The Influence of Medieval Roman Law on Peace Treaties," in Randall Lesaffer, ed., *Peace Treaties and International Law in European History: From the Middle Ages to World War One* (Cambridge: Cambridge University Press, 2004), 147, 151.
[17] Lesaffer, *supra* note 14 at 15–16.

was defined more clearly: the right of concluding treaties and alliances was limited to princes and equivalent holders of "sovereignty".[18] In this period, peace negotiations were increasingly professionalized, with the sovereigns no longer negotiating directly with one another.[19] Principles like equality, reciprocity and treatment on equal terms developed and were, at least formally, respected in both bilateral negotiations and the multilateral peace congresses of the nineteenth century.[20] With the increasingly strict distinction between the international and national legal spheres, only very few treaties combined elements from both spheres. However, the 1648 Peace Treaties of Westphalia, often cited as creating the European state system,[21] were not only treaties between the Holy Roman Empire, its estates and foreign powers; they were also a constitutional-religious settlement for the empire itself.[22] To some extent, the 1648 Treaties can be seen as embracing the same logic that infuses contemporary peace agreements and their responses to the specific challenges arising in the context of internal armed conflicts, particularly as they relate to the restoration or creation of a shared political and legal space.

As we will see, today's peace agreements and the negotiations leading to their conclusion take radically different forms from classic, interstate peace treaties and negotiations. Moreover, a legal regime comparable to international treaty law, which is rarely applicable and can only provide limited guidance in the context of internal armed conflicts, has not developed. International law has a role to play, but the currently emerging legal framework of peace negotiations at the intrastate level must take different forms.

Contemporary peace negotiations in the context of internal armed conflicts and resulting peace agreements are characterized by another important shift. These negotiations typically introduce novelty, seeking not to re-establish but to alter the *status quo ante*, which implies important conceptual challenges similar to those arising in the context of other foundational documents like

---

[18] Heinz Durchhardt, "Peace Treaties from Westphalia to the Revolutionary Era," in Randall Lesaffer, ed., *Peace Treaties and International Law in European History: From the Middle Ages to World War One* (Cambridge: Cambridge University Press, 2004), 45, 47.

[19] Ibid., 51.

[20] Heinhard Steiger, "Peace Treaties from Paris to Versailles," in Randall Lesaffer, ed., *Peace Treaties and International Law in European History: From the Middle Ages to World War One* (Cambridge: Cambridge University Press, 2004), 59, 77. As it has often been argued, an important exception was made in 1919–1920, where "there were no negotiations" (ibid.).

[21] For a critique of this view and the "myth of Westphalia", see e.g. Lesaffer, *supra* note 14 at 9. "In short, the Westphalia Peace Treaties did not lay down the basic principles of the modern law of nations; they did, however, lay down the political and religious conditions for allowing the European powers to start building a new international legal order" (10).

[22] Ibid., 10.

constitutions. The overwhelming majority of peace agreements, through-out history, emphasized restoration over novelty.[23] In other words, the par-ties' desire to achieve peace through the conclusion of a peace agreement was naturally linked to the restoration of a previous situation; no novel ele-ments were included to alter the conditions or the essence of the relationship between the parties. This dominance of peacemaking through restoration can largely be explained by a narrow definition of peace as the absence of violence in the form of armed conflict,[24] which is part of a fundamental question of peacemaking that will be explored in more detail below. The parties may still have been striving for a "better" peace and, to this end, have envisaged modify-ing their relationship; yet the peace agreement itself, through the ubiquitous focus on restoration, did not embrace novel elements. It could, at best, lay the groundwork for future modifications.[25] As Jörg Fisch makes clear, where nov-elty was emphasized in a peace agreement, it was a purely rhetorical element. This rhetoric was most visible in the peace treaties concluded in the twentieth century, such as in Versailles, where preambles and declarations teem with the intention to depart from previous treaty-making practice and to build a "better" peace; in the treaty itself, however, novelty was again submerged by restoration.[26]

While today's peace negotiations and agreements are still characterized to an important extent by the idea of restoration – re-establishment of nonviolent conditions, reconciliation between warring factions or ethnic groups, return of refugees and internally displaced persons, restitution of property, in sum, the return to a "normal" situation – this return is characteristically accompanied by some novelty. Peace negotiations in the context of internal armed conflicts must envisage a fundamental change in the parties' relationship to build a truly common future within a shared political and legal space. It is precisely this relationship that typically lies at the heart of the conflict; a facile return to

---

[23] Jörg Fisch, *Krieg und Frieden im Friedensvertrag. Eine universalgeschichtliche Studie über die Grundlagen und Formelemente des Friedensschlusses* (Stuttgart: Klett-Cotta, 1979), 325. A somewhat similar development has taken place in the context of belligerent occupation. While the laws of occupation, notably via the 1907 Hague Regulations and the 1949 Fourth Geneva Convention, traditionally emphasize the impermanent nature of occupation and the maintenance or restoration of the former politico-legal order, a shift towards the recogni-tion of transformative occupation is noticeable: inter alia because of the increasing appli-cation of international human rights law to occupations, transformative policies may, in some cases, be valid. For this debate, see generally Adam Roberts, "Transformative Military Occupation: Applying the Laws of War and Human Rights" (2006) 100 *AJIL* 580.

[24] Fisch, *supra* note 23 at 327.

[25] Ibid., 329.

[26] Ibid., 329–330.

a previous, nonviolent situation can therefore not suffice. Since violent conflict may even cause a rupture of the constitutional continuity of a state, negotiations are also more complex in this regard and may have to break new ground. They may ultimately lead to the separation of states, as in the case of the two Sudans, with the status and rights of newly created minorities outside their former home nation being of particular concern. More often, however, the integration or reintegration of a state emerging from divisive armed conflict is at stake. Peace negotiations and resulting agreements now routinely include, in addition to the cessation of hostilities and disarmament, questions of power sharing and minority rights, substantive reform of legislative and constitutional processes, the integration of military forces, reconciliation, and other legal and sociopolitical concerns of a society emerging from a violent conflict.

In this sense, peace negotiations are a privileged moment to observe the adjustment of the legal framework or even the rise of a new framework that may disregard pre-existing constitutional standards and escape some of the formalism in traditional law making. Even though the previous normative order will always inform the "new" order in some way, with peace agreements never being created in a normative vacuum,[27] many peace negotiations, especially when framed as constitutions, do not refer to the previous order or openly aim to break with the past. The Dayton Peace Agreement, for instance, did not try to work with the framework already existing in Bosnia but produced a completely new constitutional order.[28] Contriving such a discontinuity, even if exaggerated and somewhat artificially, bears significant potential. As Peer Zumbansen argues, "New beginnings offer themselves as chances of coinciding legality and legitimacy".[29] Some of the legitimacy-related challenges of concluding peace agreements thus bear resemblance to essential questions related to foundational documents, such as constitutions and declarations of independence. In the absence of a recognized foundational law, writers of constitutions, declarations of independence and peace agreements may find themselves in a situation where it is impossible to appeal to

---

[27] On the significant role of international law, see Chapter 2, Section 2.1.

[28] As Fionnuala Ni Aolain writes, the constitution negotiated at Dayton "is a Dayton constitution and not a Bosnian constitution". Fionnuala Ni Aolain, "The Fractured Soul of the Dayton Peace Agreement: A Legal Analysis" (1998) 19 *Mich J Int'l L* 957 at 971. On the Lomé Peace Agreement, which establishes a sharp line between the past and the future, see Chapter 2, Section 2.3.2. For additional examples, see Christine Bell, *On the Law of Peace, Peace Agreements and the Lex Pacificatoria* (Oxford: Oxford University Press, 2008), 152 [henceforth Bell, *Law of Peace*].

[29] Peer Zumbansen, "Transitional Justice in a Transnational World: The Ambiguous Role of Law" (2008) 4:8 CELP Research Paper Series, online: SSRN <http://papers.ssrn.com/sol3/papers.cfm?abstract_id=1313725> at 6.

a "law of laws".[30] Hannah Arendt and Jacques Derrida have theorized this apparent dilemma in the context of constitution making. In the case of the American Declaration of Independence, the power lies in the performative "We hold these truths to be self-evident",[31] or, as Arendt suggests, "in the authority which the act of foundation carried within itself".[32] Similarly, since the American Constitution is silent on the question of ultimate authority, the Declaration of Independence provides "the sole source of authority from which the Constitution, not as an act of constituting government but as the law of the land, derives its own legitimacy".[33] This appears to be a circular reasoning. However, as Bonnie Honig observes, "a community should be able to sustain this new kind of authority … assuming that it can see and be satisfied with the power and authority inherent in its own performatives".[34] In contrast, Derrida argues that "performative" utterances tend to be combined with or be presented as "constative" utterances, such as through references to God or natural laws.[35] Derrida explains this with a "prelegitimate" moment[36] inherent in every system: "La signature invente le signataire. Celui-ci ne peut s'autoriser à signer qu'une fois parvenu au bout, si on peut dire, de sa signature et dans une sorte de rétroactivité fabuleuse".[37]

One avenue to conceptually overcome or, at least, moderate the problems associated with such a prelegitimate moment is to emphasize the transitional

[30] Bonnie Honig, "Declarations of Independence: Arendt and Derrida on the Problem of Founding a Republic" (1991) 85:1 *The American Political Science Review* 97 at 101. A quite similar argument is made by James Tully with respect to constitutions more generally: "A modern constitution thus appears as the precondition of democracy, rather than a part of democracy". James Tully, *Strange Multiplicity* (Cambridge: Cambridge University Press, 1995), 69. As Claude Klein and András Sajó recall, "The great revolutionary constitutions were established in total rupture with the former constitutional regime…. Revolution remains the ultimate form of constitution-making, pointing towards the non-legal dimensions of constitutionalism". Claude Klein & András Sajó, "Constitution-Making: Process and Substance," in Michael Rosenfeld & András Sajó, eds., *The Oxford Handbook of Comparative Constitutional Law* (Oxford: Oxford University Press, 2012), 419, 426, 440. For a discussion of *pouvoir constituant*, or *verfassungsgebende Gewalt*, as opposed to *pouvoir constitué*, see ibid., 422n14.

[31] *Declaration of Independence*, 4 July 1776 (United States of America), online: National Archives <http://www.archives.gov/exhibits/charters/declaration_transcript.html>, preamble.

[32] Hannah Arendt, *On Revolution* (New York: Viking Press, 1963), 200. See also Honig, *supra* note 30 at 102.

[33] Arendt, *supra* note 32 at 194.

[34] Honig, *supra* note 30 at 102–103.

[35] Jacques Derrida, *Otobiographies: l'enseignement de Nietzsche et la politique du nom propre* (Paris: Galilée, 1984), 11 [Derrida, *Otobiographies*] ("présenter des énoncés performatifs *comme* des énoncés constatifs" [ibid., 25]).

[36] These are the words of Honig, *supra* note 30 at 107.

[37] Derrida, *Otobiographies*, *supra* note 35 at 22. Or, as Derrida also asks pointedly, "Qui signe toutes ses autorisations de signer?" (ibid., 31).

character of constitution making and peacemaking. Especially in times of change, constitution making, or rather constitution *building*, involves gradual change, which is why a traditional conception of a unidirectional constitutionalism implying finality is inadequate.[38] Even constitutions are not monolithic instruments. Arendt recognizes this "notion of a coincidence of foundation and preservation by virtue of augmentation" and argues that "the very authority of the American Constitution resides in its inherent capacity to be amended and augmented".[39] In other words, it is the adaptable character of a so-called act of foundation that contributes to the constitution of its authority, a feature that is even more obvious in the context of substantial peace agreements. While the 1999 Sierra Leonean Lomé Peace Agreement, for instance, provides for power sharing between the government of Sierra Leone and an armed rebel group, the Revolutionary United Front (RUF), the provisions contained in the agreement are intended to structure a "Government of National Unity" only until the next elections, which are to be held "as prescribed by the Constitution".[40] Although this agreement has been considered "extralegal",[41] since the signers place it, at least in some respects, above the Sierra Leonean Constitution, it is not necessarily, and not entirely, illegitimate. The inevitable prelegitimate moment does not last; the agreement is supposed to be transitional in character, and the signers authorize themselves through a doubly performative and constative reference to "the imperative need to meet the desire of the people of Sierra Leone for a definitive settlement of the fratricidal war in their country and for genuine national unity and reconciliation".[42] The foundational "We hold" of the American Declaration of Independence is thus turned into the aspirational utterance, "we are desirous of finding a transitional mechanism ... to establish sustainable peace and security".[43] Transitional constitution building and peace building should, therefore, not be viewed as the conclusion of a contract completing the conflict but rather as an ongoing process.[44]

---

[38] Ruti Teitel, "Transitional Jurisprudence: The Role of Law in Political Transformation" (1997) 106 *Yale LJ* 2009 at 2057.

[39] Arendt, *supra* note 32 at 203. See also the discussion in Ruti G. Teitel, *Transitional Justice* (Oxford: Oxford University Press, 2000), 207–209 [henceforth Teitel, *Transitional Justice*].

[40] *Lomé Peace Agreement*, 7 July 1999 (Sierra Leone), UN Doc. S/1999/777, Part Two (Governance). On the negotiations leading to the conclusion of the agreement, see Chapter 4, Section 4.1.

[41] Jeremy L. Levitt, *Illegal Peace in Africa: An Inquiry into the Legality of Power Sharing with Warlords, Rebels, and Junta* (Cambridge: Cambridge University Press, 2012), 136.

[42] *Lomé Peace Agreement*, *supra* note 40, Preamble, para 3.

[43] Ibid., Part Two (Governance) and Preamble, para 8.

[44] See also Vivien Hart, "Constitution-Making and the Transformation of Conflict" (2001) 26:2 *Peace & Change* 153 at 157.

Regarding the process of negotiations itself, a variety of new players, and most notably nonstate actors, now shape and transform the normative framework of peace negotiations. Negotiations typically bring together government representatives and one or several nonstate actors who may control some of the state's territory and claim to represent at least a part of the population. An additional layer of complexity may arise owing to uncertainty as to whether a group is or should be considered a "party" and by whom it is or should be represented at the negotiations. The numerous rebel groups in Darfur have, since the start of their concerted armed struggle in 2003, often split into subgroups or created new factions, illustrating the challenge of dealing with shifting alliances and the changing status of potential negotiating parties. In the negotiations seeking to end the armed conflict in the Balkans in the 1990s, the mediators had to decide whether to allow the Bosnian Serbs to be represented by the president of the Republika Srpska, Radovan Karadzic, and the Bosnian Serb military leader, Ratko Mladic, who had already been indicted by the International Criminal Tribunal for the Former Yugoslavia (ICTY). Ultimately, the United States decided not to negotiate with Karadzic and Mladic but insisted on negotiating only with the Serbian president Slobodan Milosevic, who was also considered to have sufficient control over the Bosnian Serbs.[45]

In addition to the question as to who may represent the belligerent parties, the participation of marginalized groups and, more generally, the involvement of civil society actors to ensure more legitimate representation of all segments of the population in intrastate negotiations are of much greater concern than in the context of classic diplomatic negotiations between states. While negotiations still tend to be largely undemocratic, the negotiating table is now likely to be more inclusive and more diverse. As will be argued, obligations pertaining to greater participation of civil society actors are emerging.

Moreover, not only have diplomatic attempts to end internal armed conflicts radically increased in quantity, especially since the 1990s,[46] peace

---

[45] For a more elaborate discussion of the choice of parties and mediators in this context, see Melanie C. Greenberg, John H. Barton & Margaret E. McGuinness, "From Lisbon to Dayton: International Mediation and the Bosnia Crisis," in Melanie C. Greenberg, John H. Barton & Margaret E. McGuinness, eds., *Words over War: Mediation and Arbitration to Prevent Deadly Conflict* (Lanham, MD: Rowman & Littlefield, 2000), 35, 64–66 [henceforth Greenberg, Barton & McGuinness, "From Lisbon to Dayton"]. See also the discussion in Chapter 3, Section 3.2.3.

[46] Human Security Report Project, *Human Security Report 2009–2010: The Causes of Peace and the Shrinking Costs of War* (New York: Oxford University Press, 2011), 66–67.

negotiations are also mediated in a very different manner than interstate negotiations and no longer exclusively rely on state diplomacy. Numerous actors
now share the field of conflict resolution. In addition to the United Nations,
regional organizations and third states offering their good offices, several nongovernmental organizations have specialized in the peaceful resolution of
armed conflicts and mediate or assist and advise parties involved in peace
negotiations, such as the Centre for Humanitarian Dialogue,[47] Conciliation
Resources,[48] the Centre for Conflict Resolution,[49] International Alert,[50] the
Carter Center,[51] the Crisis Management Initiative,[52] the Public International
Law and Policy Group[53] and Independent Diplomat.[54] Faith-based organizations also mediate peace negotiations, as exemplified by the key role of the
Catholic Church in the peace negotiations in Mozambique and Colombia.[55]
The legitimacy of the involvement of these mediators and questions concerning their neutrality bear a strong normative dimension, as does their
ambition to persuade the negotiating parties to comply with legal obligations throughout the peace negotiations. Other third parties and observers
may also ground their positions on normative considerations or even act as
outspoken norm entrepreneurs,[56] thus contributing to the construction of the
normative framework that governs peace negotiations.

[47] See <http://www.hdcentre.org>.
[48] See <http://www.c-r.org>.
[49] See <http://ccrweb.ccr.uct.ac.za>.
[50] See <http://www.international-alert.org>.
[51] See <http://www.cartercenter.org/peace/conflict_resolution/index.html>.
[52] See <http://www.cmi.fi>.
[53] See <http://publicinternationallawandpolicygroup.org>.
[54] See <http://www.independentdiplomat.org>. Other nongovernmental organizations also play
an important role in these contexts but are not involved in the negotiated resolution of conflicts. The International Center for Transitional Justice, for instance, provides technical expertise and advice regarding transitional justice in post-conflict societies. See <http://ictj.org>.
[55] The key 1992 peace agreement was mediated by the Catholic Community of Sant'Egidio
and signed in Rome; see *General Peace Agreement for Mozambique*, 4 October 1992,
online: United States Institute of Peace <http://www.usip.org/files/file/resources/collections/
peace_agreements/mozambique_1991-92.pdf>. See also Chapter 3, Section 3.2.1. The permanent presence of the Catholic Church in the peace process was explicitly acknowledged in the
Santa Fe de Ralito Accord; see *Acuerdo de Santa Fe de Ralito*, 15 July 2003, online: Oficina del
Alto Comisionado para la Paz <http://www.altocomisionadoparalapaz. gov.co/web/acuerdos/
jul_15_03.htm> at para 8.
[56] The concept of "norm entrepreneurs" developed in the field of international relations in the
1990s. As Martha Finnemore and Kathryn Sikkink explain in their discussion on a norm's
"life cycle", "norm entrepreneurs attempt to convince a critical mass of ... norm leaders ... to
embrace new norms". Martha Finnemore & Kathryn Sikkink, "International Norm Dynamics
and Political Change" (1998) 52:4 *International Organization* 887 at 895.

1.2. THE LEGAL LITERATURE – IGNORING THE PROCESS

The legal literature has started to pay more attention to the legal nature of peace agreements, their function as binding documents and their status under international law.[57] A peace agreement can be viewed as a formalized legal agreement between two or more hostile parties – here typically between a state and one or several armed belligerent groups (sub-state or nonstate) – that ends an armed conflict and sets forth terms that all parties are obliged to comply with in the future.[58] Peace agreements can also be understood as hybrid instruments, which are primarily concluded, like a contract, between a state and nonstate actors to deal with a domestic situation, but which are often internationalized to some extent through references to international law and the involvement of international mediators, witnesses or guarantors.[59] Such internationalization removes the agreement from a purely domestic context, brings it into the sphere of international legal norms and arguably confers additional legitimacy.

Moreover, as Christine Bell argues, despite the difficulties of clear legal categorization as treaties, other international agreements or constitutions,[60] many agreements signed by governments and armed opposition groups reveal the intention of the parties that the agreement be binding under international law.[61] The legal-looking structure and language of peace agreements

[57] See, in particular, Christine Bell, "Peace Agreements: Their Nature and Legal Status" (2006) 100:2 *AJIL* 373 [henceforth Bell, "Peace Agreements: Their Nature and Legal Status"].

[58] This is adapted from the definition contained in Leslie Vinjamuri & Aaron P Boesenecker, "Accountability and Peace Agreements: Mapping Trends from 1980 to 2006," *Centre for Humanitarian Dialogue* (September 2007), online: Centre for Humanitarian Dialogue <http://www.hdcentre.org/files/Accountabilityreport.pdf> at 6. Agreements may, of course, also be signed between nonstate actors, such as the ceasefire agreement signed between representatives of the Kurdish Popular Protection Units and the Free Syrian Army in Syria in February 2013. "Kurdish Militia Signs Ceasefire with Syrian Rebels," *Reuters* (20 February 2013), online: Reuters <http://www.reuters.com/article/2013/02/20/us-syria-crisis -kurds-idUSBRE91J0YE20130220>. Such agreements will, however, rarely take the form of comprehensive agreements concerning the restoration or creation of a shared political space.

[59] The term "internationalized" is meant to reflect a certain international, and not purely domestic, dimension of the agreement; it is not to be understood in the more specific meaning of the term used in the field of international investment law to describe a particular contract between a state and a foreign private company where a nationalization, in other words domestic law, cannot prevail over such an "internationalized agreement" or "internationalized contract". See e.g. *Texaco Overseas Petroleum Co & California Asiatic Oil Co v Government of the Libyan Arab Republic* (Merits) (19 January 1977), 17 ILM 4.

[60] Bell, "Peace Agreements: Their Nature and Legal Status", *supra* note 57 at 378.

[61] Ibid., 381. For a similar argument and the conclusion that the Israeli-Palestinian Oslo Accords are, if not binding as traditional treaties, legally binding international agreements, see Geoffrey R. Watson, *The Oslo Accords: International Law and the Israeli-Palestinian Peace Agreements* (Oxford: Oxford University Press, 2000), 57–102. Watson also argues with the parties' "intent to impose mutual legal obligations" (ibid., 101).

also makes it clear that the signing parties conceive of these agreements as legal documents.[62] Despite these clarifications, the question of the legal status of peace agreements in the context of internal armed conflicts is far from resolved, as has been particularly well illustrated by the discussion around the status of the Sierra Leonean Lomé Peace Agreement and possible consequences of this determination for the validity of the amnesty provision and for the exercise of jurisdiction of the Special Court for Sierra Leone.[63]

Even to a greater extent than the nature and status of peace agreements, the peace process and more precisely the negotiations leading to the conclusion of a peace agreement have not been adequately assessed from a legal perspective. While it is challenging to find legal answers – conflict and post-conflict situations certainly "illustrate the utmost challenge of legally addressing the downfall of law, of reliability, and legitimacy"[64] – I will argue that process-related norms are closely linked to and are highly determinative of substantive outcomes. Building and recognizing a common normative framework are key prerequisites in any negotiating context. Moreover, legal norms and legal obligations that are created and assumed by peace negotiators and mediators can enhance peace negotiations and contribute to the peaceful resolution of armed conflicts, including at very early stages of peace negotiations. Many actions of peace negotiators and mediators can indeed only be understood in relation to existing or emerging norms,[65] even though the regulatory environment in which peace negotiations take place remains weak. Based on this assumption, I also claim that respecting legal obligations confers legitimacy and increases the effectiveness of peace negotiations and eventually of a peace agreement. To this end, it is necessary to better comprehend how this legitimacy is ascertained by the respective norm creators and how the underlying norms are generated and evolve over time.

[62] Bell, "Peace Agreements: Their Nature and Legal Status", *supra* note 57 at 378.
[63] *Prosecutor v. Kallon & Kamara*, SCSL-2004-15-AR72(E), Decision on Challenge to Jurisdiction: Lomé Accord Amnesty (13 March 2004) (Special Court for Sierra Leone, Appeals Chamber), in particular at para 42; the reasoning of the Appeals Chamber has been heavily and convincingly criticized by Antonio Cassese, "The Special Court and International Law: The Decision Concerning the Lomé Agreement Amnesty" (2004) 2 *Journal of International Criminal Justice* 1130, in particular at 1134–1135. With respect to the status of the Sudanese Comprehensive Peace Agreement, another commentator has concluded that "[t]o deny the international legal character of the CPA, would be to deny the efficacy of this agreement and the solution that it represents". Scott P. Sheeran, "International Law, Peace Agreements and Self-Determination: The Case of the Sudan" (2011) 60:2 *ICLQ* 423 at 457. For an analysis of the Dayton Agreements and its "*unique* legal features", see Paolo Gaeta, "The Dayton Agreements and International Law" (1996) 7 *EJIL* 147.
[64] Zumbansen, *supra* note 29 at 6.
[65] This draws on Robert M. Cover, "The Supreme Court, 1982 Term – Foreword: *Nomos* and Narrative" (1983) 97:4 *Harv L Rev* 4 at 7–8.

Generally, the legal literature still tends to leave the analysis and conceptualization of the peaceful resolution of internal armed conflicts to other disciplines. Some scholars have started to examine the more general role of legal principles or "legal issues" in this context, yet mostly in a superficial manner and without grounding such an examination in a theoretical framework.[66] The nearly omnipresent orientation towards the outcome is echoed by a heavy emphasis on the analysis of peace agreements, largely neglecting the processes that lead to their conclusion. Jeremy L. Levitt, for instance, arguing for the "supremacy of law and legal reasoning" in the context of power-sharing agreements, scrutinizes the legality of three West African peace agreements against the backdrop of pre-existing domestic, regional and international law.[67] While pursuing a certainly useful doctrinal analysis that has, so far, been virtually absent from the debate on power sharing, Levitt overemphasizes the prescriptive role of these bodies of law on power-sharing agreements and appears to disregard, more generally, the typically transitional character of peace agreements.[68] Exemplifying an "idealized narrative" on the role of law in times of change,[69] and an excessively essentialist perspective of individual accountability, he offers facile answers that pre-existing domestic, regional and international law supposedly give to complex questions.[70]

Moreover, peace agreements should be considered as being part of broader normative developments. In addition to recognizing that peace agreements are normative statements that also shape international law,[71] this book argues

---

[66] See e.g. Greenberg, Barton & McGuinness, "Introduction: Background and Analytical Perspectives," in Melanie C. Greenberg, John H. Barton & Margaret E. McGuinness, eds., *Words over War: Mediation and Arbitration to Prevent Deadly Conflict* (Lanham, MD: Rowman & Littlefield, 2000), 1, 4 [henceforth Greenberg, Barton & McGuinness, "Introduction"].

[67] Levitt, *supra* note 41 at 16.

[68] Andreas Mehler, for instance, has tentatively concluded that "maybe only transitional power-sharing arrangements can have beneficial effects". Andreas Mehler, "Peace and Power-Sharing in Africa: A Not So Obvious Relationship" (2009) 108:432 *African Affairs* 453 at 473.

[69] This language draws on Teitel, *Transitional Justice, supra* note 39 at 214. Teitel argues that it would be erroneous to give too much emphasis to the stabilizing function of law in the context of societies in transition and that "law's function in these periods is largely symbolic" (ibid., 219, 221).

[70] In addition to limiting his legal analysis to power-sharing provisions, Levitt also concludes, somewhat superficially, that power sharing is necessarily "illegal" because it is intrinsically related to granting de jure or de facto amnesties to *pirates de la loi* (Levitt, *supra* note 41 at 17, 22). For a more critical view of what is referred to as the "dictates of global justice and the liberal individualistic preferences of international human rights institutions", as well as of the role of judicial review of power-sharing agreements, see Christopher McCrudden & Brendan O'Leary, "Courts and Consociations, or How Human Rights Courts May De-Stabilize Power-sharing Settlements" (2013) 24:2 *EJIL* 477 at 477.

[71] For this argument, see also Christine Bell, *Human Rights and Peace Agreements* (Oxford: Oxford University Press, 2000), 314 [henceforth Bell, *Human Rights and Peace*

that the negotiating parties, mediators and also external actors are all actively involved in a norm creative enterprise. As in Levitt's case, and contrary to the actor- and process-centred approach on which this book relies, the literature typically treats law and legal principles as static and somehow external to the negotiations. Another good illustration is a volume on peace mediation, edited by Melanie C. Greenberg, John H. Barton and Margaret E. McGuinness,[72] where these principles include sovereignty, democracy and recognition of human rights.[73] This volume, despite its rich case studies, also reflects the seemingly inevitable concentration of legal literature on the substance of peace agreements, to the detriment of a more thorough examination of the process.

A notable exception is Omar Dajani's analysis of the role of international law in the Palestinian-Israeli peace talks.[74] Dajani recalls that "'the shadow of the law' – the influence law exerts on bargaining as a result of the possible imposition of a legal remedy if negotiations fail – is diminished at the international level".[75] If international legal norms are relatively indeterminate compared with domestic norms, it is, above all, the lack of third-party adjudication and enforcement that is often associated with this diminished "shadow of the law".[76] Dajani argues that international legal norms are, despite these characteristics, highly influential, and uses the Palestinian-Israeli context to exemplify his claim.[77] International legal norms may notably contribute to legitimizing negotiations and a resulting agreement in the eyes of both domestic and international actors.[78] In other words, international law may offer a "shade" under which peace negotiations can take place in a more legitimate, and as a result more effective, way by pulling the actors involved towards this

---

Agreements]; Anne-Marie Slaughter, "Pushing the Limits of the Liberal Peace: Ethnic Conflict and the 'Ideal Polity,'" in David Wippman, ed., *International Law and Ethnic Conflict* (Ithaca, NY: Cornell University Press, 1998), 128.

[72]　Melanie C. Greenberg, John H. Barton & Margaret E. McGuinness, eds., *Words over War: Mediation and Arbitration to Prevent Deadly Conflict* (Lanham, MD: Rowman & Littlefield, 2000).

[73]　Greenberg, Barton & McGuinness, "Introduction", *supra* note 66 at 4.

[74]　Omar M. Dajani, "Shadow or Shade? The Roles of International Law in Palestinian-Israeli Peace Talks" (2007) 32 *Yale J Int'l L* 61 [henceforth Dajani, "Shadow or Shade?"]. See also Joaquin Tacsan, *The Dynamics of International Law in Conflict Resolution* (Dordrecht: Martinus Nijhoff, 1992) for one of the rare earlier studies on the role of international law in peace negotiations, in this case the Central American peace negotiations of the 1980s.

[75]　Dajani, "Shadow or Shade?", *supra* note 74 at 64.

[76]　For this argument, see ibid.

[77]　Ibid., 62–63.

[78]　Ibid., 65.

shade and spurring compliance.[79] However, if Dajani argues persuasively that "it is possible to use law more effectively to advance the cause of peacemaking",[80] and attempts to sketch a theoretical framework that can explain the functions of law in peace negotiations, he seems to view, like the dominant legal literature does, international law as static, as an independent variable that remains unaffected by the negotiations. Such an analysis would pay more attention to reality and gain much depth by recognizing that law is dynamic and rooted in human interaction, and that legal norms are negotiated and renegotiated by the actors involved at the same time as substantive issues during peace negotiations. Contrary to an inventorial, or "artefactual inquiry",[81] legal norms, therefore, ought to be treated as a dependent variable that is part of the negotiation process.

In recent years, another body of literature around the concept of *jus post bellum* has started to develop, with the objective of completing the picture of the long-standing distinction between *jus ad bellum* and *jus in bello*. Regardless of its different translations and conceptions as "law after war"[82] or "justice after war",[83] *jus post bellum* clearly builds on principles of justice in the Kantian tradition. This perspective heavily relies on just war theory, which Brian Orend describes as "a coherent set of concepts and values designed to enable systematic and principled moral judgment in wartime".[84]

---

[79] This argument bears an important resemblance to Thomas Franck's concept of "compliance pull": "Legitimacy, in turn, is the quality of a rule, or a system of rules, or a process for making or interpreting rules that pulls both the rule makers and those addressed by the rules toward voluntary compliance". Thomas M. Franck, "The Emerging Right to Democratic Governance" (1992) 86:1 *AJIL* 46 at 50 [henceforth Franck, "The Emerging Right"]. Despite this powerful argument, it should be noted that legitimacy is a very formal concept for Franck, which makes his approach less attractive for the purpose of this thesis. For an analysis and critique of Franck's focus on formality, see Jutta Brunnée & Stephen Toope, *Legitimacy and Legality in International Law: An Interactional Account* (Cambridge: Cambridge University Press, 2010), 95.

[80] Dajani, "Shadow or Shade?", *supra* note 74 at 65.

[81] Roderick A. Macdonald & David Sandomierski, "Against Nomopolies" (2006) 57 N Ir Legal Q 610 at 617. As Macdonald and Sandomierski argue, the result of such an "artefactual inquiry" is that the "dynamic *endeavour* of symbolizing human interaction as governed by rules is reduced to the end-product – the rules themselves" (ibid.).

[82] Carsten Stahn, "Jus Post Bellum: Mapping the Disciplines," in Carsten Stahn & Jann K. Kleffner, eds., *Jus Post Bellum, toward a Law of Transition from Conflict to Peace* (The Hague: Asser Press, 2008), 93, 94 [henceforth Stahn, "Jus Post Bellum"].

[83] Brian Orend, "Jus Post Bellum: The Perspective of a Just-War Theorist" (2007) 20 Leiden J Int'l L 571 at 571; similarly, Gary J. Bass translates the notion as "postwar justice"; see Gary J. Bass, "Jus Post Bellum" (2004) 32:4 *Philosophy & Public Affairs* 384 at 384.

[84] Orend, *supra* note 83 at 571. Probably the most important contemporary work on just war theory is Michael Walzer's magnum opus *Just and Unjust Wars: A Moral Argument with Historical Illustrations* (New York: Basic Books, 1977).

Theorizing these concepts and values and their relationship with international law in the peace-building context is indeed valuable. It might, for instance, contribute to the development of a comprehensive framework by transcending existing categories of law in post-conflict situations.[85] This quest for a "holistic" normative framework that takes into account the interaction between different bodies of law[86] resonates to some extent with the objectives of the legal-pluralistic approach to the peaceful resolution of internal armed conflicts that I rely on in this book. Moreover, as Orend recalls with reference to Immanuel Kant, the benefit of ending an armed conflict does not only lie in the termination of this particular conflict; it may also "contribute to and strengthen the peace and justice of the international system more broadly".[87] The *jus post bellum* approach may therefore be seen to emphasize the interaction and cross-influence between different armed conflicts and peace processes.

Despite some conceptual similarities, my legal-pluralistic perspective on peace negotiations is different from the *jus post bellum* approach in several ways. First, *jus post bellum* seems to be primarily concerned with justice or, in the words of Orend, with the "just settlement of a just war".[88] Whereas justice, and notably procedural justice, is an important concept that surfaces repeatedly in and infuses my analysis of peace negotiations, legal normativity is more agency driven and much broader than a singular conception of justice. Second, the *jus post bellum* approach, despite claims as to its applicability to nonclassical wars,[89] has been developed in the just war tradition and is still intrinsically linked to interstate armed conflict. Third, *jus post bellum* is concerned with the post-conflict phase. The primary objectives of *jus post bellum* scholars – to identify the "justice of a belligerent power's postwar conduct"[90] or to elaborate guidelines or standards according to which the winner of a war or an occupying power should act[91] – differs from focusing on the negotiated resolution of armed conflicts and the resulting emphasis on the norms that apply to and are created by the actors involved in such a process. While it is difficult and not necessarily constructive to identify the precise

---

[85] Stahn, "Jus Post Bellum", *supra* note 82 at 98–99, 105.

[86] Ibid., 105.

[87] Orend, *supra* note 83 at 575.

[88] Ibid., 580. Others argue that justice after the war is inherently linked to the vindication of human rights. See e.g. Robert E. Williams & Dan Caldwell, "*Jus Post Bellum*: Just War Theory and the Principles of Just Peace" (2006) 7 *International Studies Perspectives* 309 at 313–319.

[89] See e.g. Stahn, "Jus Post Bellum", *supra* note 82 at 106; Orend, *supra* note 83 at 577.

[90] Bass, *supra* note 83 at 385.

[91] See e.g. Orend, *supra* note 83 at 577.

moment of the "post" in *post bellum*[92] – just as it is difficult to identify the precise start and end points of peace negotiations[93] – *jus post bellum* essentially materializes when a conflict is over. This approach is, in short, not concerned with the termination of an armed conflict but rather focuses on the enterprise of peace building and state building, mainly after intervention.[94] Finally, the solutions proposed by some *jus post bellum* scholars, such as Orend's call for another Geneva Convention on *jus post bellum*,[95] stay within a narrowly defined legal-positivistic framework that seems to deny the existence, or at least underestimates the importance, of legal normativity outside formal law.

The role and respect of legal norms in the context of peace negotiations are also prominent questions in the so-called peace versus justice literature that has emerged since the 1990s with the end of the Cold War and of numerous internal armed conflicts, and the establishment of international and internationalized criminal tribunals and other transitional justice mechanisms, such as truth and reconciliation commissions, victims' reparation schemes and public apologies.[96] The distinction between emphasizing justice, which is associated with human rights, and emphasizing peace, which is primarily linked to conflict resolution, is noticeable both in the academic literature and in the different approaches of practitioners and civil society organizations working in conflict situations.[97] Pragmatic peacemakers are ready to compromise to reach a deal, whereas justice advocates warn that there can be no peace without justice and that peace negotiations and the immediate prospect of concluding a peace agreement should not prevail over justice concerns. The dominant underlying notion of peace, as I will argue, may explain to some extent the erroneous belief of having to choose between peace and

---

[92] Ibid., 573–574. Stahn also calls for a redefinition of the temporal scope of application of *jus post bellum*; see Stahn, "Jus Post Bellum", *supra* note 82 at 106.

[93] See section 1.4.

[94] Stahn, "Jus Post Bellum", *supra* note 82 at 98. For a summary of recent trends associating *jus post bellum* with transformative occupation, the conduct of legislative reform in post conflict-zones and, more generally, the consolidation of the rule of law after intervention, see ibid.

[95] Orend, *supra* note 83 at 575.

[96] This is a nonexhaustive list of not mutually exclusive mechanisms.

[97] For an overview, see Edward Kaufman & Ibrahim Bisharat, "Introducing Human Rights into Conflict Resolution: The Relevance for the Israeli-Palestinian Peace Process" (2002) 1:1 *Journal of Human Rights* 71 at 73. On the different approaches of conflict resolution and human rights actors, see Christine Bell, "Human Rights, Peace Agreements and Conflict Resolution: Negotiating Justice in Northern Ireland," in Julie Mertus & Jeffrey W. Helsing, eds., *Human Rights and Conflict: Exploring the Links between Rights, Law and Peacebuilding* (Washington, DC: United States Institute of Peace Press, 2006), 345, 346–349 [henceforth Bell, "Human Rights, Peace Agreements and Conflict Resolution"].

justice. Peace, according to this logic, is equated with the cessation of violent hostilities: stigmatizing allegedly criminal political and military leaders and aiming to incapacitate them via international arrest warrants will stop violence. Following the terminology of Johan Galtung, this absence of violence can be called "negative peace", which is different from "positive peace" and a resulting condition that is positively defined.[98] Without circumscribing the precise degrees and facets of negative and positive peace, it can be argued that the former does not fully meet the characteristic goals of transitional justice mechanisms, which go beyond short-term peace and emphasize, *inter alia*, durable peace, reconciliation, truth, justice and dignity. The infamous slogan "no peace without justice" could be translated more accurately into "striving for the long-term goals associated with transitional justice is imperative to come closer to positive peace". If the prevalent transitional justice discourse is still primarily concerned with ending impunity and ways to deal with past crimes,[99] it is worth noting that the academic literature increasingly tries to go "beyond" further entrenching the artificially constructed extremes of the pragmatic conflict resolution and the principled human rights positions that have led to a common but false perception of a peace versus justice dichotomy.[100]

---

[98] Johan Galtung, "Violence, Peace, and Peace Research" (1969) 6:3 *Journal of Peace Research* 167 at 183. Galtung explains in this article that "positive peace" is a more open concept: "I would now identify 'positive peace' mainly with 'social justice', ... but I think one could also be open to other candidates for inclusion since the definition given of violence is broad enough also to point in other directions" (ibid., 190n31). As it has been pointed out by Francisco A. Muñoz more recently, the concept of "positive peace", which has been developed since the late 1960s, "was the result of a conscious building of a peace based on justice as generator of positive and lasting values". Francisco A. Muñoz, "Imperfect Peace," in Wolfgang Dietrich, Josefina Echavarría Alvarez & Norbert Koppensteiner, eds., *Schlüsseltexte der Friedensforschung* (Vienna: LIT, 2006), 241, 248.

[99] See e.g. International Crisis Group, online: <http://www.crisisgroup.org/en/key-issues/peace-justice.aspx>.

[100] See e.g. Cecilia Albin, "Peace vs. Justice – and Beyond," in Jacob Bercovitch, Victor Kremenyuk & I. William Zartman, eds., *The SAGE Handbook of Conflict Resolution* (London: Sage, 2009), 580. Michelle Parlevliet argues that "considering human rights and conflict transformation in conjunction deepens one's analysis of what is involved in moving from violence to sustainable peace" and advocates for a "holistic approach to human rights in conflict transformation". Michelle Parlevliet, "Rethinking Conflict Transformation from a Human Rights Perspective," *Berghof Handbook for Conflict Transformation* (Berlin: Berghof Conflict Research, 2009), online: Berghof Conflict Research <http://www.berghof-handbook.net/documents/publications/parlevliet_handbook.pdf> at 2, 8 [henceforth Parlevliet, "Rethinking Conflict Transformation"]. For a helpful review of the literature, see ibid. at 23–28. Parlevliet has also argued that there exists a "synergy" between the fields of human rights and conflict management. Michelle Parlevliet, "Bridging the Divide – Exploring the Relationship between Human Rights and Conflict Management" (2002) 11:1 *Track Two* 8 at 8. Another example is Kaufman and Bisharat's attempt of "merging the concepts of human rights and conflict resolution". Kaufman & Bisharat, *supra* note 97 at 74.

At least some transitional justice issues, as instantiated by the increasing consensus among members of the international legal community as to obligations to end impunity for grave crimes, uncover the truth and envisage reparations in some form, are regularly brought to the negotiating table and may significantly shape peace negotiations. Since transitional justice is typically associated with formal institutions established by the state and certain legal obligations under international law to deal with grave violations of international human rights law and international humanitarian law, legal considerations are omnipresent. Given its close association with international law, transitional justice is certainly one of the most explicit instantiations of the introduction of international legal norms into the context of peace negotiations and the resulting development of legal obligations for negotiators and mediators. However, legal norms are simply more visible in the context of transitional justice than in other aspects of peace negotiations. Transitional justice is thus only one part of a bigger normative picture, which is why the scope and approach of this book vis-à-vis legal normativity in the context of peace negotiations is much broader. Moreover, the focus on the negotiations and process-related norms has the merit of emphasizing a greater range of aspects than the overly outcome-focused approach in the prevailing transitional justice literature.[101]

1.3. THE PEACE AND CONFLICT STUDIES LITERATURE – IGNORING NORMATIVE CONSIDERATIONS

In addition to the relevant legal literature, and despite the challenge of conducting interdisciplinary research and working with approaches using different methods and terminologies, this book also draws on the peace and conflict studies literature. Especially since the end of the Cold War, researchers in the field of peace and conflict studies have increasingly turned their attention to internal armed conflicts and their resolution. To reflect the changing realities, classic notions of diplomatic and international relations theory therefore had to be enriched with novel emphases, such as the complexities of ethnic and identity-based conflicts,[102] or power-sharing, democratization and

---

[101] Note, however, Ruti Teitel's more nuanced view, which resonates, to some extent, with the approach pursued in this thesis regarding peace negotiations. Teitel argues that "law is shaped by the political circumstances but, also challenging the prevailing realistic accounts, law here is *not mere product* but itself *structures* the transition.... Legal responses are both *performative* and *symbolic* of transition". Teitel, *Transitional Justice, supra* note 39 at 6, 9 [emphasis added].

[102] E.g. Günther Schlee, *How Enemies Are Made. Towards a Theory of Ethnic and Religious Conflicts* (New York: Berghahn, 2008); Christian P. Scherrer, *Ethnicity, Nationalism and Violence. Conflict Management, Human Rights, and Multilateral Regimes* (Aldershot: Ashgate, 2003).

constitution-building.[103] Various other aspects linked to peace negotiations and their mediation have also been described and theorized, such as bargaining strategies;[104] power dynamics, asymmetries and the use of leverage;[105] as well as techniques to build trust among the parties,[106] to neutralize or isolate spoilers,[107] and to encourage institution building.[108] I. William Zartman has elaborated the key concept of ripeness of a conflict, which he views as "a necessary but insufficient condition for negotiations to begin".[109] The general importance of timing[110] has been highlighted, as have the various levels of negotiation, such as track one and track two or official and unofficial processes,[111] and the importance of third-party intervention.[112]

The peace and conflict studies literature is indispensable to understanding the underlying conflicts and the peace processes that are used as examples in this book; to identifying and analysing the role of the actors involved, namely, the main negotiators, mediators, civil society actors and third parties; and to exploring the reasons whether or not, and for what reasons, negotiations succeeded. In addition to these complex but rather crude facts, this body of

[103] E.g. Hart, *supra* note 44. For a succinct overview over the power-sharing literature, see Andreas Mehler, "Not Always in the People's Interest: Power-Sharing Arrangements in African Peace Agreements" (June 2008) BWPI Working Paper 40, online: SSRN <http://ssrn.com/abstract=1200862> at 2–6. As Ian S. Spears concludes, "The central weakness of power-sharing is not that it fails as an idea but that it runs into so many obstacles when put into practice". Ian S. Spears, "Understanding Inclusive Peace Agreements in Africa: The Problems of Sharing Power" (2000) 21 *Third World Quarterly* 105 at 116.

[104] E.g. Timothy Sisk, *International Mediation in Civil Wars: Bargaining with Bullets* (London: Routledge, 2009), 38.

[105] E.g. I. William Zartman & Jeffrey Z. Rubin, "The Study of Power and the Practice of Mediation," in I. William Zartman & Jeffrey Z. Rubin, eds., *Power and Negotiation* (Ann Arbor: University of Michigan Press, 2000), 3; Karin Aggestam, "Mediating Asymmetrical Conflict" (2002) 7:1 *Mediterranean Politics* 69.

[106] E.g. Aggestam, *supra* note 105 at 76–77.

[107] E.g. Stephen John Stedman, "Spoiler Problems in Peace Processes" (1997) 22:2 *International Security* 5.

[108] E.g. Kirsti Samuels, "Post-Conflict Peace-Building and Constitution-Making" (2006) 6:2 *Chicago J Int'l L* 1.

[109] I. William Zartman, "Conflict Resolution and Negotiation," in Jacob Bercovitch, Victor Kremenyuk & I. William Zartman, eds., *The SAGE Handbook of Conflict Resolution* (London: Sage, 2009), 322, 329. "Ripeness occurs when the parties feel that they can no longer expect to win the conflict through escalation … and that there is a possibility of a jointly acceptable solution" (ibid.). See also I. William Zartman, *Ripe for Resolution: Conflict and Intervention in Africa*, 2nd ed. (New York: Oxford University Press, 1985).

[110] E.g. Chester A Crocker, Fen Osler Hampson & Pamela Aall, *Taming Intractable Conflicts: Mediation in the Hardest Cases* (Washington, DC: United States Institute of Peace, 2004) at 154.

[111] See e.g. Sisk, *supra* note 104 at 40.

[112] E.g. Crocker, Hampson & Aall, *supra* note 110 at 13.

literature is also instructive to capture the normative dynamics of peace negotiations. Even if peace and conflict scholars usually do not employ conventional legal terminology, some authors are explicitly concerned with issues
such as commitments,[113] legitimacy,[114] fairness[115] and a "just peace",[116] in other
words, instantiations of the normative dynamics of peace negotiations.

While it is, therefore, helpful for the purpose of this book to look to these
analyses to better grasp the dynamics of internal armed conflicts and efforts to
end them, it should be noted that most peace and conflict scholars seem to be
entirely unconcerned with normative considerations. Although its importance
is often overstated, the basic distinction between a principled approach – or,
as it is sometimes called, human rights or democratizing approach drawing
on universal norms and focused on defining ends – and a pragmatic approach
associated with conflict resolution or conflict management focused on defining means is still highly visible in the peace and conflict studies literature.[117]
Most literature in this field does not address the principled approach and does
not even make an effort to refer to norms, rules, legal obligations or other
normative considerations. If addressed at all, laws and legal principles are typically viewed as rigid,[118] alien to the parties and not flexible enough to be effective in the context of peace negotiations. Overall, the mainstream conflict
resolution scholar and practitioner appears to perceive laws and legal norms in
a formalistic manner[119] and does not consider them as constructive or helpful

---

[113] E.g. Sheeran, *supra* note 63.
[114] E.g. Kristine Höglund & Isak Svensson, " 'Damned If You Do, and Damned If You Don't': Nordic
Involvement and Images of Third-Party Neutrality in Sri Lanka" (2008) 13 *International
Negotiation* 341; Mark Peceny & William Stanley, "Liberal Social Reconstruction and the
Resolution of Civil Wars in Central America" (2001) 55:1 *International Organization* 149.
[115] E.g. Cecile Albin, *Justice and Fairness in International Negotiation* (Cambridge: Cambridge
University Press, 2001) [henceforth Albin, *Justice and Fairness*].
[116] E.g. Kevin Clements, "Towards Conflict Transformation and a Just Peace," in *Berghof
Handbook for Conflict Transformation* (Berlin: Berghof Conflict Research, 2001), online:
Berghof Conflict Research <http://www.berghof-handbook.net/documents/publications/
clements_handbook.pdf>.
[117] Bell, "Human Rights, Peace Agreements, and Conflict Resolution", *supra* note 97 at 347;
Eileen F. Babbitt, "Conflict Resolution and Human Rights: The State of the Art," in Jacob
Bercovitch, Victor Kremenyuk & I. William Zartman, eds., *The SAGE Handbook of Conflict
Resolution* (London: Sage, 2009), 613, 617; Pauline H. Baker, "Conflict Resolution versus
Democratic Governance: Divergent Paths to Peace?," in Chester A. Crocker, Fen Osler
Hampson & Pamela Aall, eds., *Turbulent Peace* (Washington, DC: United States Institute of
Peace, 2001), 753.
[118] See e.g. the discussion in Babbitt, *supra* note 117 at 617.
[119] See e.g. John H. Barton & Melanie C. Greenberg, "Lessons of the Case Studies," in Melanie
C. Greenberg, John H. Barton & Margaret E. McGuinness, eds., *Words over War: Mediation
and Arbitration to Prevent Deadly Conflict* (Lanham, MD: Rowman & Littlefield, 2000),
343, 360.

but rather as utopian or even restraining.[120] Lawyers may be consulted in the drafting process of an agreement, but, to put it somewhat cynically, they are better kept away from the negotiating table. Of course, this perception of the legal field as a static and bureaucratic science in the context of peace negotiations is not new: Robert Lansing, the secretary of state of the United States commissioned to negotiate peace after World War I, describes in his personal account of the Paris Peace Conference President Woodrow Wilson's "prejudice against the legal profession in general" and notes that Wilson did "not value the advice of lawyers except on strictly legal questions".[121]

1.4. DEFINITIONS AND CASE STUDIES – SITUATING METHODOLOGICAL CHOICES

Because of the occurrence of similar forms of violence – sometimes called internal strife, turmoil or disturbances – and the frequent internationalization of primarily internal armed conflicts, the term "internal armed conflict" calls for a definition. By tradition, the most relevant body of law, international humanitarian law, does not offer a full definition of the various types of armed conflict. Additional Protocol II to the Geneva Conventions, for instance, limits its application to armed conflicts between the armed forces of a state and organized armed groups exercising control over a part of the state's territory and being able to carry out "sustained and concerted military operations"; moreover, the Protocol states that it "shall not apply to situations of internal disturbances and tensions, such as riots, isolated and sporadic acts of violence and other acts of a similar nature",[122] distinguishing these forms of violence from armed conflicts. While the Protocol provides only scant guidance as to the precise threshold of "armed conflict", the jurisprudence of international

---

[120] This prevalent view has been confirmed to the author in conversations with conflict resolution specialists working, among others, for the United States Institute of Peace (USIP) and the Crisis Management Initiative (CMI).

[121] Robert Lansing, *The Peace Negotiations. A Personal Narrative* (Boston: Houghton Mifflin, 1921), 41. The view that law, and more specifically international law, is marginal is, of course, not limited to peace negotiations but "tends to get reinforced at moments of political crisis". Gerry Simpson, "International Law in Diplomatic History," in James Crawford & Martti Koskenniemi, eds., *The Cambridge Companion to International Law* (Cambridge: Cambridge University Press, 2012), 25, 26.

[122] *Protocol Additional to the Geneva Conventions of 12 August 1949, and relating to the protection of victims of non-international armed conflicts (Additional Protocol II)*, 8 June 1977, 1125 UNTS 609 (entered into force 7 December 1978), art 1(1) and 1(2). In this regard, Additional Protocol II provides more guidance than common article 3 to the 1949 Geneva Conventions, which only refers to an "armed conflict not of an international armed conflict".

criminal tribunals has tried to further delineate the boundaries of what constitutes an armed conflict. The ICTY notably added the condition of "protracted armed violence" as a necessary threshold criterion,[123] and it ruled that every conflict must be evaluated individually on its intensity and on the level of organization of the warring parties.[124]

This need for individual evaluation of every conflict reflects the conviction that drawing pre-existing and pre-established definite boundaries is neither required nor constructive here. While more detailed definitions with formal criteria have been elaborated in the field of conflict and peace research,[125] peace negotiations typically try to end violent situations in continuous flux and of varying degree of intensity. Commonly used criteria of 25 or 1,000 battle-related deaths per year, for instance, may be necessary and useful in the context of quantitative conflict and peace research but might lead to unnecessary formal limitations for the purpose of this book and run counter to its intention of being inclusive and of addressing peace processes comprehensively.[126] Moreover, since the question as to whether specific instruments, such as Additional Protocol II, apply to a certain conflict at a given moment is largely irrelevant for this analysis, the less technical term "internal armed conflict" was preferred over "noninternational armed conflict" and "armed conflict not of international character". As a result, I do not rely on a single existing definition, although several provide useful elements that allow the development of a working definition characterized by low threshold criteria. Thus, besides the general exclusion of interstate armed conflicts, essential attributes are the occurrence of substantial violence, no matter over which period of time or whether this violence ceased for certain periods of time, and some level of organization of the parties involved, one of which will usually be, but does not have to be, the government of a state.

---

[123] *Prosecutor v. Dusko Tadić*, IT-94-1, Decision on the Defence Motion for Interlocutory Appeal on Jurisdiction (2 October 1995) (International Criminal Tribunal for the Former Yugoslavia, Appeals Chamber) at para 70.

[124] For more information on this discussion, see Sylvain Vité, "Typology of Armed Conflicts in International Humanitarian Law: Legal Concepts and Actual Situations" (2009) 91:873 *Int'l Rev Red Cross* 69 at 76–77.

[125] See e.g. Uppsala Conflict Data Program (UCDP) & Centre for the Study of Civil Wars, International Peace Research Institute, Oslo (PRIO), *UCDP/PRIO Armed Conflict Database Codebook*, version 4-2011, online: Uppsala University <http://www.pcr.uu.se/digital Assets/63/63324_Codebook_UCDP_PRIO_Armed_Conflict_Dataset_v4_2011.pdf>.

[126] It would, for instance, not seem sensible to refer to a long-lasting conflict and to have to constantly adjust the analysis because specific years not recorded in an armed conflict database because of lower numbers of battle-related deaths are, in fact, precluded from consideration for methodological reasons.

Similarly as in the case of a definition of "internal armed conflict", this book does not work with a particular already existing concept of "peace" or "peace process".[127] Peace may indeed have different connotations in different contexts,[128] and the objectives of peace negotiations cannot be expected to be identical. Without defining and redefining peace in each situation, this book tries to embrace the perspective of the parties involved and to respect their perception of peace. Generally, however, the meaning of "peace" goes beyond the mere absence of violence. In the context of internal armed conflicts, it is typically insufficient to conclude a cessation of hostilities or truce to deal with the conflict and achieve more than short-term, or negative, peace. More comprehensive negotiations dealing with fundamental political questions are usually necessary to open the door for attaining long-term, or positive, peace.[129] Throughout the book, the term "negotiations", which denotes "persistent peace initiatives ... likely to be more significant than an isolated peace initiative",[130] will be used rather than the term "process", both to reflect the focus on the period prior to the conclusion of an agreement and to avoid an association with an even more comprehensive endeavour that also encompasses the implementation of an agreement.[131]

With respect to the cases referred to in this book, a notable prevalence of situations where peace negotiations resulted in a written agreement is linked to the fact that an agreement, with its typical form of a legal document and its legal-like language, is not only easily accessible to the researcher but may also serve as an indicator of the legal norms present and absent in the negotiations. These agreements, regardless of their success or failure, are " 'snap-shots' of possible frameworks for moving away from violent conflict".[132] Generally,

---

[127] For the problematic definition of a "peace process", see Christine Bell, *Peace Agreements and Human Rights* (Oxford: Oxford University Press, 2003), 16–19.

[128] See, for instance, the concepts explored in a volume edited by Wolfgang Dietrich et al., eds., *Peace Studies: A Cultural Perspective* (New York: Palgrave Macmillan, 2011); for the meanings of *shalom* in Hebrew and *salaam* and *sulh* in Arabic, see Kaufman & Bisharat, *supra* note 97 at 73.

[129] On the concept of negative and positive peace, see e.g. Galtung, *supra* note 98 at 183.

[130] John Darby & Roger Mac Ginty, "Introduction: What Peace? What Process?," in John Darby & Roger MacGinty, eds., *Contemporary Peacemaking: Conflict, Violence and Peace Processes* (New York: Palgrave Macmillan, 2003), 1, 2.

[131] My conception of "peace process" is therefore larger than, for instance, Christine Bell's, who states that "peace agreements result from peace processes". Bell, *Law of Peace*, *supra* note 28 at 19. It is worth mentioning that in her seminal work, Bell mainly focuses on peace agreements and their implementation, whereas I am concerned with the prior processes of negotiating such agreements.

[132] International Council on Human Rights Policy, "Negotiating Justice? Human Rights and Peace Agreements" (2006), online: International Council on Human Rights Policy <http://www.ichrp.org/files/reports/22/128_report_en.pdf> at 2.

negotiations may be concluded by a comprehensive document, a cessation of hostilities agreement, a framework agreement or even a verbal accord,[133] or come to an end without the parties reaching an agreement at all. The success or failure of negotiations as well as the form of terminating a negotiating process are, as a result, irrelevant for their inclusion as examples in this study. It should be noted that the often numerous efforts to negotiate an end to a specific conflict will not necessarily be examined in their entirety. By focusing on the most revealing periods, my accounts of the various negotiations therefore bear no claim of substantive comprehensiveness. The inclusion not only of a textual analysis of agreements but also of a discourse analysis of negotiating processes themselves, in addition to a theoretical approach relying on legal pluralism, is intended to counter the risk of overemphasizing the outcome to the detriment of the process and of overlooking implicit norms that the negotiators and mediators may either not want to make explicit in an agreement or may not necessarily be conscious of.

Several internal armed conflicts and conflict-resolution processes will be used to illustrate the normative claims made, namely, Darfur, North–South Sudan, northern Uganda, Côte d'Ivoire, Colombia, Sri Lanka, Sierra Leone, Mozambique, Bosnia and Israel-Palestine.[134] Even if any selection remains limited and subjective to a certain extent, these situations have been chosen as they possess several common features. First of all, the conflicts and attempts to negotiate their end fall into roughly the same time period. Most of these conflicts are either still ongoing or were terminated after the end of the Cold War, which is representative of the fact that more and more internal armed conflicts are currently being ended by negotiations. While the majority of conflicts ended in a military victory up to the 1980s, the negotiated resolution has become the dominant mode of conflict termination since the 1990s,[135] making this period the most instructive for my research. My focus therefore

[133] The United Nations Department of Political Affairs, on its "UN Peacemaker" site, distinguishes eight types of peace agreements: (1) truce, cessation of hostilities, ceasefire and armistice agreements; (2) preliminary agreements; (3) pre-negotiation agreements; (4) framework agreements; (5) interim agreements; (6) sub-agreements; (7) comprehensive agreements; and (8) implementation agreements. See online: UN Peacemaker <http://peacemaker.un.org> (section Peace Agreements). UN Peacemaker is, according to its own description, an "online mediation support tool for international peacemaking professionals".

[134] Despite the fact that it eludes a clear categorization, the Israeli-Palestinian conflict remains mostly an intrastate rather than an interstate conflict and shares many characteristics with other ethno-political conflicts. For this argument, see also Kaufman & Bisharat, *supra* note 97 at 74.

[135] For detailed numbers, see Hartzell & Hoddie, *supra* note 5 at 10; Human Security Report Project, *Human Security Report 2012*, *supra* note 10 at 175.

lies on processes that were ended in the 1990s or 2000s or that are still going on. Whereas it may be useful to put conflict-resolution processes into a historical perspective, the contemporary processes, as argued above, are radically distinct from their precursors.

Moreover, the type of conflict, apart from being primarily intrastate armed conflicts, has not been significant for the selection. Most conflicts are driven by multiple concerns;[136] thus, a categorization, commonly made in the peace and studies literature, into ethnic conflicts, conflicts fought because of political or ideological reasons or over resources is not necessary, nor would it be constructive here. While it may be more likely that similar challenges can be perceived in the context of conflicts sharing certain attributes, the normative dynamics are not necessarily different, and the emergence and relevance of legal norms in the negotiating phase is not tied to a certain type of conflict. Furthermore, only those conflicts where there has been not only an isolated but a discernibly sincere attempt to negotiate an end to them have been included, that is, where genuine negotiations have taken or are taking place. Conflicts that were ended by a military victory were not automatically excluded, but a negotiating process must have been attempted at some point.

The conflicts selected are also representative of a significant trend in the context of the negotiated resolution of internal armed conflicts, namely, the increasingly important involvement of external actors, such as international and regional organizations, third states, nongovernmental organizations and institutions like the International Criminal Court (ICC). Their function may be to assist as mediators or provide other support (technical, logistical) to the negotiations, deploy a peacekeeping mission or adjudicate international crimes. While the conflicts do not lose their characteristic of being primarily intrastate, this kind of internationalization shows that peace negotiations are seldom purely internal.

The background of the respective conflict and the relevant actors involved will only be addressed insofar as it is necessary to embark on the reflective analysis of the normative dynamics of peace negotiations. These short overviews do not always follow the same model but are dependent on the arguments that the respective situation is meant to illustrate. Regarding the negotiations in Mozambique and Bosnia, for instance, the emphasis will be put on the role of the mediators; as for northern Uganda, more time will be spent on the ICC and the normative effect that it has had on the negotiations. Other processes,

---

[136] For a similar approach, see Chandra Lekha Sriram, *Peace as Governance: Power-Sharing, Armed Groups and Contemporary Peace Negotiations* (New York: Palgrave Macmillan, 2008), 5.

such as the one aiming to end the conflict in Darfur, will play a more prominent role in the context of the discussion on civil society involvement and associated emerging obligations.

It should be noted that I have refrained from conducting in-depth empirical research for several reasons. First, actual peace negotiations are not easily accessible to the academic researcher and, therefore, do not lend themselves to empirical research based on direct observation. They heavily rely on personal trust and are sometimes conducted secretly over a significant period of time. As a result, secondary materials had to suffice. Second, one of the main objectives of this book is to explore and confirm at the theoretical level, on the one hand, the usefulness of a pluralistic understanding of law to better understand peace negotiations and, on the other hand, to enlighten and further develop this theoretical approach through the analysis of peace negotiations. To pursue this both theory-testing and theory-generating endeavour, it was reasonable to primarily conduct and ground the research in the more theoretical, and not at a specific-empirical, level. Third, conducting "thick" empirical research would inevitably have restricted the range of examples and would have radically narrowed my perspective to the description and analysis of a more specific content. Instead, the inclusion of several geographically and typologically diverse conflict-resolution processes was considered more fruitful to discern normative trends and arising obligations. The focus on process trumps a description of content, which would, in the words of Jeremy Webber, "appear more like a snapshot in time ... immediately subject to mutation and change".[137] A static account of the legal norms governing a given context cannot, indeed, capture the more complex and fluid normative dynamics of peace negotiations, where the role of the actors involved and the norm-creation processes themselves are constantly contested and renegotiated.

This approach also mirrors one of the theoretical foundations on which this book relies: that legal norms arise through human interaction. In the context of peace negotiations, this interaction is not limited to the actors most immediately involved, the (former) belligerents. Peace negotiations are always internationalized enterprises. These processes cross-influence and borrow from each other,[138] notably through the work of international mediation

---

[137] Jeremy Webber, "Naturalism and Agency in the Living Law," in Marc Hertogh, ed., *Living Law: Reconsidering Eugen Ehrlich* (Oxford: Hart, 2009), 201, 205 [henceforth Webber, "Naturalism and Agency"].

[138] By way of example, the African National Congress supported the peace process in Northern Ireland and therefore influenced the Irish Republican Army and Sinn Féin, which, then, supported the Basque peace process. See International Council on Human Rights Policy, *supra* note 132 at 12.

organizations, and are conducted in the shadow of other external actors, such as foreign governments or international tribunals. It is not only a truce or a more comprehensive peace agreement but also the underlying normative structure that are constantly negotiated and renegotiated. A focused but broad perspective is therefore necessary to explore these dynamics. In an effort to sketch a more comprehensive picture, the aspects analysed are drawn from different processes in their various stages. Formal outcome documents are only one source; press releases and media reports as well as studies conducted by peace researchers may be equally or even more revealing about the role of legal norms, underlying legal obligations and commitments, as well as the legal consciousness of the actors involved. Together, these sources allow the identification of the various norm-application and norm-creation processes and a comprehension of the meaning of emerging norms.

Where precisely in this normative enterprise should my research and my approaches be situated? While I do not consider myself a norm advocate or entrepreneur, either of whom might argue for a stricter application of the rule of law or the adoption of "the laws of peace negotiations", I am aware that my focus on certain norms is inevitably subjective and influenced by certain beliefs. In this sense, my "mode"[139] is certainly not exclusively descriptive; to the contrary, participating in and contributing to the normative debate are implied characteristics of my endeavour. My approach hence embraces but is not limited to an identification of the symbolic aspects and functions of legal norms[140] in the context of peace negotiations but rather bears resemblance to what Jeremy Webber has called "exhortation".[141] Although I primarily employ descriptive language, I certainly go beyond the role of a mere observer. My attempt to discern collective norms and interactional obligations is, however, not equivalent to proposing a specific norm or outcome, or to speaking of law "in the singular".[142] The terms used throughout the book are meant to mirror this conviction. By way of example, like many legal pluralists, I avoid the term

---

[139] I am following here Jeremy Webber's terminology. Jeremy Webber, "Legal Pluralism and Human Agency" (2006) 44 *Osgoode Hall LJ* 167 at 193 [henceforth Webber, "Legal Pluralism and Human Agency"].

[140] Madonald and Sandomierski argue that "the symbolic aspect of normativity, the message that a particular means of conceiving of rules gives to citizens, is as important as any instrumental measure" (*supra* note 81 at 631).

[141] Webber, "Legal Pluralism and Human Agency", *supra* note 139 at 194.

[142] Webber seems to oversimplify the two modes – exhortatory and descriptive – and to exaggerate the finality of the exhortatory mode. Going beyond description does not necessarily and always imply, as Webber claims, to "speak of law in the singular, for we are appealing to our audience to adopt a particular way of resolving disagreements" (Webber, "Legal Pluralism and Human Agency", *supra* note 139 at 194).

"law", which is traditionally associated with the state,[143] and prefer the more open and less loaded notion of "legal norms" instead. Similarly, "legal system" implies a closed and finite structure,[144] whereas the "normative framework", the "normative dynamics" or the "legal culture"[145] of and surrounding peace negotiations stand for openness and the potential of change.

By trying to capture the normative dynamics of peace negotiations and to detect certain norms, clarifying their use and relevance and confirming the value of the legal-theoretical approach employed, I certainly seek to enhance the "grip" of legal norms in this context. Based on the belief that legal norms may be viewed as primarily facilitating human conduct and interaction, the goal of such a constructivist approach is to make peace negotiations more effective, thus preventing future violence and contributing to more robust societies.[146]

In line with the premises that it is the normative role of the actors contributing to peace negotiations that is decisive and that the discourse of these actors is not only illustrative but constitutive of the normative framework, Chapter 2 will analyse the discourse on legal norms in the context of peace negotiations. This actor-centred perspective also infuses the discussion on peace mediation. Mediators, as it will be argued, symbolize the archetypical normative actor that is constantly involved in the process of norm-creation and -application while inspired and directed by largely external normative influences, such as international legal norms and related obligations. It is not only the mediators' conduct that is affected by this normatization; their role is particularly significant from a legal perspective because they introduce legal obligations in the negotiations and propose them to the negotiating parties. The subsequent discussion will focus on two sets of obligations. The first relates to the involvement in peace negotiations of civil society actors, who have significant norm creative capacities; the second concerns transitional justice, one of the most contentious debates between law and politics in the context of peace negotiations. It will be argued that it is the engagement with and internalization of such normative propositions by the respective actors that is determinative of the normative framework of peace negotiations and that, as a manifest instantiation of this internalization, legal obligations are emerging.

---

[143] See e.g. Webber, "Naturalism and Agency", *supra* note 137 at 203.

[144] This relies on the argument made by H. Patrick Glenn. See e.g. H. Patrick Glenn, *Legal Traditions of the World*, 3rd ed. (Oxford: Oxford University Press, 2007), at xxiii, xxv; "La tradition juridique nationale" (2003) 55:2 RIDC 263.

[145] For this terminology, see e.g. Webber, "Legal Pluralism and Human Agency", *supra* note 139 at 192.

[146] The constructivist approach of Jutta Brunnée and Stephen Toope, in particular their "interactional theory of international legal obligations", will be explored in more detail in Chapter 5, Section 5.2.

2

Analysing the Discourse on International Legal Norms – a Nascent Shift from Outcome to Process

As it has been argued in the preceding chapter, the interactions between the various actors involved are decisive for the role that legal norms play in the context of peace negotiations aiming to end internal armed conflicts. Since legal norms are grounded in social practice and human interaction,[147] the construction of legal normativity and legal normativity itself is, therefore, inherently dialogical in character. As Fuller argued, law is an activity, and legal norms are all but a completed project; they are purposive, aspirational, a continuous challenge.[148] Based on the hypothesis that discourse is not only illustrative but constitutive of the normative framework, the objectives of this chapter are to assess the importance attached to international law in peace negotiations by negotiators and mediators as well as to explain two related phenomena: the emergence of process-oriented legal norms in the context of peace negotiations and the disconnect between the often presumed importance of international law and its relatively inconsequential weight in practice.

---

[147] Macdonald & Sandomierski, *supra* note 81 at 620; Martha Finnemore & Stephen J. Toope, "Alternatives to 'Legalization': Richer Views of Law and Politics" (2001) 55:3 *International Organization* 743.

[148] Fuller, *The Morality of Law, supra* note 1 at 106 and 145. See also Brunnée & Toope, *supra* note 79 at 22.

2.1. ASSUMPTIONS ABOUT THE IMPORTANCE OF INTERNATIONAL LAW FOR PEACE NEGOTIATIONS

International law[149] has not been overly concerned with peace and peacemaking, but rather with lawful ways to engage in armed conflict,[150] and it does not deal explicitly with the peaceful resolution of internal armed conflicts. Nevertheless, also because it has undergone an important transformation since the 1980s,[151] international law can be expected to be highly influential in this context, notably via international human rights law and international criminal law.[152] First, international law, because of its externality to the parties, can facilitate the conduct of peace negotiations by offering the parties a more neutral language and internationally accepted standards regarding legitimate and illegitimate conduct and demands.[153] In the context of the Israeli-Palestinian conflict, for instance, it has been argued that "only international law can provide impartial definitions of acceptable behaviour that are universally endorsed".[154] Human rights, in particular, may "serve as a trust-building measure"[155] and enable the parties to address "reconcilable

[149] If the focus is on international law here, several regional organizations, such as the African Union, the Council of Europe and the Organization of American States, have created legal regimes that may be resorted to in the context of the peaceful resolution of internal armed conflicts. The term "international law" should, therefore, not be understood narrowly but rather as being inclusive of these international, regional normative frameworks.

[150] See Martti Koskenniemi, "International Law in the World of Ideas," in James Crawford & Martti Koskenniemi, eds., *The Cambridge Companion to International Law* (Cambridge: Cambridge University Press, 2012), 47, 58.

[151] Bell, *Law of Peace, supra* note 28 at 31.

[152] Christine Bell also points out the relevance of the development of peacekeeping mechanisms that present themselves as an important tool to make the actors engaged in an internal armed conflict comply with commitments established under a ceasefire agreement (ibid., 39–40).

[153] For this argument, see e.g. Jorge L. Esquirol, "Can International Law Help? An Analysis of the Colombian Peace Process" (2000–2001) 16 *Conn J Int'l L* 23 at 23; International Council on Human Rights Policy, *supra* note 132 at 110; Christine Bell, Colm Campbell & Fionnula Ni Aolain, "Justice Discourses in Transition" (2004) 13:3 *Soc & Leg Stud* 305 at 323, who also argue that in the context of Northern Ireland, international law scrutiny of the state's behaviour was not as robust as it might have been, which is somewhat paradoxically linked to the place of the United Kingdom as a leading Western democracy (ibid.). For a criticism of this view, arguing that the negotiating parties may, in fact, be "fighting a very aggressive campaign of lawfare", see Paul R. Williams, "Lawfare: A War Worth Fighting" (2010) 43:1&2 *Case W Res J Int'l L* 145 at 146. On the concept of lawfare, see Section 2.4.1.

[154] Susan M. Akram et al., "Introduction" in Susan M. Akram et al., eds., *International Law and the Israel-Palestinian Conflict* (New York: Routledge, 2011), 1, 4. See also Richard Falk, who argues, in a "deliberately 'utopian'" way, that "the acceptance of international law is the best way to achieve peace and security in Israel-Palestine". Richard Falk, "International Law and the Peace Process" (2005) 28:3 *Hasting Int'l & Comp L Rev* 331 at 331–332.

[155] Kaufman & Bisharat, *supra* note 97 at 77.

interests underlying [their] positions such as mutual fears of discrimination and domination".[156] As it has also been maintained in this context, continuously avoiding human rights considerations may prolong a peace process.[157] It is worth highlighting that international human rights law has been increasingly applied in times of armed conflict, exposing government wrongs and making it more difficult for states to present themselves as legitimate and armed opposition groups as inherently illegitimate.[158]

Second, internal armed conflicts often represent a threat to international peace and security and generate grave violations of international human rights and humanitarian law and are therefore automatically a concern to the international legal community as a whole. Some domestic legal orders do not provide specific responses to deal with genocide, crimes against humanity and war crimes.[159] The international criminal legal order, in particular because of the establishment of a permanent international criminal court and the increased exercise of universal jurisdiction by third states, may provide such responses and have some bearing on domestic ways of dealing with current or past atrocities. Similarly, rehabilitation and compensation of victims of grave crimes, the return of refugees and displaced persons as well as restitution of property are often framed through rights-based language. Human rights can offer objective standards[160] and, as it has been argued, play a facilitative[161] and legitimizing role.[162] They can also be seen to provide the basis for international involvement.[163] Numerous peace agreements concluded in the context of an internal conflict accentuate this international dimension, with the parties asserting their intention that the agreement be binding under international law.[164]

Third, since the domestic legal order in conflict or post-conflict situations is dysfunctional,[165] or its legitimacy is challenged, legal norms recognized at the international level may often be referred to as the only available or

---

[156] International Council on Human Rights Policy, *supra* note 132 at 109.

[157] Kaufman & Bisharat, *supra* note 97 at 77.

[158] On this argument, see Bell, *Law of Peace*, *supra* note 28 at 33.

[159] Moreover, in the immediate aftermath of a major conflict, the domestic judicial system may simply be unavailable.

[160] Bell, "Human Rights, Peace Agreements, and Conflict Resolution," *supra* note 97 at 353.

[161] Ibid., 348.

[162] Ibid., 355.

[163] International Council on Human Rights Policy, *supra* note 132 at 112.

[164] Bell, "Peace Agreements: Their Nature and Legal Status", *supra* note 57 at 381. Bell also offers a list of examples, including the agreements in Angola, Burundi, the DRC, Guatemala, Mozambique, etc. (ibid.). See also Bell, Campbell & Ni Aolain, *supra* note 153 at 309; John Quigley, "The Israel-PLO Interim Agreements: Are They Treaties?" (1997) 30 *Cornell Int'l LJ* 717 at 740.

[165] As Christine Bell argues, "Domestic constitutionalism post-agreement is by its nature dysfunctional" (*Law of Peace*, *supra* note 28 at 275).

legitimate formal source of law. In the words of Ruti Teitel, international law is "continuous and enduring" and "frequently invoked as a way to bridge shifting understandings of legality".[166] The often disputed legal status of negotiating nonstate actors is a case in point. International humanitarian law, under which armed opposition groups might have acquired some form of international legal subjectivity,[167] is a fairly common reference to determine and legitimize, at least implicitly, the controversial participation of representatives of nonstate actors in the negotiations.[168] Turning to a legal order that is somehow external to and pre-exists the specific conflict in question and involving external actors in the negotiations are part of a long tradition in peace treaty making. Interstate peace treaties, which traditionally rely on the equality of sovereign states without proper enforcement mechanisms, have often included third parties to enhance the authority and binding character of the treaty. In Europe in the Middle Ages, and up to the mid-sixteenth century, it was common that the parties ratify treaties by oath and submit themselves to ecclesiastical jurisdiction, with excommunication and interdicts being possible sanctions for perjury.[169] Even the very earliest known peace treaties, concluded in the third millennium BC in Mesopotamia, assign the governance of such treaty relations to gods.[170] Similarly, because of the very nature of contemporary intrastate peace agreements, which can usually not be concluded in the form of an international treaty,[171] and the typical imbalance of power between the negotiating parties, external actors routinely get involved. The United Nations, regional organizations like the European Union, the African Union and the Economic Community of West African States, and regional powers or other states may sign an agreement as witnesses or guarantors. While these signatures do not

---

[166] Teitel, *Transitional Justice, supra* note 39 at 20.

[167] For a discussion on the applicability of common article 3 of Additional Protocol II to the Geneva Conventions to nonstate actors, see Liesbeth Zegveld, *Accountability of Armed Opposition Groups in International Law* (Cambridge: Cambridge University Press, 2002), 9–18. See also Bell, *Law of Peace, supra* note 28 at 130–132.

[168] For a discussion in the Colombian context, see Esquirol, *supra* note 153 at 39–61.

[169] Lesaffer, *supra* note 14 at 23–24.

[170] Dennis J. McCarthy, *Treaty and Covenant: A Study in Form in the Ancient Oriental Documents and in the Old Testament* (Rome: Biblical Institute Press, 1978), 32. In the 1280 BC treaty concluded between Hattusilis III of Hatti and Ramses II of Egypt, the gods are explicitly called upon to guarantee the treaty and to curse the violator (ibid., 48).

[171] Article 3 of the Vienna Convention on the Law of Treaties states that the Convention "does not apply to international agreements concluded between states and other subjects under international law or between such other subjects of international law". *Vienna Convention on the Law of Treaties*, 23 May 1969, 1155 UNTS 331 (entered into force 27 January 1980). This does not mean that peace agreements concluded between states and nonstate actors cannot be legally binding international agreements. For this discussion, see Chapter 1, Section 1.2. Bell, *Law of Peace, supra* note 28 at 128–136.

confer a status comparable to ecclesiastical jurisdiction in the Middle Ages and early modern times, with direct and foreseeable sanctions to be applied by this third party in case of noncompliance, they fulfil similar functions with respect to enhancing the binding character of the agreement for the primary parties.

International law does not only inspire peace processes in a unidirectional manner. Armed conflicts and their control and resolution have, indeed, contributed significantly to the development of international law.[172] Especially long-standing conflicts, like the Israeli-Palestinian one, have further defined numerous key concepts in the field of international humanitarian law and refugee law. However, the victims of these conflicts have rarely received appreciable benefits of this normative expansion.[173] The international legal framework is, nevertheless, part of interactional negotiation processes; it is under continuous deliberation, at the same time as substantive peace agreements are being negotiated.

2.2. DISCOURSE ANALYSIS IN CONTEXT

In addition to international legal norms that have an impact on peace negotiations, the normative role of the actors involved in peace negotiations are decisive. Since the legal-normative framework of peace negotiations is not generated apart from the subjective understanding of the negotiators, mediators and external actors, the use of existing and the emergence of novel legal norms in the context of peace negotiation is intrinsically linked to these actors. Their discourse does not only illustrate the emergence of these norms; based on the assumption that language is constructive, this discourse can be considered constitutive[174] and therefore contributes to the process of norm-creation.

---

[172] For this argument, see also Bell, *Human Rights and Peace Agreements, supra* note 71 at 314.

[173] Akram et al., *supra* note 154 at 1. The authors argue that "there is a yawning gap between the extraordinary contribution that the Middle East conflict has made towards developing international law (primarily through UN resolution, diplomatic statements, and scholarly comments), and the strange muteness by those who manage the conflict to meaningfully insist that any final settlement of the Middle East conflict must be shaped by the recognized rights of those who live there" (ibid., 3).

[174] Margaret Wetherell, "Themes in Discourse Research: The Case of Diana," in Margaret Wetherell, Stephanie Taylor & Simeon J. Yates, eds., *Discourse Theory and Practice: A Reader* (London: Sage Publications, 2001), 14, 15–16. Discourse analysis is the study of language in use; according to a broader definition, it encompasses the study of human meaning-making. See also Margaret Wetherell, Stephanie Taylor & Simeon J. Yates, "Introduction" in ibid. at 3. Focusing on the discourse in the context of peace negotiations may be encountered with criticism, since the discourse may only be lip service, with the negotiators or mediators inconsequentially claiming to uphold human rights and the rule of law. As a matter of fact, words are never sufficient by themselves; they do, however, illustrate and build up a continued reflection on a certain issue.

"In this normative world, law and narrative are inseparably related. Every pre-
scription is insistent in its demand to be located in discourse – to be supplied
with history and destiny, beginning and end, explanation and purpose".[175]
Drawing on this notion of narratives as conceived by Robert Cover, it is the
discourse that gives meaning to legal norms in the context of peace negotiations. Analysing the discourse, an instantiation of human interaction, hence
exposes the construction and use of as well as the relevance attached to legal
norms. In the context of peace negotiations, the discourse maps out the possible range of agreement and, in the long run, determines the sustainability
and impact of an agreement.

As it has been argued in the field of discourse analysis, discourse should
be seen as a joint production:[176] it is relational. In the words of Norman
Fairclough, "'discourse' might be seen as some sort of entity or 'object',
but it is itself a complex set of relations including relations of communication between people who talk, write and in other ways communicate with
each other".[177] This view is shared by a similar constructivist emphasis of
legal-theoretical approaches on human interaction and the continuous creation and re-creation of legal normativity.

If narrative and discourse are intertwined and have so far been referred to
without much precision, these terms do have somewhat different connotations. Narratives are associated with storytelling: they are viewpoints and experiences told in the form of a story, over which an individual or a collective can
claim ownership. Compared with this more specific genre, "discourse" does
not emphasize specific authorship, implies a lesser degree of coherence and is
also more inclusive than the notion of "narrative"; the former includes the latter, but the reverse is not necessarily the case.[178] By way of example, the text of
peace agreements, statements reported in the media, codes of conduct of peace
mediation organizations and personal accounts of negotiations are all part of
the discourse. They would only deserve the label "narratives" if they resemble
a story, if they have, for instance, a beginning and an end. For the purpose of
this study, it will not be necessary to identify the precise "degree of 'narrative-
ness' in a discourse",[179] or to reduce discourse to a technical, social scientific

---

[175] Cover, *supra* note 65 at 5.
[176] See Wetherell, *supra* note 174 at 18.
[177] Norman Fairclough, *Critical Discourse Analysis: The Critical Study of Language*, 2nd ed.
(Harlow: Longman/Pearson, 2010), 3.
[178] "There is some property or set of properties that makes a given discourse a narrative rather
than something else". Peter Brooks, "Narrative in and of the Law," in James Phelan & Peter J.
Rabinowitz, eds., *A Companion to Narrative Theory* (Malden, MA: Blackwell, 2005), 415.
[179] James Phelan & Peter J. Rabinowitz, eds., *A Companion to Narrative Theory* (Malden,
MA: Blackwell, 2005), 548.

concept merely denoting the "how" for telling a story, as it is, for instance, the case in structuralist narratology.[180] All these accounts are pertinent to analyse which actor or group of actors relies on which terms and concepts, acts as a deliberate norm advocate or contributes to the construction of legal norms in a more implicit and not necessarily conscious and coherent manner. Since the legal narratology movement has tended to confer an "oppositional" over-tone to stories,[181] such as those told by victims, it is worth highlighting that the focus here does not lie on stories offering an alternative to an "official" account of peace negotiations or a different idea of peace altogether.[182] In the following, the notion "discourse" and its underlying theoretical concepts will therefore be privileged over "narratives", without wholly disqualifying the use of the word "narrative" or relevant insights from narratology.

This book, like most discourse research, relies heavily on texts, notably peace agreements, statements reported in the media, documents published by nongovernmental organizations on their websites and other publicly accessi-ble documents. Legal literature has focused on the outcome and an analysis of the text of peace agreements and their usually prescriptive language drawing, to a varying degree, on formal international law.[183] Several studies have exam-ined, *inter alia*, the impact that human rights nongovernmental organizations have had on the language employed in peace agreements.[184] The finalized texts of peace agreements and the reliance of the drafters on formal inter-national law are certainly instructive and will also be the point of departure here. However, very little attention has been paid in the literature to the less developed and not necessarily coherent but arguably more germane discourse of the negotiating parties, peace mediators and external actors with respect to international law or legal norms more generally.[185] Compared with the texts

---

[180] See ibid., 544.

[181] See e.g. Brooks, *supra* note 178 at 415–416. On "counter-storytelling" and the argument that such storytelling can benefit members of "outgroups", see Richard Delgado, "Storytelling for Oppositionists and Others: A Plea for Narrative" (1989) 87 *Mich L Rev* 2411.

[182] See, for instance, the volumes edited by Dietrich et al, *supra* note 128 and by Toyin Falola & Hetty ter Haar, eds., *Narrating War and Peace in Africa* (Rochester, NY: Rochester University Press, 2010).

[183] See e.g. Bell, "Peace Agreements: Their Nature and Legal Status", *supra* note 57.

[184] See e.g. Michael O'Flaherty, "Sierra Leone's Peace Process: The Role of the Human Rights Community" (2004) 26:1 *Hum Rts Q* 29.

[185] This distinction is not equivalent to the debate between conflict resolution and human rights fields that is frequently seen as opposing pragmatists who focus on the process and idealists who focus on outcomes (see, for instance, the discussion in Christine Bell, "Peace Agreements and Human Rights: Implications for the UN," in Nigel D. White & Dirk Klaasen, eds., *The UN, Human Rights and Post-Conflict Situations* (Manchester: Manchester University Press, 2005), 241, 245 [henceforth Bell, "Peace Agreements and Human Rights: Implications for the UN"]). It rather builds on the argument that mainstream legal analysis has unduly focused on ends and neglected the means.

of peace agreements, this discourse transpiring during the negotiations is less tangible and less accessible. It will nevertheless be given its due weight here, in line with the emphasis on the dynamics of peace negotiations over a particular outcome. Meanings evolve, and narratives change over time,[186] which requires a focus on discursive practices during the process.

While any discourse analysis is subjective to some extent, this one is selective in several aspects. First, only a few peace negotiation contexts have been chosen, mostly for which some secondary literature was already available. The objective was, nevertheless, to cover different conflicts and conflict-resolution processes, including Colombia, Darfur, northern Uganda, Bosnia, Côte d'Ivoire and Israel-Palestine. Second, the discourse analysed is mainly a discourse of elites. While this may be expected and considered natural in the context of still largely elite-driven peace negotiations, it is important to be aware of this dimension. Power relations and the capacity to frame a certain discourse as authoritative may also lead to certain inaccuracies, especially in the absence of a signed agreement. As explored in the mediation literature, the structure of the mediation process and the ways in which mediators ask questions and make summaries inevitably contribute to emphasizing some narratives and to crafting one dominant story, on which an agreement will ultimately be grounded.[187] The differing accounts of Israeli, US and Palestinian officials of what "really" happened during the 2000 negotiations at Camp David is a good example of how negotiators and mediators will, consciously or unconsciously, propagate different versions of particular events and contribute to the construction of certain beliefs. As Jeremy Pressman argues, the dominant version does, however, not necessarily correspond to the most accurate one.[188] Some actors may also choose

---

[186] As Sara Cobb and Hussein Yusuf argue, "Reconciliation is a process by which persons *change the stories* and the narratives they tell at both the interpersonal and the institutional level. Thus, narrative can provide a lens on reconciliation processes that could help design and explain how peacemaking works as it focuses on the processes that support the evolution of meaning itself". Sara Cobb & Hussein Yusuf, "Narrative Approach to Peacemaking in Somalia," in Susan Allen Nan, Zachariah Cherian Mampilly & Andrea Bartoli, eds., *Peacemaking: From Practice to Theory*, vol. 1 (Santa Barbara, CA: Praeger, 2012), 328, 331.

[187] David Spencer & Michael Brogan, *Mediation Law and Practice* (Cambridge: Cambridge University Press, 2006), 94. Cobb and Rifkin speak of the colonization of alternative stories by the dominant story. Sara Cobb & Janet Rifkin, "Practice and Paradox: Deconstructing Neutrality in Mediation" (1991) 16:1 *Law & Soc Inquiry* 35 at 52–53.

[188] If Israel and the United States "have a significant edge in the public relations battle over rhetoric, images, and symbols", Pressman concludes that "the evidence suggests that the Palestinian narrative of the 2000–2001 peace talks is significantly more accurate than the Israeli narrative". Jeremy Pressman, "Visions in Collision, What Happened at Camp David and Taba?" (2003) 28:2 *International Security* 5 at 7, 37.

not to contribute directly to the peace negotiation discourse, as illustrated by the desire of some smaller civil society organizations in Sri Lanka to avoid "peace" and "peace-building" terminology and even to emphasize their "un-NGOness" because of the perceived association, in the eyes of the broader public, of "NGOs" with an elitist network funded and manipulated by foreign agencies.[189] Third, what should also be recalled in the context of a discussion of peace negotiations is that violence is generally destructive to storytelling and disrupts "the capacity of people to narrate their experience".[190] Analysing the discourse in the context of armed conflicts is, in this sense, inevitably imperfect. Third, only publicly available documents have been taken as examples. While more accessible, reliable and also more influential on other contexts than the discourse not documented in writing, they are only part of the discourse through which norms are constructed in peace negotiations. The discourses at the negotiating table and those intended for the general public often differ drastically.[191] Moreover, it should be kept in mind that the level of consciousness of the relevant actor regarding the normative impact of his or her discourse varies: from outright, deliberate norm advocacy or entrepreneurship by international human rights organizations to the more instinctive and implicit normative conduct by facilitative mediators or the negotiating parties.[192] Based on discourse analysis theory,[193] it can

---

[189] Oliver Walton with Paikiasothy Saravanamuttu, "In the Balance? Civil Society and the Peace Process 2002–2008," in Jonathan Goodhand, Jonathan Spencer & Benedikt Korf, eds., *Conflict and Peacebuilding in Sri Lanka: Caught in the Peace Trap?* (London: Routledge, 2011), 183, 192–194. See also the discussion in Chapter 4, Section 4.5.

[190] Cobb & Yusuf, *supra* note 186 at 332. The German writer Uwe Timm relates how pointedly his brother, a member of the Waffen-SS, closes his diary in 1943, considering it "nonsensical" to record the unspeakable: "Hiermit schließe ich mein Tagebuch, da ich es für unsinnig halte, über so grausame Dinge, wie sie manchmal geschehen, Buch zu führen". Uwe Timm, *Am Beispiel meines Bruders* (Cologne: dtv, 2009), 147. The indescribable nature of war is also palpable in Leo Tolstoy's *War and Peace*, where the Emperor Alexander I exclaims: "What a terrible thing war is: what a terrible thing! *Quelle terrible chose que la guerre!*" Leo Tolstoy, *War and Peace*, translated by Louise Maude and Aylmer Maude (New York: Alfred A. Knopf, 1992), vol. 1, 324.

[191] As the lead negotiator of the Colombian government pointedly stated in the context of the negotiations with the FARC in early 2013, "One thing is what the FARC says publicly as part of its platform … and another thing is what it says at the table". "Colombia, FARC Say Peace Talks Advancing," *Reuters* (10 February 2013), online: Reuters <http://www.reuters.com/article/2013/02/10/us-colombia-rebels-talks-idUSBRE9190DM20130210>.

[192] Human rights advocacy and mediation are, of course, not mutually exclusive functions. See, for instance, the argument in Parlevliet, "Rethinking Conflict Transformation," *supra* note 100 at 18.

[193] Jonathan Potter & Margaret Wetherell, "Unfolding Discourse Analysis," in Margaret Wetherell, Stephanie Taylor & Simeon J. Yates, eds., *Discourse Theory and Practice: A Reader* (London: Sage, 2001), 198, 199.

indeed be argued that the process of norm-creation through discourse does not necessarily have to be intentional or a conscious construction. Discourse does not have to be overly reflective to be constitutive: "discourse is initiatory, celebratory, expressive, and performative, rather than critical and analytic".[194] Therefore, even though the actors and the normative dimensions of their interaction are at the heart of this discourse analysis, the level of normative consciousness of these actors is largely irrelevant.[195]

2.3. "HARD" REFERENCES TO INTERNATIONAL LEGAL NORMS IN PEACE AGREEMENTS

Exploring the discourse on existing international legal norms contained in the text of peace agreements recognizes the relevance of this discourse and of the kind of norms it refers to. Peace agreements, through the language they contain with respect to international law, mirror a prevalent conviction that international law has certain functions to fulfill in this context. This conviction manifests itself in the act of drafting and signing peace agreements, in other words, in specific situations at certain moments in time. The textual analysis of references to what can be seen as an existing, relatively formal legal framework acknowledges the continued relevance of law largely made by the state and the community of states and is useful to explore the importance that is attached to international law by peace negotiators and mediators. Recurring themes include references to international legal norms relating to human rights, transitional justice, women and refugees.

The examination of references to international legal norms in peace agreements will rely on a twofold approach. First, databases that have been established by peace research organizations, namely, the Peace Agreements Database of the University of Ulster's Transitional Justice Institute[196] and the United Nations' peace agreements database,[197] will be used to carry out a quantitative analysis of the number of peace agreements that contain references to international legal norms and of the kinds of references made as well as to discern possible normative trends. The objective here is not to establish statistically relevant findings but to get a general sense of written references to international legal norms in peace agreements. Drawing definite conclusions from such a quantitative approach could only be done with much caution;

---

[194] Cover, *supra* note 65 at 13.
[195] Fuller, "Human Interaction and the Law," *supra* note 3 at 9.
[196] Peace Agreements Database, Transitional Justice Institute (University of Ulster) <http://www.peaceagreements.ulster.ac.uk/>.
[197] UN Peacemaker <http://peacemaker.un.org>.

meaningful numbers, whether in absolute or in percentage terms, are difficult to ascertain, mostly because of the great variety of agreements included
in these databases. Pre-negotiation, framework and substantive as well as
implementation agreements will, naturally, not resort to the same kind of
international legal norms in the same manner. Moreover, by way of example,
the Peace Agreements Database of the Transitional Justice Institute contains
more than 640 peace agreements,[198] which encompass interstate and intrastate
agreements and separately listed partial agreements, as well as proposed agreements that were not accepted by all relevant parties.

As a result, in addition to relying on an only partly revealing quantitative
approach, the text of several peace agreements and the language that has been
used will be examined more closely by quoting and comparing relevant references. These agreements, which are all framework or substantive agreements,
include the Comprehensive Peace Agreement (Sudan), the Darfur Peace
Agreement, the Accord de Linas-Marcoussis (Côte d'Ivoire), the Annexure
[*sic*] to the Agreement on Accountability and Reconciliation (Northern
Uganda) and the Dayton Peace Agreement (Bosnia).

Several areas can be distinguished where international legal norms are
referred to, the most important one being international human rights law.
For the sake of this analysis, the broad "rights" category will be divided into
references to international or regional human rights instruments and related
enumerations of rights; provisions dealing with individual accountability and
amnesties, which are linked to human rights but which are distinct because of
their more specific focus and their largely backward-looking nature; arrangements to ensure the return of refugees and displaced persons, a common challenge in the context of internal armed conflicts; and references to the rights
of women and concerns related to gender issues, as called for in Security
Council Resolution 1325.

2.3.1. *Human Rights – Relying on a Widely Recognized Framework*

Several international and regional instruments are resorted to in peace agreements seeking to end internal armed conflicts. These instruments, like the
Universal Declaration of Human Rights and the African Charter on Human
and Peoples' Rights, are sometimes recalled symbolically to mark the end
of a period of massive human rights violations and the beginning of a new
rights-based and rights-honouring future. They may also be called upon to
confer additional legitimacy to an agreement by putting it on normative

---

[198] See <http://www.peaceagreements.ulster.ac.uk/>.

foundations based on international standards. Some instruments, like the European Convention on Human Rights, may not only provide important normative guidance but also be incorporated into domestic law via a substantive agreement. It should be kept in mind that because of their very nature, human rights are often considered a useful element to be included in peace agreements, notably in order to guarantee accrued protection to the weaker party. The representatives of national minorities might, for instance, insist on specific human rights guarantees, without which a peace agreement would lose its essence. Human rights provisions may therefore not only be included on account of an idealist, or principled, Kantian position that emphasizes the universality of rights; they may also be included for very pragmatic reasons.[199]

Many peace agreements invoke specific international or regional human rights conventions and treaties and also enumerate specific rights. Some agreements also foresee the establishment of an enforcement mechanism, such as a national human rights institution. Relevant factors have been identified in the literature for ways in which human rights are dealt with in peace agreements.[200] These factors include differences in human rights abuses committed during the conflict; different degrees of internationalization of the peace process, the cultural background of the parties and their faith in a rights-based approach; and the strength of civil society and its position vis-à-vis human rights.

In the following discussion, only agreements containing this kind of human rights language will be considered, even though many agreements that do not explicitly refer to human rights deal, in their substance, with human rights issues. Provisions on power sharing, the electoral system and institutional reform, and access to natural resources typically address questions of injustice and inequality,[201] without necessarily using the language and logic of international human rights instruments. Although it is not always quantifiable, the impact of international human rights law may thus be much more significant than reflected by the language employed in peace agreements.

To get a sense of the numbers, peace agreements contained in two databases have been compared. Out of the more than 640 peace agreements concluded since 1990[202] and listed in the Transitional Justice Institute's Peace Agreements

[199] Bell, *Human Rights and Peace Agreements, supra* note 71 at 302–303.

[200] See International Council on Human Rights Policy, *supra* note 132 at 37. The following is a nonexhaustive list. See also Bell, *Human Rights and Peace Agreements, supra* note 71 at 37.

[201] See also International Council on Human Rights Policy, *supra* note 132 at 3, 16.

[202] Of these 640 agreements, around 75 are interstate agreements. The year 1990 was chosen as starting date because, in the words of the Transitional Justice Institute, "it broadly marks the end of the Cold War and the beginning of the peace agreement era". <http://www.peaceagreements.ulster.ac.uk/about.html>. A comparison with the UN databank confirms this assumption: only 30 out of the 295 intrastate agreements were concluded before 1990.

Database, 132 provide for a human rights framework,[203] in other words, more than every fifth agreement. Thirty-eight of these agreements also establish or envisage establishing a human rights institution. The peace agreements database of the United Nations[204] lists 295 intrastate agreements (of a total of 394 agreements), of which nearly every second agreement, to be precise 143, deals with human rights.

This means that a significant number of peace agreements concluded since 1990 in the context of internal armed conflicts contain references to international human rights law or establish a human rights framework. Some peace agreements establish this framework by incorporating international or regional human rights conventions. The 1995 Dayton Peace Agreement provides, for instance, that the European Convention on Human Rights and its protocols "apply directly in Bosnia and Herzegovina" and "have priority over other law".[205] Moreover, the agreement establishes several human rights institutions, such as a new Constitutional Court and a Commission on Human Rights, which consists of an internationally appointed ombudsman and a Human Rights Chamber.[206] This strong stance on human rights cannot be explained only by the fact that the conflict had been characterized by massive human rights violations, with the parties now realizing that a robust human rights framework would be necessary to ensure a nonviolent future for Bosnia; it can rather be attributed to the heavy involvement of international actors and notably the insistence of the United States to include human rights into the agreement.[207] The influence of regional institutions is also manifest: as Bell has pointed out, the design of the Commission on Human Rights bears resemblance to the one of the former European Commission and Court of Human Rights of the Council of Europe.[208] Despite this fairly strong embeddedness

[203] More precisely, the database lists agreements containing "provisions providing for a human rights framework to guide the post-conflict period, for example by making provision for a bill of rights or for incorporation of human rights standards". <http://www.peaceagreements.ulster .ac.uk/glossary.html>. This implies, for instance, that mere references to human rights instruments are insufficient for inclusion of an agreement under this heading.

[204] See <http://peacemaker.un.org>.

[205] *General Framework Agreement for Peace in Bosnia and Herzegovina (Dayton Peace Agreement)*, 14 December 1995, 35 ILM 75, online: Office of the High Representative and EU Special Representative <http://www.ohr.int/dpa/default.asp?content_id=379>, Annex 4, art II 2.

[206] Ibid., Annex 4, art VI and Annex 6. As Bell argues, "While human rights institutions and mechanisms abound, their remit and jurisdiction is overlapping and confused and the mechanisms for enforcement are unclear" (Bell, *Human Rights and Peace Agreements, supra* note 71 at 221).

[207] Bell, *Human Rights and Peace Agreements, supra* note 71 at 313. The Dayton Peace Agreements (*supra* note 205) also established an enforcement mechanism in Annex 6, ch 2, Part B. The role of the United States in mediating the Dayton Peace Agreement will be explored in more detail in the Chapter 3 (see particularly Sections 3.1.2 and 3.2.2).

[208] Bell, *Human Rights and Peace Agreements, supra* note 71 at 224.

within the logic of international human rights law, key provisions of the Dayton Peace Agreement relating to political representation based on ethnic identity have been invalidated by the European Court of Human Rights.[209] This raises serious questions with respect to the role of both national and regional courts in reviewing power-sharing agreements that are concluded in the context of major political transitions. However, in its discussion of the admissibility of the case, the court emphasized that – leaving aside the responsibility for *including* the contested constitutional provisions – Bosnia and Herzegovina could nevertheless be held responsible for *maintaining* them.[210] This can be read both as a commitment to recognizing the transitional and somewhat exceptional nature of the Dayton Peace Agreement and as a reminder that, in the court's view, such arrangements gradually lose their temporary justification.

Other peace agreements refer to human rights rather laconically but, at the same time, in an open-ended way. Mentioning national, regional or international instruments may thus substitute a more particular elaboration of a human rights framework. The Lomé Peace Agreement, for instance, provides that:

> the basic civil and political liberties recognized by the Sierra Leone legal system and contained in the declarations and principles of Human Rights adopted by the UN and OAU, especially the Universal Declaration of Human Rights and the African Charter on Human and Peoples' Rights, shall be fully protected and promoted within Sierra Leonean society.[211]

An enumeration of a few specific rights follows, including the right to take part in the governance of one's country.[212] The Lomé Peace Agreement is also notable for the parties agreeing to create an "autonomous quasi-judicial national Human Rights Commission",[213] yet without further specifying the outlook of such a commission or procedural aspects as to its creation.

With respect to human rights provisions, the 2006 Darfur Peace Agreement, which was mediated mainly by the African Union and signed in Abuja between the Sudanese government and, in the end, only one faction of the Sudan Liberation Movement/Army represented by Minni Minawi,[214] resembles the

---

[209] For a critical discussion of the Court's 2009 judgment in *Sejdić and Finci v. Bosnia and Herzegovina*, see McCrudden & O'Leary, *supra* note 70.

[210] *Sejdić and Finci v. Bosnia and Herzegovina*, nos 27996/06 and 34836/06 (22 December 2009) (European Court of Human Rights, Judgment of the Grand Chamber) at para 30.

[211] *Lomé Peace Agreement*, *supra* note 40, art XXIV.1.

[212] Ibid., art XXIV.2.

[213] Ibid., art XXV.

[214] For a concise summary of the shortcomings of the Abuja process, in particular the lack of sufficient communication with the people of Darfur by the mediators and the unsuccessful pressure on the rebel leaders, which undermined the African Union's authority, see Laurie

Lomé Peace Agreement. In the preamble of the Darfur Peace Agreement, the parties highlight the emblematic value of human rights by "condemning all acts of violence against civilians and violations of human rights, and stressing full and unconditional acceptance of their obligations under international Humanitarian Law, international human rights law, and relevant UN Security Council Resolutions".[215] The chapter on power sharing includes most of the language on human rights, where direct reference is made to international instruments: "The Parties reiterate their commitment to respect and promote human rights and fundamental freedoms as detailed below and in international human rights covenants ratified by the GoS [Government of Sudan]".[216] An extensive enumeration of specific rights, such as the right to life, the right to a fair trial and the right to freedom of religion and expression, follows, and the two International Covenants on Civil and Political Rights (ICCPR) and on Economic, Social and Cultural Rights (ICESCR) are explicitly mentioned.[217]

In the 2005 North–South Sudanese Comprehensive Peace Agreement, the Sudanese government and the Sudan People's Liberation Army (SPLA) did not explicitly commit to promoting and protecting human rights. They did, however, confirm the authoritative status and standard-setting role of human rights and humanitarian law by relating it to violations of the agreement: "the following acts shall constitute violations to this Agreement: ... violation of human rights, humanitarian law and obstruction of freedom of movement".[218]

Nathan, "Towards a New Era in International Mediation" *Crisis States Research Centre* (May 2010), online: Crisis States <http://www.crisisstates.com/download/Policy%20Directions/ Towards%20a%20new%20era%20in%20international%20mediation.pdf> at 3. See also Sean P. Brooks who describes the "deadline diplomacy" promoted by the international community and the shifting role of the mediators from facilitators to formulators and manipulators. Sean P Brooks, "Enforcing a Turning Point and Imposing a Deal: An Analysis of the Darfur Abuja Negotiations of 2006" (2008) 13 International Negotiation 413 at 425–429. For an analysis of the Darfur negotiations and their links with the North-South process, see International Crisis Group, "A Strategy for Comprehensive Peace in Sudan" (26 July 2007), online: International Crisis Group <http://www.crisisgroup.org/home/index.cfm?id=4961&l=1> at 8–10.

[215] *Darfur Peace Agreement*, 5 May 2006, online: United Nations Development Programme Sudan <http://www.sd.undp.org/doc/DPA.pdf>, preamble.

[216] Ibid., art 3 at para 24.

[217] Ibid., art 3 at para 28(a).

[218] *Agreement on Permanent Ceasefire and Security Arrangements Implementation Modalities between the Government of the Sudan (GoS) and the Sudan People's Liberation Movement/ Sudan People's Liberation Army (SPLM/SPLA) during the Pre-Interim and Interim Periods*, 31 December 2004, art 10.1.6. This agreement is one of the key documents leading to the 2005 Comprehensive Peace Agreement, in which it appears as Annexure 1: *Comprehensive Peace Agreement between The Government of The Republic of The Sudan and the Sudan People's Liberation Movement/Sudan People's Liberation Army*, 9 January 2005, online: United Nations Mission in Sudan <http://unmis.unmissions.org/Portals/UNMIS/Documents/ General/cpa-en.pdf> [*Comprehensive Peace Agreement*].

Respecting the said rights, as an underlying obligation, hence became part of the contractual relationship between the parties signing the agreement.

Again, it can be hypothesized that the inclusion of references to human rights in these peace agreements is related to the fairly strong involvement of external actors in the negotiations, at least at the final stages. The Lomé Peace Agreement, the Darfur Peace Agreement and the Sudanese Comprehensive Peace Agreement were all signed as witnesses by up to a dozen envoys or representatives of international and regional organizations, as well as of foreign governments.

As it has already been mentioned, the number of peace agreements containing references to human rights and the language used do not always reflect an accurate picture of the importance of human rights in a peace process. While the 1992 General Peace Agreement for Mozambique, for instance, contains only few references to human rights,[219] it should be recalled that at the time the agreement was negotiated, a new constitution was elaborated that included a comprehensive bill of rights.[220] The fact that an agreement does not contain any references to human rights might therefore be related not only to the decision of the negotiators and mediators not to attach much importance to human rights but also to the nature and functions of an agreement. However, a correlation between the constitution-making nature of a peace process, especially when sponsored by international actors committed to promoting democratic values and the liberal peace,[221] and the inclusion of human rights can be assumed. This means that in a case like Dayton, where international actors are heavily involved in developing a comprehensive constitution-like agreement that designs new institutions of governance, the lack of references to human rights would come as a greater surprise and probably be perceived as a more obvious lacuna than in the case of a locally mediated cease-fire agreement.

It is worth pointing out that since the negotiations and agreements in the Israeli-Palestinian process will be analysed in more detail in Section 2.3.2, these agreements contain no or only very short and vague references to human rights. A comprehensive study of the agreements concluded in the 1990s revealed that "human rights" are only referred to in secondary items

---

[219] *General Peace Agreement for Mozambique, supra* note 55. Protocol III of the agreement guarantees, inter alia, freedom of the press, freedom of association and expression and political activity, and liberty of movement.

[220] International Council on Human Rights Policy, *supra* note 132 at 25.

[221] For a rich volume that deals, among other things, with the intellectual foundations and critiques of the liberal peace and explores possible alternatives, see Susanna Campbell, David Chandler & Meera Sabaratnam, eds., *A Liberal Peace? The Problems and Practices of Peacebuilding* (London: Zed Books, 2011).

and annexes but not in the main documents.[222] The Oslo Accords do allude to human rights, but rather parenthetically. The Interim Agreement provides that "Israel and the [Palestinian] Council shall exercise their powers and responsibilities pursuant to this Agreement with due regard to internationally-accepted norms and principles of human rights and the rule of law".[223] As it will be explored in more detail in Section 2.4.1, the highly asymmetrical nature of the conflict and the very different stance of the negotiating parties on human rights and their relevance for resolving the conflict are mainly responsible for the almost complete absence of human rights language in Israeli-Palestinian agreements.[224] It can, nevertheless, be concluded that besides such notable exceptions, human rights are regularly referred to and provide an at least symbolic normative basis for peace agreements.

2.3.2. *Transitional Justice – Balancing Retrospectivity and Prospectivity in an Agreement*

Because serious crimes, including genocide, crimes against humanity and war crimes, are often perpetrated and remain unpunished in the context of internal armed conflicts, numerous peace agreements explicitly address and attempt to deal with these crimes. Transitional justice mechanisms indeed epitomize the role of legal norms in peace agreements and are among the most obvious illustrations of the "indivisibility of forward- and backward-looking measures".[225]

Only a few international treaties explicitly address these issues. The Genocide Convention, also part of customary international law, requires states to punish anyone who commits genocide.[226] Similar obligations arise under the Torture Convention and the Apartheid Convention. Only Additional Protocol II to the Geneva Conventions contains a specific provision on amnesties: "At the end of

---

[222] Mohammed Abu-Nimer & Edward Kaufman, "Bridging Conflict Transformation and Human Rights: Lessons from the Israeli-Palestinian Peace Process," in Julie A. Mertus & Jeffrey W. Helsing, eds., *Human Rights & Conflict: Exploring the Links between Rights, Law, and Peacebuilding* (Washington, DC: United States Institute of Peace, 2006), 277, 298–301.

[223] *Israeli-Palestinian Interim Agreement on the West Bank and Gaza Strip*, 28 September 1995, UN Doc. A/51/889, art XIX.

[224] It can be hypothesized that the "discouraging human rights record" of the Palestinian Authority (Watson, *supra* note 61 at 252) might also be a factor that has not contributed to making the Palestinian side push for the inclusion of stronger human rights language into the agreements.

[225] Bell, *Human Rights and Peace Agreements*, *supra* note 71 at 311.

[226] *Convention on the Prevention and Punishment of the Crime of Genocide*, 9 December 1948, 78 UNTS 277 (entered into force 12 January 1951), art 4. The obligation is not based on the principle of universal jurisdiction, but of territorial jurisdiction, which means that *genocidaires* must be tried by the state where the genocide was committed or by an international criminal tribunal; see Article 6 of the Convention.

hostilities, the authorities in power shall endeavour to grant the broadest possible amnesty to persons who have participated in the armed conflict, or those deprived of their liberty for reasons related to the armed conflict, whether they are interned or detained".[227] As the International Committee of the Red Cross (ICRC) has commented, despite this encouragement to grant amnesties in the aftermath of a noninternational armed conflict, the amnesty provision "could not be construed to enable war criminals, or those guilty of crimes against humanity, to evade punishment".[228] The developments at the international level since the 1990s with respect to providing accountability for the gravest crimes have also affected peace negotiations. International criminal law, and notably the Rome Statute of the ICC, addresses more specifically the question of individual accountability for genocide, crimes against humanity, war crimes and the crime of aggression. While related obligations may have arisen under customary international law, the international criminal legal framework can be expected to have the most immediate impact on situations where the ICC may exercise its jurisdiction. It must, nevertheless, be concluded that international instruments do not provide clear guidance as to the establishment of transitional justice mechanisms and are sometimes not consistent with each other.[229]

Most provisions in peace agreements relating to transitional justice refer to individual criminal accountability and to amnesties, as well as to modes of establishing truth and bringing about reconciliation. These provisions exemplify that the dual past- and future-oriented function of peace agreements is not a given but must be established and carefully balanced, through negotiations, in every context. The actors involved may not attach the same importance to dealing with a violent past and may not have the same opinion as to its significance in paving the way for a more peaceful future. Moreover, representatives of the negotiating parties, such as top government officials or leaders of armed groups, may be concerned about individual accountability for the crimes committed and therefore about their personal future and comfort. Even if there cannot be a choice between peace and justice,[230] aspects relating

---

[227] *Additional Protocol II, supra* note 122, art 6(5).

[228] International Committee of the Red Cross (Jean-Marie Henckaerts & Louise Doswald-Beck), *Customary International Humanitarian Law, Volume I: Rules* (Cambridge: Cambridge University Press, 2005), 612. See also Bruce Broomhall, who argues that the amnesty provision "is intended primarily to discourage the prosecution under ordinary criminal law". Bruce Broomhall, *International Justice and the International Criminal Court: Between Sovereignty and the Rule of Law* (Oxford: Oxford University Press, 2003), 96.

[229] For a more detailed analysis of the relevant provisions originating from these overlapping international legal regimes, see Bell, *Human Rights and Peace Agreements, supra* note 71 at 260–270.

[230] On the existence, both in theory and in practice, of an oversimplifying peace and justice dichotomy, see Chapter 5.

to transitional justice, and, in particular, individual accountability, are frequently among the most delicate issues to be negotiated. While the question as to whether, in some circumstances, amnesties are prohibited under international law as well as the argument that associated legal obligations are emerging will be explored in more detail in Section 5.1, it can be asserted at this point that the intensified discourse on transitional justice is reflected in the text of a significant number of peace agreements.

According to the UN database, transitional justice is part of 115 of the 295 agreements. These agreements include the Ugandan Annexure to the Agreement on Accountability and Reconciliation, the Accord de Linas-Marcoussis and the Accord politique de Ouagadougou (Côte d'Ivoire), the Darfur Peace Agreement, and the Dayton Peace Agreement. The Transitional Justice Institute's database reveals that out of the more than 640 agreements included, 63 address the question of amnesty or pardon, in other words, roughly every tenth agreement. These provisions may look very different. Some peace agreements enact, or foresee enacting, a comprehensive amnesty. In the 2002 Luena Memorandum of Understanding, for instance, the [Angolan] "Government guarantees … the approval and publication … of an Amnesty Law for all crimes committed in the context of the armed conflict between the UNITA military forces and the Government".[231] Some agreements provide amnesty only to the members of a specific group, with the apparent goal of demobilizing and reintegrating former combatants of nonstate armed groups. A good example is the 1990 accord between the Colombian government and the M-19, the first of the Colombian guerrilla groups to start a process of negotiations.[232] The accord provides that "el Gobierno Nacional, a partir de la fecha, aplicará el Indulto a los miembros del M-19 y dará inicio a los programas de reinserción social y productivos acordados".[233] It is worth highlighting the syntactic structure of

---

[231] *Memorando de Entendimento Complementar ao Protocolo de Lusaka para a Cessação das Hostilidades e Resolução das Demais Questões Militares Pendentes nos Termos do Protocolo de Lusaka (Luena Memorandum of Understanding)*, 4 April 2002 (Angola), UN Doc. S/2002/483, ch II, 2.1.

[232] Mauricio García Durán, Vera Grabe Loewenherz & Otty Patiño Hormaza, "The M-19's Journey from Armed Struggle to Democratic Politics" (2008) Berghof Transitions Series, online: Berghof Conflict Research <http://www.berghof-conflictresearch.org/documents/publications/transitions_m19.pdf> at 6.

[233] *Acuerdo político entre el gobierno nacional, los partidos políticos, el M-19, y la iglesia católica en calidad de tutora moral y espiritual del proceso [Accord between the National Government, the Political Parties, the M-19 and the Catholic Church in the capacity of a moral and spiritual guide for the process]*, 9 March 1990 (Colombia), online: UN Peacemaker <http://peacemaker.un.org/sites/peacemaker.un.org/files/CO_900309_Acuerdo%20Pol%C3%ADtico%20Entre%20El%20Gobierno%20Nacional%20los%20Partidos%20Pol%C3%ADticos%20y%20El%20M-19.pdf>, art 8.

this succinct clause: since the same sentence provides for the pardoning of M-19 members and the initiation of social reintegration programs, the agreement underscores the parties' understanding that the amnesty will help the former combatants return to civil life. This agreement, concluded in March 1990, paved the way for the 1991 Constitution, which also allowed guerrilla movements, including the M-19, to become political parties.[234]

Other agreements contain references to international criminal law and specific limitations to the amnesties provided, thus excluding the application of amnesty in the case of grave violations of international human rights and humanitarian law. An amnesty provision that is meant to encourage the return of refugees and displaced persons can be found in an annex to the Dayton Peace Agreement:

> Any returning refugee or displaced person charged with a crime, other than a serious violation of international humanitarian law as defined in the Statute of the International Tribunal for the Former Yugoslavia since January 1, 1991, or a common crime unrelated to the conflict, shall upon return enjoy an amnesty. In no case shall charges for crimes be imposed for political or other inappropriate reasons or to circumvent the application of the amnesty.[235]

This clause illustrates well the dual backward- and forward-looking nature of transitional justice provisions. Amnesty is to be granted, but only "upon return"; past crimes, with notable exceptions, should be forgotten so that refugees and displaced persons can go back to their former lives.

The Accord de Linas-Marcoussis, concluded in 2003 between the main political parties and armed groups from Côte d'Ivoire, even foresees in the annex "Programme du gouvernement de réconciliation", in the section "Droits et libertés de la Personne humaine", to bring alleged criminals before international criminal justice institutions:

> Sur le rapport de la Commission internationale d'enquête, le gouvernement de réconciliation nationale déterminera ce qui doit être porté devant la justice pour faire cesser l'impunité. Condamnant particulièrement les actions

---

[234] For an analysis of this process, see García Durán, Grabe Loewenherz & Patiño Hormaza, *supra* note 232. The authors argue that one "lesson is that a legal normalisation through transitional methods is required which permits the political engagement of those who abandon arms. Amnesties and mechanisms for access to electoral processes should be fast and flexible, in order to facilitate the guerrillas' incorporation into politics and into the current legal regime" (ibid., 35). For an analysis of the 1991 Constitution, see also Farid Samir Benavides Vanegas, "Law as a Peace Treaty: The Case of the M-19 and the 1991 Colombian Constitution," online: University of Massachusetts Amherst <http://www.umass.edu/legal/Hilbink/250/Benavides.pdf>.

[235] *Dayton Peace Agreement, supra* note 205, Annex 7, art VI.

des escadrons de la mort et de leurs commanditaires ainsi que les auteurs d'exécutions sommaires sur l'ensemble du territoire, la Table Ronde estime que les auteurs et complices de ces activités devront être *traduits devant la justice pénale internationale.*[236]

Moreover, in the section "Regroupement, Désarmement, Démobilisation", the parties agree on a broad although not absolute amnesty:

Le gouvernement de réconciliation nationale prendra les mesures nécessaires pour la libération et l'amnistie de tous les militaires détenus pour atteinte à la sûreté de l'Etat et fera bénéficier de la même mesure les soldats exilés. La loi d'amnistie n'exonérera en aucun cas les auteurs d'infractions économiques graves et de *violations graves des droits de l'homme et du* droit international humanitaire.[237]

These provisions show that the accord does not draw a clear line between the past and the future as, for instance, the Lomé Peace Agreement does. Transitional justice in the Accord de Linas-Marcoussis symbolizes both a new beginning and a connection to the past. By providing for "la libération et l'amnistie de tous les militaires détenus", the parties seek to move on in order to build a common, peaceful future. Some categories of grave crimes are, however, excluded, with the parties signalling their conviction that grave violations of international humanitarian law, for instance, ought not to be forgotten but must be punished. The international legal order is not only represented through the mentioning of "violations graves des droits de l'homme et du droit international humanitaire", for which no amnesty is to be granted. The previous reference to "justice pénale internationale" is especially remarkable, not only as an evident recourse to international legal norms and international institutions, but also because the agreement was concluded in January 2003, without any prospect as to the establishment of an international or hybrid tribunal with jurisdiction over the crimes committed in Côte d'Ivoire and only six months after the entry into force of the Rome Statute. The clause can be read in the context of the then rapidly developing importance of international criminal justice institutions, above all the ICC. Although Côte d'Ivoire had not ratified the Rome Statute, it

---

[236] *Accord de Linas-Marcoussis*, 24 January 2003 (Côte d'Ivoire), online: United States Institute of Peace <http://www.usip.org/files/file/resources/collections/peace_agreements/cote_divoire_01242003en.pdf>, Annexe (Programme du gouvernement de réconciliation), art VI.3 (emphasis added).

[237] Ibid., art VII.5 (emphasis added). This clause was repeated in the *Accord politique de Ouagadougou*, 4 March 2007 (Côte d'Ivoire), online: United Nations Mission in Côte d'Ivoire <http://www.onuci.org/pdf/ouagaaccord.pdf>.

accepted ICC jurisdiction under article 12(3) of the statute a few months after the Accord de Linas-Marcoussis had been signed.[238]

It can be argued that the negotiating parties, mediators and third parties signing the agreement as witnesses had learned from the futile situation in Sierra Leone a few years earlier. The Lomé Peace Agreement granted a comprehensive amnesty and pardon to all combatants and collaborators, mentioning specifically Foday Sankoh and the members of four armed groups. This far-reaching and heavily debated provision merits being quoted at length:

Article IX: Pardon and Amnesty

1. In order to bring lasting peace to Sierra Leone, the Government of Sierra Leone shall take appropriate legal steps to grant Corporal Foday Sankoh absolute and free pardon.

2. After the signing of the present Agreement, the Government of Sierra Leone shall also grant absolute and free pardon and reprieve to all combatants and collaborators in respect of anything done by them in pursuit of their objectives, up to the time of the signing of the present Agreement.

3. To consolidate the peace and promote the cause of national reconciliation, the Government of Sierra Leone shall ensure that no official or judicial action is taken against any member of the RUF/SL, ex-AFRC, ex-SLA or CDF in respect of anything done by them in pursuit of their objectives as members of those organisations, since March 1991, up to the time of the signing of the present Agreement. In addition, legislative and other measures necessary to guarantee immunity to former combatants, exiles and other persons, currently outside the country for reasons related to the armed conflict shall be adopted ensuring the full exercise of their civil and political rights, with a view to their reintegration within a framework of full legality.[239]

Several points are remarkable with respect to this provision. It is noticeable that the agreement does not mention why or for which acts amnesties or pardons are to be granted, besides the vague reference to "*anything done by them [all combatants and collaborators] in pursuit of their objectives*".[240] Moreover, the terms chosen are somewhat confusing. While the

[238] Republic of Côte d'Ivoire, *Declaration Accepting the Jurisdiction of the International Criminal Court* (18 April 2003), online: International Criminal Court <http://www.icc-cpi.int/NR/rdonl yres/74EEE201-0FED-4481-95D4-C8071087102C/279844/ICDEENG.pdf>.

[239] *Lomé Peace Agreement, supra* note 40, art IX.

[240] Ibid. (emphasis added).

title mentions "pardon" and "amnesty", the first two paragraphs concerning Foday Sankoh and "all combatants and collaborators" speak of "absolute and free pardon", and the third paragraph concerns members of four
armed groups, against whom "no official or judicial action" is to be taken as
well as "other persons" to whom "immunity", still another concept, is to be
"guaranteed".

The wording of the provision hence surprises in several ways. On the one
hand, the granting of pardon to someone is usually preceded by the recognition of a particular wrong. It does not repress the memory of the irrevo-
cable,[241] but it implies forgiveness of the offender.[242] Amnesty, on the other
hand, which comes from the Greek *amñstía*, implies forgetting, oblivion,
and "seeks to efface psycho-social traces 'as if nothing had happened,'
imposing silence about the memory of the unforgettable".[243] Yet forgetting
does not imply forgiving, and forgiving does not imply forgetting.[244] While
employing different and somewhat confusing terms, the provision appears
primarily to seek to ensure that no investigations or prosecutions be carried
out with respect to "anything done" in relation to the armed conflict, in
order to "consolidate the peace and promote the cause of national reconciliation". This last sentence suggests that the drafters believed that not granting "immunities" to former combatants, for instance, would obstruct efforts
to achieve peace and promote reconciliation. A sharp separation is drawn
between the past and the future, with the date of the signing of the agreement being the disconnecting cardinal point: the past is to be forgotten,
and, as the language employed reveals, even forgiven, to give way to a more
peaceful, common future.

The inclusion of this comprehensive pardon and amnesty provision reveals,
above all, that the issue of transitional justice was a major concern for the parties. The past was dealt with explicitly and self-consciously in the agreement,
even if the result was the expression of the plain understanding of the parties
that the past would and should be forgotten, be separated from and not determine the future. A new era was supposed to start on 7 July 1999. This "ban
on recalling"[245] in the Lomé Peace Agreement is part of a long tradition, with

---

[241] Peter Krapp, "Amnesty: Between and Ethics of Forgiveness and the Politics of Forgetting"
(2005) 6:1 *German Law Journal* 185 at 191.
[242] Leila Nadya Sadat, "Exile, Amnesty and International Law" (2006) 81 *Notre Dame L Rev* 955
at 964, n 23.
[243] Krapp, *supra* note 241 at 191.
[244] Jacques Derrida, "To Forgive: The Unforgivable and the Imprescriptible," in John D. Caputo,
Mark Dooley & Michael J Scanlon, eds., *Questioning God* (Bloomington: Indiana University
Press, 2001), 21, 23, 26.
[245] This language is borrowed from Krapp, *supra* note 241 at 187.

the first historically recorded amnesty being granted in Athens in 403 BC, the main objective of which being reconciliation.[246] Even earlier peace treaties, such as the Egyptian-Hittite Treaty of Kadesh, concluded around 1280 BC, while being silent on questions of guilt, contain an unspoken but consciously desired mutual amnesty.[247]

Any discussion of the pardon and amnesty provision of the Lomé Peace Agreement would not be complete without considering the famous disclaimer of the special representative of the UN secretary-general that was added, in handwriting, to one of the copies after the agreement had been signed.[248] The disclaimer reportedly stipulated that the amnesty and pardon in Article IX of the agreement shall not apply to the international crimes of genocide, crimes against humanity, war crimes and other serious violations of international humanitarian law. Despite the uncertain legal nature and value of this disclaimer, it reflects the growing awareness at the time that blanket amnesties for grave crimes ought not to be granted in a peace agreement and that the United Nations would not support an agreement containing such an amnesty provision. The disclaimer set an important precedent and can be seen as evidence of the United Nations' "ever more critical attitude towards the unlimited granting of amnesties in a process of national reconciliation".[249]

The Ugandan Annexure to the Agreement on Accountability and Reconciliation, concluded in February 2008 between the Ugandan government and the Lord's Resistance Army (LRA) and aiming to end the conflict ravaging

---

[246] Adriaan Lanni, "Transitional Justice in Ancient Athens: A Case Study" (2010) 32:2 *U Pa J Int'l L* 551, in particular at 566–567; Nicole Loraux argues that "c'est précisément parce qu'ils se souvenaient du passé que les Athéniens ont interdit à quiconque de le rappeler". Nicole Loraux, *La cité divisée: L'oubli dans la mémoire d'Athènes* (Paris: Payot et Rivages, 1997), 275. On the history of amnesties in peace treaties, see generally Fisch, *supra* note 23 at 35–278. Fisch concludes that tacit and at times explicit amnesties were habitual in the Greek-Hellenistic time period between 422 and 180 BC. Ibid. at 63. See also Jon Elster, *Closing the Books: Transitional Justice in Historical Perspective* (Cambridge: Cambridge University Press, 2004), 3–21; Krapp, *supra* note 241 at 187.

[247] Fisch, *supra* note 23 at 59. Fisch explains that "indirekt wird das gewollte Vergessen im ägyptischen Vertrag fassbar" (ibid. at 60).

[248] The handwritten disclaimer was added to one of the copies, but neither the United Nations nor others seem to have retained a copy of this document. See Patricia Hayner, "Negotiating Peace in Sierra Leone: Confronting the Justice Challenge" *Centre for Humanitarian Dialogue & International Centre for Transitional Justice* (December 2007), online: International Centre for Transitional Justice <http://www.ictj.org/static/Africa/SierraLeone/HaynerSL1207.eng .pdf> at n 3 [henceforth Hayner, "Negotiating Peace in Sierra Leone"].

[249] Carsten Stahn, "United Nations Peace-Building, Amnesties and Alternative Forms of Justice: A Change in Practice?" (2002) 84:845 *Int'l Rev Red Cross* 191 at 201 [henceforth Stahn, "United Nations Peace-Building"].

northern Ugandan since the mid-1980s,[250] also contains plain language with respect to international criminal law and, specifically, the ICC:

> RECALLING their [the parties'] commitment to preventing impunity and promoting redress in accordance with the Constitution and international obligations, and recalling, in this connection, the requirements of the Rome Statute of the International Criminal Court (ICC) and in particular the principle of complementarity.[251]

This reference can be explained by the need to formally address the involvement and future role of the ICC in northern Uganda, especially after the issuance of international arrest warrants against five leaders of the LRA. While the parties recall Uganda's obligations under the Rome Statute, the principle of complementarity, according to which the ICC only complements national criminal justice systems,[252] is also highlighted and hints at the parties' understanding that the exercise of jurisdiction by the ICC over crimes committed in northern Uganda might be challenged. This is particularly remarkable since it was the Ugandan government, in December 2003, that triggered ICC jurisdiction over the crimes allegedly committed by the LRA by referring the situation in the northern part of the country to the ICC prosecutor based on Article 14 of the Rome Statute.[253]

In northern Uganda, the not only potential but very real involvement of the ICC thus made the parties put the question of justice and individual accountability high on the agenda in the negotiations. It can be argued that the readiness of the LRA and the Ugandan government to agree that "[a] special division of the High Court of Uganda shall be established to try individuals who are alleged to have committed serious crimes during

---

[250] For the origins of the conflict, see generally Tim Allen, *Trial Justice, the International Criminal Court and the Lord's Resistance Army* (London: International African Institute, 2006).

[251] *Annexure to the Agreement on Accountability and Reconciliation*, 19 February 2008 (Uganda), online: UN Peacemaker <http://peacemaker.un.org/sites/peacemaker.un.org/files/UG_080219_Annexure%20to%20the%20Agreement%20on%20Accountability%20and%20Reconciliation.pdf>, preamble.

[252] According to article 17(1)(a) of the Rome Statute, one of the key provisions relating to complementarity, a case is inadmissible when "the case is being investigated or prosecuted by a State which has jurisdiction over it, unless the State is unwilling or genuinely unable to carry out the investigation or prosecution". *Rome Statute of the International Criminal Court*, 17 July 1998, 2187 UNTS 90, UN Doc. A/CONF.183/9 (entered into force 1 July 2002), art 17 [henceforth *Rome Statute*].

[253] International Criminal Court, "Press Release: President of Uganda Refers Situation Concerning the Lord's Resistance Army (LRA) to the ICC" (29 January 2004), online: International Criminal Court <http://www.icc-cpi.int/en_menus/icc/press%20and%20media/press%20releases/2004/Pages/president%20of%20uganda%20refers%20situation%20concerning%20the%20lord_s%20resistance%20army%20_lra_%20to%20the%20icc.aspx>.

the conflict"²⁵⁴ and to even include fairly detailed provisions on the investigations and prosecutions to be carried out²⁵⁵ was directly related to this threatening shadow cast by the ICC. The text of the Annexure suggests that the parties responded to this shadow and attempted to attenuate it. Moreover, with respect to national procedures, the Annexure is also noteworthy for containing provisions on traditional justice,²⁵⁶ which reflects the different opinions as to the role and place of rituals like *mato oput* against the backdrop of prosecutorial-type trials. Although, like other agreements dealing with transitional justice, the Annexure contains references to international criminal law, the question as to whether justice ought to be delivered through international or national institutions is therefore not clearly resolved.

With respect to the Israeli-Palestinian context, it is, again, worth noting that the agreements do not contain any comprehensive mechanism to address transitional justice issues. Only some provisions, for instance, on prisoner release and on the protection of Palestinian informers "who were in contact with the Israeli authorities",²⁵⁷ address some immediate concerns and are intended to contribute to confidence building between the parties.

In conclusion, international law can have a prominent place in peace agreement provisions dealing with crimes perpetrated during the conflict and is introduced into these agreements mostly via international criminal law, albeit in very different ways. The number of peace agreements containing provisions on transitional justice and the agreements analysed in more detail above suggest an increasingly shared understanding among negotiators and mediators that crimes committed during internal armed conflicts are to be addressed in peace negotiations and that international law has a role to play in this regard. A generalized mode of relying on international law does, however, not exist. What may appear as a static body of law for the negotiating parties and be represented by distant institutions, like the ICC, is in practice referred to and utilized very differently and even treated quite creatively.

2.3.3. *Refugees and Internally Displaced Persons – Returning to "Normality"*

The return of refugees and internally displaced persons is often a highly controversial point of peace negotiations, especially when disputes over land

---

²⁵⁴ *Annexure to the Agreement on Accountability and Reconciliation, supra* note 249, art 7.
²⁵⁵ Ibid., art. 10–15.
²⁵⁶ Ibid., arts 19–22. The Annexure also addresses the question of reparations. Ibid., arts 16–18.
²⁵⁷ *Agreement on the Gaza Strip and the Jericho Area (Cairo Agreement)*, 4 May 1994, UN Doc. A/49/180, art XX. For a more detailed analysis, see Bell, *Human Rights and Peace Agreements, supra* note 71 at 280–283.

and resources are among the causes of an internal armed conflict. On the one hand, a hasty return of a great number of refugees and displaced persons may add to an already delicate situation and reawaken local disputes over land, thus endangering a fragile peace agreement.[258] In the long term, on the other hand, return is a sign and part of the resolution of an armed conflict: "return is a signifier of 'normalisation' and a test of the capacity of political and legal institutions to deliver to communities viable alternatives to violent conflict".[259] The negotiating parties and mediators must balance these important risks and objectives, and peace agreements often contain quite nuanced language with respect to refugees and displaced persons. Similar to the question as to how to deal with crimes committed during the conflict, the domestic legal framework is in many situations ill prepared to deal with massive displacement, which is why some peace agreements have recourse to international provisions.

International law offers some guidance on the return and non-return (protection against non-refoulement) of refugees via the Refugee Convention,[260] as well as through general human rights provisions relating to the freedom of movement. Article 12 of the ICCPR provides specifically that "everyone ... shall ... have the right to liberty of movement and freedom to choose his residence" and that "no one shall be arbitrarily deprived of the right to enter his own country".[261] One is hard-pressed, however, to find more specific stipulations, such as obligations for states to facilitate the return of refugees and displaced persons following armed conflict. Several initiatives have been made to fill at least some of the existing normative gaps, in particular with respect to internally displaced persons. The Guiding Principles on Internal Displacement, developed by the UN secretary-general's special representative on internally displaced persons in the 1990s, provide a framework that aims to guide states in their treatment of internally displaced persons, among others by setting forth guarantees for safe return. Principle 28, for instance, notes that "competent authorities have the primary duty and responsibility to establish conditions ... which allow internally displaced persons to return

---

[258] International Council on Human Rights Policy, *supra* note 132 at 59.

[259] Ibid.

[260] *Convention Relating to the Status of Refugees*, 28 July 1951, 189 UNTS 137 (entered into force 22 April 1954), in particular arts 1 and 33. The Palestinian refugees, insofar as they are assisted by the United Nations Relief and Works Agency, form a specific category and are not protected under the Refugee Convention. On the specific status of the Palestinian refugees, see Lex Takkenberg, *The Status of Palestinian Refugees in International Law* (Oxford: Oxford University Press, 1998).

[261] *International Covenant on Civil and Political Rights*, 19 December 1966, 999 UNTS 171 (entered into force 23 March 1976), arts 12.1, 12.4 [henceforth *ICCPR*].

voluntarily".[262] Moreover, the reintegration of returned or resettled internally displaced persons must be facilitated.[263] While, generally speaking, such standards are certainly valuable, it seems that they have not been overly inspiring for negotiations on the possible return of refugees and internally displaced persons.

It is, as always, useful to read and assess peace agreements and their respective provisions, in this case on the return of refugees and displaced persons, in their proper context. By way of example, the manner and time frame of the return of refugees and displaced persons cannot easily be anticipated or regulated in the immediate aftermath of an internal armed conflict. Specifically negotiated provisions might have little impact or might, in reality, not be necessary anymore. Refugees may return prior to the conclusion of a peace agreement, as it was, for instance, the case in Mozambique.[264] Moreover, the return of refugees and concrete timetables might actually be a more important concern of neighbouring states,[265] the governments of which possibly trying to raise this issue in the negotiations and convincing the parties to agree on an "ordered" return. The common assumption that peace depends on the return of refugees and displaced persons and that peace agreements should, as a result, address this issue, has also been criticized. As Howard Adelman has concluded, "Refugee repatriation is neither a necessary nor a causal condition of peace.... Peace may be in process without refugee repatriation, and refugee repatriation need not even be a manifestation of peace".[266] Yet the importance of addressing the issue of refugees and displaced persons can be related to the type of armed conflict.[267] In the case of ethnic conflict, people are frequently displaced intentionally, as in Bosnia or Rwanda, and not just as a by-product of violent conflict over power, as in Angola or Mozambique.[268] As a result, it can be hypothesized that provisions dealing with the return of

---

[262] Commission on Human Rights, *Report of the Representative of the Secretary-General, Mr. Francis Deng, submitted pursuant to Commission resolution 1997/39. Addendum: Guiding Principles on Internal Displacement*, UN Doc. E/CN.4/1998/53/Add.2 (1998), principle 28.

[263] Ibid.

[264] International Council on Human Rights Policy, *supra* note 132 at 69.

[265] Howard Adelman, "Refugee Repatriation," in Stephen John Stedman, Donald Rothchild & Elizabeth M. Cousens, eds., *Ending Civil Wars: The Implementation of Peace Agreements* (Boulder, CO: Lynne Rienner, 2002), 273, 292–293.

[266] Ibid., 273. Another study also found "little correlation between whether provision for repatriation is made in the peace agreement and whether it happens in practice". International Council on Human Rights Policy, *supra* note 132 at 69.

[267] Adelman, *supra* note 265 at 283–289. Adelman also points to the type of peace, i.e. negative or positive, intended by the agreement. Ibid. at 289–290.

[268] Ibid., 285.

refugees and displaced persons will be found more regularly and ought to play a more prominent role in peace agreements intending to end ethnic conflicts.

These caveats might lead to the assumption that few peace agreements deal with the return of refugees and displaced persons, and that even fewer frame such a return in rights language or base it on international legal norms. The databases show, in fact, that a significant number of peace agreements do: 44 out of the more than 640 peace agreements listed in the Transitional Justice Institute's Peace Agreements Database explicitly refer to refugees;[269] in the UN database, the agreements addressing refugees total 93, out of 245 intrastate agreements.

It seems that few substantive agreements attempt to deal with the question of refugees and displaced persons – and their return – comprehensively. The Lomé Peace Agreement shows that the return of refugees and displaced persons is, as a rather technical matter, only agreed to in principle, with the details to be discussed at a later stage. In this document, the parties agreed to "design and implement a plan for voluntary repatriation and reintegration of Sierra Leonean refugees and internally displaced persons, including non-combatants, in conformity with international conventions, norms and practices".[270] While the Lomé Peace Agreement contains only this rather vague reference and does not elaborate further on either the kind of "international conventions, norms and practices" or their implementation in the Sierra Leonean context, other agreements provide for a specific right to return to the country. The language of the Dayton Peace Agreement, for instance, goes beyond a general right to return by providing that "all refugees and displaced persons have the right freely to return to their homes of origin".[271] The agreement is also notable for containing provisions for property restitution – and compensation if restitution is not possible – and for establishing a Commission for Refugees and Displaced Persons.[272]

As for the Mozambique 1992 General Peace Agreement, it provides for a "right to choose to reside anywhere in the national territory and to leave or return to the country" but specifies that refugees and displaced persons should "preferably" return to their "original places of residence".[273] While the parties agreed to involve UN agencies and other organizations, they deferred the

---

[269] See <http://www.peaceagreements.ulster.ac.uk/glossary.html>.

[270] *Lomé Peace Agreement, supra* note 40, art XXII.

[271] *Dayton Peace Agreement, supra* note 205, Annex 7, art I.1.

[272] However, no funds were made available for compensation. International Council on Human Rights Policy, *supra* note 132 at 69.

[273] *General Peace Agreement for Mozambique, supra* note 55, Protocol III, arts III–IV. See also International Council on Human Rights Policy, *supra* note 132 at 65.

more detailed organization of assistance to refugees and displaced persons to a later stage.

The Darfur Peace Agreement contains not only explicit rights language regarding refugees and internally displaced persons but also direct references to international law:

> Displaced and war-affected persons will enjoy the same human rights and fundamental freedoms as any citizen under the law of the Sudan. In particular, the relevant authorities have a responsibility to ensure that such persons enjoy freedom of movement and of choice of residence, including the right to return and to reestablish themselves at their places of origin or habitual residence. The treatment of displaced and war-affected persons in and from Darfur will conform to international humanitarian law, human rights law and guiding principles, as set out in the Declaration of Principles.[274]

The same agreement also provides that "displaced persons have the right to restitution of their property, whether they choose to return to their places of origin or not, or to be compensated adequately for the loss of their property, in accordance with international principles".[275] Moreover, it contains some interesting language with respect to the implementation, through a Compensation Commission, of the restitution of property or compensation:

> Taking note of … the customary practices of tribal restitution in Darfur, the Commission shall work out principles for appropriate restitution or other compensation. In doing so, the Commission shall take into account, among other considerations: (a) International principles and practices, national law and customary law and practices.[276]

This acknowledgement in the text of a peace agreement of the multiple relevant normative orders, including customary practices, is quite remarkable, even if it remains unclear how exactly the Commission is to elaborate appropriate and workable "principles".

In sum, international law is being referred to in the field of refugees and displaced persons in some peace agreements. The impact of these references appears to be necessarily limited, since, as it has been pointed out above, the return of refugees and displaced persons is frequently not under the direct control or discretion of the negotiating parties. Important principles emanating from international law, such as freedom of movement or the right to restitution or compensation, do nevertheless find their way into agreements and

---

[274] *Darfur Peace Agreement, supra* note 215, art 21 at paras 176–177.
[275] Ibid., art 21 at para 194.
[276] Ibid., art 21 at para 205.

can be expected to shape the post-conflict society and the way the return of refugees and displaced persons is handled by the respective authorities.

2.3.4. *Promoting and Protecting the Rights of Women – (En)Gendering Peace*

Women have typically been entirely absent from peace negotiations. They rarely occupy positions of political leadership and are even more rarely part of the army or armed groups. Since peace negotiations are usually conducted between representatives of the belligerent parties, peacemaking, like war making, has been an almost exclusively male-dominated field. Even if women may contribute considerably to an armed conflict, either as combatants themselves or as supporters to the fighting forces, or actively promote and lobby for peace, common perceptions of women as passive victims of the conflict usually keep them away from the negotiating table.[277] Moreover, gender relations are infrequently considered as lying at the heart of an armed conflict.[278]

The situation has been changing since the 1990s as a result of the increasing awareness that women are not only affected intensely, and in specific ways, by armed conflicts but that they can and ought to play a more active role in the process of conflict resolution. Corresponding to this awareness, gender-related human rights considerations relevant to armed conflicts and their resolution, such as the fundamental principle of equality and the right to participate in political decision making as well as responses to gender-based violence, have started to be claimed and applied more thoroughly. With a view to ensuring

[277] Anne Itto, "Guests at the Table? The Role of Women in Peace Processes" (2006) 18 *Accord* 56, online: Conciliation Resources <http://www.c-r.org/our-work/accord/sudan/women.php> at 56–58. Itto also provides several concrete examples of the way in which women contributed to the armed conflict in Sudan as well as its resolution. A quite extraordinary example of the possible peacemaking role of women is related by Antonia Potter: "In the Solomon Islands and Papua New Guinea, mediators called on women to disarm their men physically, which many of them did, a feat that armed peacekeepers might not have been able to achieve in a way that preserved dignity and allowed the broader process to continue". Antonia Potter, "Gender Sensitivity: Nicety or Necessity in Peace-Process Management?" (2008), online: Oslo forum <http://www.osloforum.org/sites/default/files/Antonia%20Potter%20Gender%20sensitivity%20 WEB.pdf> at 64. Similar dynamics can be discerned in the field of transitional justice, where women have typically been excluded from processes establishing such mechanisms. For an overview of feminist critiques of transitional justice processes, see Christine Bell & Catherine O'Rourke, "Does Feminism Need a Theory of Transitional Justice? An Introductory Essay" (2007) 1 *International Journal of Transitional Justice* 23.

[278] United Nations Division for the Advancement of Women, *Peace Agreements as a Means for Promoting Gender Equality and Ensuring the Participation of Women*, paper prepared by Christine Chinkin, UN Doc. EGM/PEACE/2003/BP.1 (31 October 2003), online: United Nations <http://www.un.org/womenwatch/daw/egm/peace2003/reports/BPChinkin.PDF> at 13.

the future inclusion of women in the domestic political sphere, specific references to women in peace agreements are especially important in the context of agreements having quasi-constitutional or constitutional quality.[279]

Although several international instruments could provide guidance on women and gender issues, they are rarely referred to explicitly in peace agreements. However, the general influence of equality provisions contained in human rights law instruments, such as the ICCPR, the ICESCR and the Convention on the Elimination of all Forms of Discrimination against Women (CEDAW),[280] is sometimes noticeable. In the ICCPR, every state party agrees to "respect and to ensure to all individuals within its territory and subject to its jurisdiction the rights recognized in the present Covenant, without distinction of any kind, such as … sex"[281] and to "undertake to ensure the equal right of men and women to the enjoyment of all civil and political rights".[282] With respect to political participation, CEDAW specifies that the

> States Parties shall take all appropriate measures to eliminate discrimination against women in the political and public life of the country and, in particular, shall ensure to women, on equal terms with men, the right:
>
> (a) To vote in all elections and public referenda and to be eligible for election to all publicly elected bodies;
> (b) To participate in the formulation of government policy and the implementation thereof.[283]

These instruments thus set out general principles and rights with respect to political participation of women without particularizing their participation or applying it to the context of peace negotiations. The most relevant document concerning women and their role in societies emerging from violent conflict consists therefore in UN Security Council Resolution 1325 (2000). In this resolution, the Security Council specifically highlighted the "important role of women in the prevention and resolution of conflicts and in peace-building"

---

[279] Christine Bell & Catherine O'Rourke, "Peace Agreements or Pieces of Paper? The Impact of UNSC Resolution 1325 on Peace Processes and their Agreements" (2010) 59 *ICLQ* 941 at 948 [henceforth Bell & O'Rourke, "Peace Agreements or Pieces of Paper?"].

[280] For a list of peace agreements containing references to CEDAW, see ibid. at n 57.

[281] ICCPR, *supra* note 261, art 2.

[282] Ibid., art 3.

[283] *Convention on the Elimination of All Forms of Discrimination against Women*, 18 December 1979, 1249 UNTS 13 (entered into force 3 September 1981), art 7. For an overview of peace agreements addressing the respective provisions of CEDAW, see Miriam J. Anderson, "Gender and Peacemaking: Women's Rights in Contemporary Peace Agreements," in Susan Allen Nan, Zachariah Cherian Mampilly & Andrea Bartoli, eds., *Peacemaking: From Practice to Theory*, vol. 1 (Santa Barbara, CA: Praeger, 2012), 344, 372–375.

and called, inter alia, for a broader participation of women in peace processes. The Security Council also

> *Urges* Member States to ensure increased representation of women at all decision-making levels in national, regional and international institutions and mechanisms for the prevention, management, and resolution of conflict;
>
> . . .
>
> *Calls on* all actors involved, when negotiating and implementing peace agreements, to adopt a gender perspective, including, inter alia:
>
> (a) The special needs of women and girls during repatriation and resettlement and for rehabilitation, reintegration and post-conflict reconstruction;
> (b) Measures that support local women's peace initiatives and indigenous processes for conflict resolution, and that involve women in all of the implementation mechanisms of the peace agreements;
> (c) Measures that ensure the protection of and respect for human rights of women and girls, particularly as they relate to the constitution, the electoral system, the police and the judiciary.[284]

Thanks to these fairly detailed provisions proclaimed by the Security Council in a unanimously adopted resolution, peace agreements, especially those in which UN representatives are involved as mediators, can be expected to be more gender sensitive.

Regarding the absolute numbers, 59 peace agreements, out of the 295 intra-state agreements included in the UN database, specifically address the situation and role of women; the Transitional Justice Institute's Peace Agreements Database lists 47, out of more than 640 agreements. These agreements include the Darfur Peace Agreement, the Lomé Peace Agreement and the Sudanese Comprehensive Peace Agreement.[285] While modest, the impact of Resolution 1325 is nevertheless discernible. A study showed that the percentage of peace agreements containing a reference to women rose markedly

---

[284] UN SCOR, 55th Year, 4213rd Mtg, UN Doc. S/RES/1325 (2000), paras 1, 8 [SC Res 1325]. Related subsequent Security Council resolutions are SC Res 1820, 1888, 1889 and 1960.

[285] This section will focus on these agreements. For a good study of the inclusion of women's rights and gender in peace agreements, which analyses the 1996 Mindanao, the 1997 Chittagong Hills Tract, the 1999 East Timor, the 2001 Bougainville, the 2005 Aceh and the 2006 Nepal agreements, see Cate Buchanan et al., "From Clause to Effect: Including Women's Rights and Gender in Peace Agreements" (Centre for Humanitarian Dialogue, 2012), online: HD Centre <http://www.hdcentre.org/uploads/tx_news/24ClausereportwebFINAL.pdf>.

subsequent to the adoption of this resolution.[286] A few agreements, such as the 2008 Agreement on a Permanent Ceasefire between the Government of Uganda and the LRA,[287] also mention it specifically, without necessarily dealing in substance with the issues addressed by the Security Council.

In the Darfur Peace Agreement, women and gender issues are referred to numerous times throughout the text. The parties, among other things, guarantee equality of women and men,[288] highlight the various special concerns and needs of women, since the war has had a "particularly deleterious impact on women",[289] and recognize the "need for special measures to ensure women's equal and effective participation in decision-making at all levels".[290] "Special consideration" is also given to the "active and visible participation by women" in the Darfur-Darfur Dialogue and Consultation, a reconciliation mechanism to be composed of all stakeholders from Darfur.[291] With respect to representation of Darfurians in the executive, the government of Sudan expressly commits itself to making special efforts "to ensure that women are represented" in the nominations to be made.[292] The agreement thus applies in its substance several gender-related provisions contained in human rights instruments and Security Council Resolution 1325 and also refers specifically to the ICCPR and ICESCR, though not to CEDAW, in this regard.[293]

Other peace agreements are less outspoken on the question of political participation and representation but contain more general language with respect to the recognition of women's needs and their role in the post-conflict period. The Lomé Peace Agreement, much shorter than the Darfur Peace Agreement, contains a single and rather elusive provision on women:

> Given that women have been particularly victimized during the war, special attention shall be accorded to their needs and potentials in formulating and implementing national rehabilitation, reconstruction and development programmes, to enable them to play a central role in the moral, social and physical reconstruction of Sierra Leone.[294]

[286] Bell & O'Rourke, "Peace Agreements or Pieces of Paper?," *supra* note 279 at 955–956.

[287] *Agreement on a Permanent Ceasefire*, 23 February 2008 (Uganda), online: UN Peacemaker <http://peacemaker.un.org/sites/peacemaker.un.org/files/UG_080223_Agreement%20on%20a%20Permanent%20Ceasefire.pdf>, art 6.1.

[288] *Darfur Peace Agreement*, *supra* note 215, art 3 at para 28(a).

[289] Ibid., art 17 at para 109.

[290] Ibid., art 1 at para 15.

[291] Ibid., art 31 at para 461(e).

[292] Ibid., art 8 at para 69(d).

[293] Ibid., art 3 at para 28(a).

[294] *Lomé Peace Agreement*, *supra* note 40, art XXVIII.2.

In contrast to a rights-based approach rooted in international human rights law, this agreement therefore emphasizes the "needs and potentials" of women and depicts them primarily as victims of the conflict.

In the otherwise extensive Sudanese Comprehensive Peace Agreement, only some women- and gender-related concerns materialize; detailing power and wealth sharing along regional interests was clearly deemed more important during the negotiations than addressing other dimensions, such as gender.[295] The few provisions, however, draw directly on international human rights law and its principles. In the 2004 Protocol on Power Sharing, which was reproduced as chapter 2 of the Comprehensive Peace Agreement, the parties commit to ensuring the equal rights of men and women and, in this context, specifically refer to the ICCPR and the ICESCR.[296] In the 2002 Machakos Protocol, reproduced as chapter 1, the parties agree to work together to "establish a democratic system of governance taking into account ... gender equality",[297] without identifying any specific measures. With similar generality, the Agreement on Permanent Ceasefire and Security Arrangements Implementation Modalities, annexed to the Comprehensive Peace Agreement, provides for the Demobilization, Disarmament, Re-Integration and Reconciliation Programme to be "gender sensitive".[298]

While gender scholarship and advocacy relating to armed conflicts has become hugely identified with accountability for and prevention of sexual and gender-based violence against women and girls,[299] very few peace agreements

---

[295] Itto, *supra* note 277 at 58.

[296] *The Protocol between the Government of the Sudan (GOS) and the Sudan People's Liberation Movement (SPLM) on Power Sharing*, 26 May 2004, art 1.6.2.16; reproduced as chapter 2 (Power Sharing) of the *Comprehensive Peace Agreement, supra* note 217.

[297] *Comprehensive Peace Agreement, supra* note 217, Chapter 1: The Machakos Protocol, Part A: Agreed Principles, 1.5.1. The original agreement, the *Machakos Protocol* (20 July 2002), lists this provision as article 1.6. of part A (Agreed Principles).

[298] Ibid., Annexure 1, art 24.8.

[299] Institutional responses within the United Nations have, for instance, led to the establishment of the Office of the Special Representative of the Secretary-General on Sexual Violence in Conflict (see S/RES/1888 (2009) at para 4) and of the network "UN Action", which unites the work of 13 UN entities (for more information, see Stop Rape Now <http://www.stoprapenow .org/about/>). It is worth mentioning that sexual and gender-based violence against men and boys has only recently achieved some attention. For a critique of responses by the United Nations, see Sandesh Sivakumaran, "Lost in Translation: UN Responses to Sexual Violence against Men and Boys in Situations of Armed Conflict" (2010) 92:877 *IRRC* 259. One of the reasons, as Rosemary Grey and Laura J. Shepherd have pointed out, may be that "dominant representations of sexual violence in war in the relevant scholarly literature tend to envision the body of the victim of such violence as female in form". Rosemary Grey & Laura J. Shepherd, "'Stop Rape Now?': Masculinity, Responsibility, and Conflict-related Sexual Violence" (2012) 16:1 *Men and Masculinities* 115 at 129.

address this issue, even in the context of conflicts characterized by widespread sexual and gender-based violence.[300] The Security Council's call "on all parties to armed conflict to take special measures to protect women and girls from gender-based violence, particularly rape and other forms of sexual abuse, and all other forms of violence in situations of armed conflict"[301] and its emphasis of the responsibility of states to prosecute those responsible for gender-based crimes[302] have not been echoed in many peace agreements. In the Darfur Peace Agreement, the government of Sudan commits, at least, to investigating "all crimes, including those committed against women and children".[303] The Ugandan Annexure to the Agreement on Accountability and Reconciliation is among the few agreements including specific language on gender-based violence.[304] In this agreement, the parties also agreed that investigations shall "give particular attention to crimes and violations against women and children committed during the conflict".[305]

In sum, the discourse on women in peace agreements has been changing, albeit slowly. As Bell and O'Rourke concluded in 2010, "There is little evidence of systematic inclusion of women in peace agreement texts, or systematic treatment of issues across peace agreements within conflicts".[306] Moreover, most references to women appear to be rather unsubstantial and are infrequently derived from normative principles established by international law.

An interesting quantitative analysis that concerns the time period addressed by references to women in peace agreements might shed some light on the current trends. Miriam J. Anderson concludes that only few references are linked to conflict-related issues, such as gender-based violence (7 out of the 135 agreements that were studied between 1989 and 2005), and to the period of transition, such as gender quota in transitional institutions (9 agreements); a greater number of agreements contain references aiming to affect the status of women in the long term (28 agreements), such as the establishment of specific

---

[300] For an overview, see UNIFEM, "Women's Participation in Peace Negotiations: Connections between Presence and Influence" (August 2010), online: UN Women <http://www.unwomen.org/wp-content/uploads/2012/10/03A-Women-Peace-Neg.pdf> at 20. See also Bell & O'Rourke, "Peace Agreements or Pieces of Paper?," *supra* note 275 at 965, n 73.

[301] SC Res 1325, *supra* note 284 at para 10.

[302] Ibid., at para 11.

[303] *Darfur Peace Agreement, supra* note 215, art 26 at para 277.

[304] *Annexure to the Agreement on Accountability and Reconciliation, supra* note 251, e.g. art 4(f).

[305] Ibid., at para 13(c).

[306] Bell & O'Rourke, "Peace Agreements or Pieces of Paper?," *supra* note 279 at 968. The 2010 UNIFEM report concluded similarly that "gender-blind peace agreements are still the norm, not the exception". UNIFEM, *supra* note 300 at 2. Christine Chinkin also highlights the challenges of gender mainstreaming in the negotiation of peace agreements in her paper prepared for the United Nations Division for the Advancement of Women, *supra* note 278 at 8.

institutions dealing with women's issues.[307] These numbers suggest that when references to women find their way into peace agreements, the texts tend to deal with underlying structural issues in a forward-looking, often aspirational way, notably by emphasizing the equality of women and men. Such provisions reflect the important opportunities that peace negotiations and agreements represent: an agreement may not only symbolize a concerted attempt to end an armed conflict but may also aspire to solve structural problems and generate fundamental changes in a post-conflict society.

2.4. DISCOURSE IN THE PROCESS

The act of referring to, or being silent on, international legal norms in the text of a peace agreement is always preceded by a process. Without rejecting the importance of formal international law that is mainly tied to the state and the community of states, I argue that an agreement-focused analysis cannot portray the complete normative picture. The process of negotiating what will constitute the text of an agreement can less easily be understood in terms of a conclusive, act- and outcome-centred "what", but rather in terms of an actor-centered "who" and "how".

The discourses transpiring during peace negotiations will therefore be analysed across the boundaries of specific conflicts and peace processes and along the three main groups of actors involved in peace negotiations, namely, the negotiators, mediators and influential external actors. Some of these actors do not define their normative allegiance as being primarily connected to state law, or existing international legal norms, although they may allude to and interact with formal norms projected by the respective state or the community of states. It is in this stage that the full meaning of the hypothesis that discourse is not only illustrative but constitutive of the normative framework materializes most decisively. Without any claim to exhaustiveness or socio-scientific measurability, it can be asserted that these examples of the respective discourses on legal norms reveal broader normative trends: it is indeed through their discourse in the process that the various actors introduce, build on and develop or reject and eliminate normative propositions. This interaction constructs a discursive and normative framework and maps out zones of possible agreement.

2.4.1. *The Negotiators' Strategic References to International Legal Norms*

Those actors who are directly involved in the negotiations rarely seem to be preoccupied with international law. The political and military leaders, who

[307] Anderson, *supra* note 283 at 345–348.

typically sit at the negotiating table, want to have "free hands" in the resolution of what is usually perceived as a purely political problem. If legal norms, whether national or international, are typically considered a constraint, they may nevertheless be referred to by the negotiators, especially when considered more constraining and thus disadvantageous for the other party. In this sense, legal norms are used primarily for strategic purposes, which corresponds to an instrumentalism[308] captured by the concept of "lawfare"[309] and also by David Kennedy's argument that the law of armed conflict has become a "strategic legal vernacular".[310]

In northern Uganda, for instance, international legal norms and proceedings, and their strategic use, have been considered a major stumbling block for the peace process. On the one hand, in particular since the issuance

---

[308] Nathaniel Berman speaks of a "strategic instrumentalization" of the distinction of the spheres of war and not-war. Nathaniel Berman, "Privileging Combat? Contemporary Conflict and the Legal Construction of War" (2004) 43:1 *Colum J Transnat'l L* 1 at 7.

[309] I am referring to the concept without an inherently pejorative connotation that associates lawfare with the strategic, irresponsible and even unfair use of law, in particular by opponents to a presumably legitimate government. For different meanings and uses of the concept, see Wouter G. Werner, "The Curious Career of Lawfare" (2010) 43:1&2 *Case W Res J Int'l L* 61. David Kennedy describes the word as it has been coined by the American military: "law as a weapon, law as a tactical ally, law as a strategic asset, an instrument of war". David Kennedy, "Lawfare and Warfare," in James Crawford & Martti Koskenniemi, eds., *The Cambridge Companion to International Law* (Cambridge: Cambridge University Press, 2012), 158, 160 [henceforth Kennedy, "Lawfare and Warfare"]. For many commentators, lawfare is different from the ordinary application of international law: according to Paul R. Williams, for instance, "'lawfare' is conducted when a party uses or misuses law or legal mechanisms with the intent of securing a political or military advantage over the opposing party. Importantly, the ordinary application of international law and the law of armed conflict – international humanitarian law – does not constitute 'lawfare'" (Williams, *supra* note 153 at 145). Williams also cites several examples of what he considers lawfare – that may be waged before, during or after an armed conflict – including the proceedings of Serbia against Kosovo in the International Court of Justice and attempts of the Sudanese government to include provisions on demobilization and demilitarization, presented as standard legal language to the armed opposition groups from Darfur, in a ceasefire agreement (ibid., 149–151). For a sharp criticism of the currently predominant use of the term lawfare, which "seems to be little more than a rhetorical gambit to attack challenges to the legality of the behavior of the military forces of Israel or the US", see William A. Schabas, "Gaza, Goldstone, and Lawfare" (2010) 43:1&2 *Case W Res J Int'l L* 307 at 310. For the more general tendency that Gerry Simpson has called "juridified diplomacy" and that consists in the "translation of political conflict into legal doctrine, and occasionally, the resolution of these conflicts in legal institutions", in particular through war crimes trials, see Gerry Simpson, *Law, War and Crimes: War Crimes Trials and the Reinvention of International Law* (Cambridge: Polity Press, 2007), 132.

[310] David Kennedy, *Of War and Law* (Princeton, NJ: Princeton University Press, 2006), 119. Drawing on David Kennedy, it can also be argued that a purely strategic use of legal norms may contribute to weakening the integrity of the respective legal norms and their normative force (ibid., 135).

of arrest warrants against the leaders of the LRA by the ICC, international criminal proceedings have been portrayed as restraining and used by outsiders to influence the peace process, with the warrants having been characterized as "a very obnoxious situation" by LRA negotiators.[311] On the other hand, the avenue of international criminal proceedings has been used by the Ugandan government as a strategic tool. In 2007, when the LRA leaders had already made a withdrawal of the warrants a precondition for engaging in a peace process, President Museveni stated that "if [the LRA leaders] go through the peace process then we can use alternative justice, traditional justice, which is a bit of a soft landing for them. But if they persist and stay in exile then they will end up in The Hague for their crimes".[312] It should be highlighted that the primary negotiating parties have not contested or discussed in any way substantive provisions of international criminal law nor its general validity but rather the initiation of particular proceedings, at a given time, against the LRA leaders.

In the situation of Darfur, the involvement of the ICC has not only been criticized with respect to the possible correlation between the timing of the issuance of arrest warrants and the peace process; it was the institution itself and its underlying legal order that came under fire. The ICC indictments against senior members of the Sudanese government have been depicted as a Western conspiracy and direct impediment to peace in the region, notably by the indicted Sudanese President Omar al-Bashir himself.[313] To explain his rejection of ICC jurisdiction, and the ICC as an authoritative institution altogether, Al-Bashir reportedly stated, "We have refused to kneel to colonialism, that is why Sudan has been targeted".[314] While "peace first, justice later" became a prevalent maxim in Uganda, international criminal law, brought in

---

[311] Henry Mukasa, "Kony to Meet his Peace Team," *New Vision* (21 August 2008), online: New Vision <http://www.newvision.co.ug/PA/8/13/645737>. See also Will Ross, "Ugandans Ask ICC to Spare Rebels," *BBC News* (16 March 2005), online: BBC <http://news.bbc.co.uk/2/hi/africa/4352901.stm>.

[312] "Uganda's President Hopes Rebels Choose 'Soft Landing'," *Reuters* (4 June 2007), online: Reuters <http://www.reuters.com/articles/latestCrisis/idUSL04425927>.

[313] See e.g. "ICC Indictment Could Ruin North-South Sudan Peace – UN," *Sudan Tribune* (6 November 2008) online: Sudan Tribune <http://www.sudantribune.com/spip.php?article29167>; Nick Grono & David Mozersky, "Sudan and the ICC: A Question of Accountability" (31 January 2007), online: International Crisis Group <http://www.crisis-group.org/en/regions/africa/horn-of-africa/sudan/op-eds/sudan-and-the-icc-a-question-of-accountability.aspx>. See also "Bashir Calls ICC Arrest Warrant a 'Conspiracy'," *The Telegraph* (5 March 2009), online: Telegraph <http://www.telegraph.co.uk/news/worldnews/africaandindianocean/sudan/4942470/Sudan-President-Omar-al-Bashir-calls-ICC-arrest-warrant-a-conspiracy.html>.

[314] "Bashir Calls ICC Arrest Warrant a 'Conspiracy'," *supra* note 313.

through ICC proceedings, was depicted quite straightforwardly as an obstacle to peace in the case of Darfur.

In Darfur, international law has also been referred to by nonstate actors to justify participation in peace negotiations. In 2010, for instance, the government of Sudan, arguing that a ceasefire agreement had to be signed first, did not allow Khalil Ibrahim, the leader of one of the main rebel movements (Justice and Equality Movement), to return from Libya to Darfur, as requested by the mediator. A spokesperson of this movement dismissed this line of reasoning and argued that "international law grants [us] this right as rebel group participating in a peace process".[315]

The question of rights anchored in international law surfaced recurrently at the Israel-Palestinian Permanent Status Negotiations, with the Palestinian negotiators typically giving more emphasis to rights than the Israeli side. By way of example, during a rather technical discussion on security issues and control over the Palestinian electromagnetic sphere in September 2000, the Israeli discourse, as transcribed by the PLO Negotiation Support Unit, implied a more practical, needs-based approach: "whatever needs you may have in it, we shall do our best to accommodate [them] – before signing the agreement".[316] The discourse of the Palestinian negotiator's response reflects a more principled approach: "you use a phrase which I don't like – that you'll take care of my commercial needs. I'm talking about my rights. Give me your security concerns, and let's discuss it.... we will accommodate Israeli needs, not the other way around".[317] The Israeli-Palestinian context thus illustrates that international law, and more specifically international human rights law, is typically relied on and referred to by the weaker negotiating party. "International legality" has even been described as the Palestinians' "most valuable currency".[318] It is interesting to note that claiming violations of international law is part of the bargaining and does not necessarily purport to an unconditional relief of such violations. While Palestinian negotiators, for instance, have frequently denounced Israeli settlements in the West Bank as "illegal", they also signalled that a solution consisting of a partial maintenance of the status quo

---

[315] "JEM Rebels Head to Doha for Talks on Darfur Peace Process," *Sudan Tribune* (12 November 2010), online: Sudan Tribune <http://www.sudantribune.com/spip.php?article36906>.

[316] As cited in Omar Dajani, "'No Security without Law': Prospects for Implementing a Rights-Based Approach in Palestinian-Israeli Security Negotiations," in Susan M. Akram et al., eds., *International Law and the Israeli-Palestinian Conflict* (New York: Routledge, 2011), 184, 194.

[317] As cited in ibid.

[318] Robert Malley & Hussein Agha, "Camp David: The Tragedy of Errors," *New York Review of Books* (9 August 2001), online: NYREV <http://www.nybooks.com/articles/archives/2001/aug/09/camp-david-the-tragedy-of-errors/?pagination=false>.

in exchange of other land could be acceptable.[319] Similarly, if defending the right to return of Palestinian refugees, the negotiators were open to discussing mechanisms that would offer other options to the refugees and limit the numbers of refugees returning to Israel.[320]

For the more powerful party, international law may appear as the antithesis to a negotiated solution, or even as a threat. It seems, for instance, that the Israeli delegation has persistently rejected any commitments to international human rights standards in the negotiations.[321] With respect to the Palestinian right to return, a member of the Israeli delegation negotiating the 1993 Oslo Accords stated: "When supporters of the Palestinians speak of implementing their 'right of return' to Israel, they are not speaking of peaceful accommodation with Israel; rather, they are using a well-understood code phrase for the destruction of Israel".[322] Instead of discussing the refugee issue on the basis of international law, Israel would challenge the applicability or relevance of international law and offer a negotiated compromise.[323] As a legal adviser to the Israeli government and member of Israeli negotiating teams has argued with respect to the alleged right to return of Palestinians: "The text of paragraph 11 (of Resolution 194) provides no support for the claim that there is a 'right' to return under international law. The paragraph does not mention the word 'right'; it simply states that the refugees 'should be permitted' to return".[324]

If Israel, as the more powerful party, has been reluctant to accept rights claims made by the Palestinians, it is interesting to note that arguments based on rights have not been completely absent in the Israeli discourse, with Israel's "right to exist" materializing most often. Ehud Barak, for instance, would not speak of the Palestinian nonrecognition of Israel's existence as a state but refer to the Palestinians not accepting "the moral and juridical *right* of the State of Israel to exist as a Jewish state".[325]

It appears that relying on rights-based language derived from international law in the context of peace negotiations is rarely equivalent to obtaining guidance in good faith. More frequently, international law is employed and framed by one of the negotiating parties in an unconstructive way and is thus part of a

[319] See, for instance, the citations in ibid.
[320] Ibid.
[321] Kaufman and Bisharat refer to the negotiations of the 1998 Wye River Memorandum. Kaufman & Bisharat, *supra* note 97 at 79 and n 53.
[322] Joel Singer, "No Palestinian 'Return' to Israel" (2001) 87 ABA J 14 at 14.
[323] See, for instance, the conclusion in Matthew Kalman, "The Palestinian Right of Return in International Law – The Israeli Perspective" (2008) 8 Nexus 43 at 58.
[324] Daniel Taub, as cited in ibid., 54.
[325] Ehud Barak interviewed by Ari Shavit, "Eyes Wide Shut," *Ha'aretz* (magazine) (6 September 2002), 8 at 11 as quoted in Pressman, *supra* note 188 at 13 (emphasis added).

calculation where it can help or hinder one's negotiation strategy. Transitional justice, in particular, has a "malleable quality, and is sufficiently indeterminate to make it particularly susceptible to strategic instrumentalism".[326] It is, nevertheless, significant that international legal norms are part of the negotiating parties' discourse, even if to different degrees. Through their discourse during the negotiations, representatives of governments and nonstate actors signal their stance on international law and identify possible norms on which an agreement may be built. At the same time, they make an often unconscious but highly significant contribution as norm generators and norm applicants to the development of the legal-normative framework of peace negotiations.

2.4.2. Cautious Peace Mediators

Peace mediators typically frame their approach towards legal norms with caution. On the one hand, mediators do not want to unduly restrict their mediation strategy by strict adherence to generalized prescriptive norms or dissuade the negotiating parties through an overly legalistic approach that could be seen as not leaving enough room for negotiation. On the other hand, the endorsement of international legal norms, and most importantly of international human rights law, international humanitarian law and international criminal law, has become increasingly audible in the discourse of mediators.

In the absence of a functioning national legal order readily available, peace mediators are actively involved in shaping the legal-normative framework of peace negotiations. Even if the negotiating parties are the primary norm generators, an internal armed conflict, which affects large portions of or the whole population and possibly threatens regional and international peace and security, cannot be compared with a private dispute between relative equals. Moreover, protective norms and fundamental values of concern to the global community as a whole may be at stake. As will be argued in more detail in Chapter 3, peace mediators form an epistemic community and increasingly acknowledge that existing legal norms, notably those projected by the international legal order, are relevant for peace negotiations. The discourse of international and regional organizations,[327] as well as of nongovernmental organizations illustrates well this normative consciousness and ambition of mediating organizations.

---

[326] Bell, *Law of Peace, supra* note 28 at 257.

[327] For the involvement of regional organizations as mediators, see Ole Elgström, Jacob Bercovitch & Carl Skau, "Regional Organisations and International Mediation: The Effectiveness of Insider Mediation" (2003) 3:1 *African Journal on Conflict Resolution* 11 at 15–16. Regarding regional organizations, it should be noted that they have typically been

The United Nations, as the only truly global organization having a clear mandate in the field of international peace and security, plays a central role with respect to mediation in the context of internal armed conflicts. Mediation efforts have been made in numerous situations, including, in recent years, in Côte d'Ivoire, Darfur and Sri Lanka.[328] Moreover, UN representatives can be expected to introduce existing international legal norms into peace negotiations, also because their own conduct ought to correspond to normative standards the organization itself stands for and that are usually anchored in international law. The official discourse of the United Nations reveals an increasing normatization, since the late 1990s, of the involvement of the organization as a peace mediator, and the organization has become much more outspoken with respect to transitional justice and "mainstreaming human rights" in the context of the peaceful resolution of armed conflicts. As the secretary-general noted in 1999 after having issued guidelines to his envoys and representatives:

> These guidelines ... are, I believe, a useful tool with which the United
> Nations can assist in brokering agreements *in conformity with law* and in a

established with the primary purpose of managing conflicts among their member states. In addition to this formally legitimized position with respect to interstate conflicts, regional organizations, such as the Organization for Security and Co-operation in Europe (OSCE), have also become involved in the resolution of intrastate conflicts. On the OSCE, see e.g. Dennis J. D. Sandole, *Peace and Security in the Postmodern World: The OSCE and Conflict Resolution* (New York: Routledge, 2007). For an analysis of the norm-based work of the OSCE High Commissioner on National Minorities in Macedonia, see Steven R. Ratner, "Does International Law Matter in Preventing Ethnic Conflict?" (2000) 32 *International Law and Politics* 591 [henceforth Ratner, "Does International Law Matter"]. The African Union has mediated several negotiations, such as those leading to the 2006 Darfur Peace Agreement. See Chapter 3, Section 3.1.2. The Economic Community of West African States (ECOWAS) has become increasingly involved in conflict resolution processes in the region and has developed quite significant institutional capacities in this regard. According to Mariama Conteh, a Dakar-based adviser for the Crisis Management Initiative, ECOWAS has become the "natural, authoritative mediator in the region". Interview of Mariama Conteh (17 September 2012). The Association of Southeast Asian Nations (ASEAN), although the sole regional intergovernmental organization established in August 1967, has not played a significant role and only intervened occasionally as a mediator. See Kwei-Bo Huang, "The Transformation of ASEAN as a Third-Party Mediator in Intra-Regional Disputes of Southeast Asia," in Jacob Bercovitch, Kwei-Bo Huang & Chung-Chian Teng, eds., *Conflict Management, Security and Intervention in East Asia: Third-Party Mediation in Regional Conflict* (New York: Routledge, 2008), 147.

[328] A complete list of recent situations in which the United Nations led or supported mediation is included in the report of the secretary-general, *Strengthening the Role of Mediation in the Peaceful Settlement of Disputes, Conflict Prevention and Resolution, Report of the Secretary-General*, UN Doc. A/66/811 (25 June 2012) at para 22 [henceforth *Strengthening the Role of Mediation*].

manner which may provide the basis for lasting peace. They are a significant step in the direction of *mainstreaming human rights*.[329]

The secretary-general's 2004 report on the *Rule of Law and Transitional Justice in Conflict and Post-Conflict Settings* is even more explicit in its insistence that "peace agreements and Security Council resolutions and mandates ... [r]espect, incorporate by reference and apply *international standards for fairness, due process and human rights* in the administration of justice".[330]

Other sources also mirror the normative consciousness of the UN and circumscribe its mediation endeavours. On its UN Peacemaker site, an online tool for international peacemaking professionals, the UN plainly states its understanding that "peacemaking is [b]ound by [i]nternational [l]aw" and that "[a] peace agreement that is founded on the principles of international law and human rights provides a firm foundation for subsequent peacebuilding efforts".[331] Moreover, UN peacemaking activities are guided by a legal framework that is assembled in the UN Peacemaker's "Legal Library" and constituted of international treaties and conventions, such as the UN Charter, the 1949 Geneva Conventions and the international human rights conventions.[332] This normative consciousness of the United Nations clearly extends beyond its own representatives and envoys. As the discourse shows, the United Nations asserts that international law is not only binding for its own mediators but that it also provides a normative basis for all peace mediators. According to the *Guidance for Effective Mediation* issued by the secretary-general in 2012, all mediators "must be briefed and familiar with the applicable international law and normative frameworks" and should "ensure that the parties understand the demands and limits of applicable conventions and international laws".[333]

Similarly, the discourse of some peace mediation organizations on international legal norms transcends specific contexts and infuses their work more generally. Fundamental documents, such as codes of conduct and mission statements, reveal a normative commitment similar to the United Nations'.

[329] United Nations, "Press Release: Secretary-General Comments on Guidelines Issued to Envoys," UN Doc. SG/SM/7257 (10 December 1999) (emphasis added) [henceforth UN, "SG Comments on Guidelines"].

[330] *The Rule of Law and Transitional Justice in Conflict and Post-Conflict Societies, Report of the Secretary-General*, UN Doc. S/2004/616 (23 August 2004), at paras 64 (a) and (b) (emphasis added). This report was endorsed by the UN Commission on Human Rights, *Human Rights and Transitional Justice*, Human Rights Resolution 2005/70 of 20 April 2005, 61st Session, UN Doc. E/CN.4/RES/2005/70.

[331] See <http://peacemaker.un.org> (section Peacemaking Resources).

[332] Ibid.

[333] *Strengthening the Role of Mediation, supra* note 328, Annex I, Guidance for Effective Mediation at para 42.

Part of the mission of the Centre for Humanitarian Dialogue (HD Centre), for instance, a conflict mediation organization, is to "support only those solutions that offer the best prospect for a just and lasting peace, *in line with international law*".[334] Independent Diplomat, an organization that offers "advice and assistance in diplomatic technique and strategy", states that it "only helps those who support democracy, *human rights and the rule of law*".[335] As for International Alert, this peace-building nongovernmental organization explicitly refers in its code of conduct to international human rights:

> We are committed to pressing for *international human rights standards* to be recognised and incorporated in settlement agreements and for the establishment and development of effective institutions for the protection, promotion and implementation of civil, political, economic, social and cultural rights. We are also committed to supporting measures which address the problems of impunity and injustice, historical truth and compensation for victims.[336]

Through such references to international legal norms, mediating organizations also assert certain values and principles, notably with respect to upholding these norms in the context of peace negotiations. Other organizations, such as the Crisis Management Initiative, Conciliation Resources, the Centre for Conflict Resolution and the Carter Center's Conflict Resolution Program, are, however, less outspoken on this matter.

In sum, peace mediation organizations are generally cautious about making declarations on international legal norms in the context of peace negotiations.[337] The discourse nevertheless brings to light significant normative trends. Some organizations clearly state their stance on international legal norms and their proposed role in the context of peace negotiations in the organization's code of conduct or mission statement. These documents are particularly revealing and fill an important gap in the otherwise very careful discourse of mediators, who rarely comment in public on ongoing or past negotiations.[338]

---

[334] Centre for Humanitarian Dialogue, "Who We Are," online: HD Centre <http://www.hdcentre.org/about> (emphasis added). HD Centre also proclaims that "the HD Centre's operational work suggests that justice and the rule of law play a central role in sustainable conflict resolution". See <http://www.hdcentre.org/projects/justice-peacemaking>.

[335] Online: Independent Diplomat <http://www.independentdiplomat.org> (emphasis added).

[336] International Alert, "Code of Conduct" (1998), online: International Alert <http://www.international-alert.org/pdf/coc_full.pdf> at 5 (emphasis added).

[337] This cautiousness is related to and can be explained by the established influence of fundamental principles of mediation, including neutrality, impartiality and confidentiality, which will be explored in more detail in Chapter 3.

[338] A review of the transcripts of thirty-three interviews conducted in 2006 and 2007 by the United States Institute of Peace with individuals who were involved in negotiating the Sudanese Comprehensive Peace Agreement, including officials from the United States and Norway and

2.4.3. *The Purposeful Discourse of External Actors*

The discourse of external actors on international legal norms is highly diverse, given the wide range of these actors' possible status and interests vis-à-vis the negotiations. The following examples are intended to illustrate this diversity and reflect those discourses that can be expected to be influential. International, regional and nongovernmental organizations, as well as third states having particular concerns, for instance, because of their geographical vicinity to the conflict zone, may affect the negotiations significantly, even if they are not directly involved in the negotiations. Furthermore, although the discourses of these actors may not produce tangible results in a specific context, they are an important part of the more general discourse on international legal norms and contribute to the construction of the normative framework of peace negotiations.

The discourse of some external actors is openly anchored in international law, with some actors even advocating for the respect of and contributing to the progress of international law in a norm entrepreneurial manner. Some, typically Western, governments and human rights organizations regularly call on other governments and armed groups to respect international law and the rule of law, not only with regard to respecting the laws of war but also when an agreement is being negotiated. International human rights law, international humanitarian law and international criminal law are the branches of law that are most often relied on by these actors. The long-standing approach of European states of upholding international law, and in particular international humanitarian and human rights law, in the context of the Israeli-Palestinian peace process[339] illustrates the importance attached to international law in peace negotiations by some third parties and observers. To cite only one example of the discourse of the government of the United Kingdom: "respect for human rights and full observance of Israel's international obligations in that regard is the key. A real obstacle to the creation of a better climate is Israel's

---

representatives of nongovernmental organizations, reveals the limited importance attached to legal considerations by these actors. In the interviews, only a few references to human rights violations committed in Sudan and to the applicability of Sharia law in the south were made. While the interview questions were most likely not geared to revealing normative concerns, the virtually total absence of references to international legal norms is, nevertheless, striking. The transcripts are available online: "Oral Histories: The Sudan Experience Project," online: United States Institute of Peace <http://www.usip.org/publications/oral-histories-the -sudan-experience-project>.

[339] Lynn Welchman, "The Middle East Peace Process and the Rule of Law: Irreconcilable Objectives?," in Eugene Cotran & Mai Yamani, eds., *The Rule of Law in the Middle East and the Islamic World: Human Rights and the Judicial Processes* (London: I. B. Tauris, 2000), 51, 52.

continuing refusal to acknowledge that the provisions of the relevant international agreements are applicable to the Occupied Territories".[340] On the other
end of the spectrum is the United States, whose conflict resolution initiatives
can generally be described as not being based on international law.[341] A widely
shared commitment of influential external actors to an approach rooted in
international law can therefore not be discerned. The attitudes of external
actors vary and may be seen as lying along a rights-power axis,[342] similar as in
the case of negotiators.

In Uganda, the discourse of external actors on international law has concerned, to a great extent, the ramifications of the involvement of the ICC.
Especially when the arrest warrants against five LRA leaders were unsealed,
both international and local nongovernmental organizations voiced their fears
concerning the introduction of international criminal law, in this situation
incarnated by the ICC prosecutor, and condemned the "intervention" of the
court. Members of the Acholi Religious Leaders' Peace Initiative even pre-
dicted that "this kind of approach is going to destroy all efforts for peace".[343]
As in the case of the negotiating parties, the discourse was not directed at
international criminal law per se and rarely targeted the ICC as an institution
but rather denounced the ill-timed issuance of international arrest warrants.
In this sense, the discourse focused more on procedure and timing than on
the general relevance of international law and, for instance, the substantive
applicability of international criminal law.

Some organizations have attempted to elaborate universally valid guidelines to make peace negotiations more effective, and with respect to addressing transitional justice concerns in peace agreements, types of "permissible"
and "impermissible" amnesties have been identified.[344] The International
Council on Human Rights Policy, for instance, has concluded that while
amnesty "is still permissible and in some cases desirable ... serious violations

---

[340] As cited in ibid., 53.

[341] See e.g. Akram et al., *supra* note 154 at 6.

[342] Akram et al. speak of "rights against power" (ibid.).

[343] UN Office for the Coordination of Humanitarian Affairs, "UGANDA: Peace Groups and
Government Officials Worried about ICC Probe into LRA" (30 January 2004), online: IRIN
<http://www.irinnews.org/Report.aspx?ReportId=48356>. Similar concerns were raised by the
Ugandan Amnesty Commission, which has pertinent expertise in the field of reintegrating
former LRA fighters into society, but which also saw its raison d'être being put in danger by the
involvement of the ICC.

[344] See e.g. International Council on Human Rights Policy, *supra* note 132 at 84; Centre for
Security Studies, ETH Zurich, "Dealing with the Past in Peace Mediation" (September
2009), online: Centre for Security Studies (CSS), ETH Zurich <http://www.isn.ethz.ch/isn/
Digital-Library/Publications/Detail/?ord538=grp2&size538=10&ots591=eb06339b-2726-928e-0
216-1b3f15392dd8&lng=en&id=114851> at 6.

of international law must be investigated, prosecuted and punished"[345] and has issued recommendations to mediators regarding human rights:

> Mediators should consider how to take a proactive role in securing human rights frameworks. This is particularly important where the negotiations are isolated from NGO or civil input.... Mediators should carefully consider the implications for their own role and international obligations, in being complicit in an amnesty provision which violates international law. This may affect the mediators' notion of strict "impartiality" regarding the demands of the parties. Mediators can dissent from amnesty provisions which are not in compliance with international law.[346]

An interesting case in point is the Colombian peace process, where international law, or rather the way it is conceived and utilized not only by the primary parties but also by influential commentators, does not appear to have facilitated the peaceful resolution of the armed conflict.[347] The use of international humanitarian law by the guerrillas has been described as "purely strategic"[348] and international law as being "routinely invoke[d] ... to frustrate negotiations and compromise".[349] Jorge Esquirol has argued that while "any legal argument is inherently linked to some political position", only one interpretation of international law is held to be valid in Colombia, in other words an argument put forward by those reluctant to politically compromise.[350] Draft agreements, such as the so-called Mainz Agreement of 1998 and the 2005 Justice and Peace Law have been criticized both by domestic and international actors for their inconsistency with international law.[351] Moreover, if supported, these documents were defended merely on political, not legal, grounds.[352] Esquirol has persuasively concluded that in the Colombian context, international law has been monopolized by orthodox commentators whose approach undermines the potential of law being used as a device for peace.[353] A less state- and sovereignty-centred approach to international law could, among other things,

---

[345] International Council on Human Rights Policy, *supra* note 132 at 90.

[346] Ibid., 94, 97.

[347] José E. Arvelo, "International Law and Conflict Resolution in Colombia: Balancing Peace and Justice in the Paramilitary Demobilization Process" (2005–2006) 37 *Geo J Int'l L* 411 at 413.

[348] Esquirol, *supra* note 153 at 70.

[349] Ibid., 24.

[350] Ibid., 61.

[351] Catalina Díaz, "Colombia's Bid for Justice and Peace," in Kai Ambos, Judith Large & Marieke Wierda, eds., *Building a Future on Peace and Justice: Studies on Transitional Justice, Peace and Development, The Nuremberg Declaration on Peace and Justice* (Berlin: Springer, 2009), 469, 476.

[352] Esquirol, *supra* note 153 at 64.

[353] Ibid., 74. "Peace negotiations are thus narrowly close to illegal and thus illegitimate" (ibid., 73).

allow civil society to be more involved in the elaboration of humanitarian accords and peace agreements,[354] a claim that is, of course, valid not only in the Colombian context.

2.5. THE DISCOURSE ON INTERNATIONAL LEGAL NORMS – FROM PRESCRIPTION TO FACILITATION?

A summary assessment of the discourse of peace negotiators, mediators and external actors shows that the process of developing the normative frame-work of peace negotiations through the discourse of these actors is an ongo-ing, and certainly not coherent or structured, endeavour. International legal norms may be referred to for various purposes and at all stages of a peace process: to justify and legitimize participation, notably of nonstate actors, at the negotiations; to build the substance of and provide a legal basis for a peace agreement; and to provide mechanisms for its implementation, for instance, through the establishment of human rights commissions. Peace negotiations may not yet have become "legally saturated" and have turned into a "legal institution" comparable to war;[355] yet international legal norms undoubtedly, and increasingly, shape peace negotiations and make themselves felt in this context.[356] What can also be concluded is that legal norms are rarely seen as facilitating the process of negotiations: international law is rather construed as restrictive and not as facilitative. This can explain why conflict resolution theorists and practitioners are wary of legal norms and their claimed rigid and bureaucratic character.[357] As it has been argued convincingly in the context of the Israeli-Palestinian negotiations, the discourse reflects an orthodox view on international law that tends to create binary oppositions.[358] While human rights language, for instance, may be pushed for by some actors, rights- and principle-based approaches are often seen to be of diminished importance because of their perceived support for the cause of only one negotiating party, usually the weaker one in terms of political and military power, which is possibly trying to replace warfare by lawfare. Sometimes, the negotiating parties therefore prefer to keep a low profile on international law, and such approaches may be set aside as a whole in the negotiations.[359] The urge to

---

[354] Ibid., 81.

[355] This draws on the argument made by Kennedy, "Lawfare and Warfare," *supra* note 309 at 162.

[356] As David Kennedy argues, "the opportunities for law to make itself felt in the experience of those participating in modern war ... have multiplied dramatically" (ibid.).

[357] Babbitt, *supra* note 117 at 617.

[358] Michelle L. Burgis, "A Discourse of Distinction? Palestinians, International Law, and the Promise of Humanitarianism" (2009) 15 *Palestine Yearbook of International Law* 41 at 56.

[359] See e.g. Akram et al., *supra* note 154 at 34.

obtain guidance from legal norms for the negotiations or the conclusion of a peace agreement appears to be a rare phenomenon.

The prevalent discourse of the negotiators, mediators, and external actors on international law, as well as its missing analysis in the literature,[360] can also explain the disconnect between the oftentimes claimed importance of international law[361] and its limited significance for peace negotiations in reality. It appears that mainly implicit assumptions that shape the discourse are responsible for the unrealized potential of legal norms to contribute to the peaceful resolution of armed conflicts. This kind of approach can also be seen as diminishing the scope for negotiated settlement and bottom-up peace processes.[362]

It would be important not to entrench a common tendency that consists in a prescriptive and strategic application of existing legal norms in the context of peace negotiations. We should rather value the constitutive and facilitative role of legal norms and de-emphasize their regulative nature; in this latter meaning, norms are mainly ends oriented and can hardly facilitate negotiations. If legal norms appear to play already a more prominent role in peace negotiations, it is through such an outcome- or end-oriented lens that emphasizes the inclusion of specific language into the text of a peace agreement. However, since norms will rarely lead to definite outcomes,[363] and since means and ends are inherently interrelated,[364] it can be argued that a more careful attention, from a legal point of view, to the means will engender procedural justice

---

[360] The Israeli-Palestinian and Colombian examples illustrate that the legal literature has started to pay more attention to the discourse around the importance and use of international law in the context of peace negotiations. However, the analysis largely focuses on legal commentators, who are usually mere observers in a peace process. While the legal discourse of the negotiating parties themselves may not be as developed as the academic discourse, it is still striking that the former does not seem to have been reflected on in any significant way.

[361] See Section 2.1.

[362] Bell, "Peace Agreements and Human Rights: Implications for the UN," *supra* note 185 at 263.

[363] This relies on Friedrich V. Kratochwil, "How Do Norms Matter?," in Michael Byers, ed., *The Role of Law in International Politics* (Oxford: Oxford University Press, 2000), 35, 48.

[364] For an elaborate theoretical argument on this relationship, see Lon Fuller, "Means and Ends," in Kenneth I. Winston, ed., *The Principles of Social Order: Selected Essays of Lon L. Fuller* (Durham, NC: Duke University Press, 1981), 61. Roderick A. Macdonald makes a similar argument: "[since] means cannot be divorced from ends, it follows that one cannot adequately understand how choices about means are made without grounding the question in particular contexts and particular times. Analytical tools and conceptual devices are culturally determined. It is simply inappropriate to assume that they can be projected in some idealized form through time and space". Roderick A. Macdonald, "The Swiss Army Knife of Governance," in Pearl Eliadis, Margaret M. Hill & Michael Howlett, eds., *Designing Government: From Instruments to Governance* (Montreal: McGill-Queen's University Press, 2005), 203, 207. For the importance of "process pluralism", see Carrie Menkel-Meadow, "Peace and Justice: Notes on the Evolution and Purposes of Legal Processes" (2006) 94 *Geo LJ* 553.

and also the materialization of more valuable ends.[365] It would therefore be beneficial to shift the common legalistic and outcome-focused approach to a process-oriented perspective that is also more faithful to the complex relationship between means and ends.

If the discourse of mediators and external actors still relies to a large extent on formally recognized international legal norms, which are often encountered with suspicion by other actors involved in peace negotiations, the developing normative consciousness and normative conduct of mediators is, at least in some cases, not directed at a specific outcome but primarily at the process, with legal norms being considered constructive from a process perspective. A good illustration is the new round of negotiations between the Colombian government and the Fuerzas Armadas Revolucionarias de Colombia (FARC) that started in October 2012. In the weeks before the launch of the negotiations, some external actors prepared for the upcoming discussions on individual accountability for crimes committed during the conflict. Although the United Nations was not to be directly involved as a mediator, the principled position of the organization regarding transitional justice was clearly voiced by the special envoy of the UN High Commissioner for Human Rights. As quoted in a news report, Todd Howland emphasized that "it is quite clear in the international legal framework that an amnesty or a pardon cannot be included", but he nuanced this seemingly inflexible position by adding that "it's not clear how far you must go with criminal law".[366] This statement confirms that, according to the United Nations, international law prohibits certain measures, such as amnesties for grave violations of international human rights law and humanitarian law, and that this prohibition must be respected in a peace process; yet besides certain red lines, there is flexibility with respect to other transitional justice mechanisms. Similarly, the Colombian president Santos identified the outer range of a possible agreement on individual accountability. When asked if he would give amnesties to members of the FARC, Santos bluntly answered, "I cannot". He cited the Rome Statute of the ICC, to which Colombia is a party, as part of his reasoning. While implying that the negotiations would be conducted in the "shadow" of the ICC, he also affirmed that "we have to sit down and negotiate, what type of transitional justice we can apply to this case. And that's part

---

[365] See also Babbitt, *supra* note 117 at 617.

[366] "UN Recommends that Colombia Peace-Process Takes into Account Victims of Ongoing Conflict," *United Press International* (13 September 2012), online: United Press International <http://www.upi.com/Top_News/Special/2012/09/13/UN-urges-Colombia-not-to-concede-to-FARC/UPI-47681347565546/>.

of the negotiation".[367] As a result, and in addition to the possible integration of FARC members into civilian life, the establishment of a truth commission and the human rights of the victims were included into the agenda of the negotiations.[368]

The point here is that through their discourses, the respective actors constantly create and redevelop the legal-normative framework of peace negotiations. While crafted in a specific context, this framework is not entirely spontaneous or self-sufficient[369] but influenced by international legal norms and the experiences and lessons from other peace negotiation contexts. Peace mediators and their discourses can contribute most meaningfully to the construction of useful and coherent but not standardized and prescriptive norms that shed light on the bargaining range and serve as guideposts for the negotiating parties along the way. With respect to the discourse on legal norms, it should also be recalled that this discourse oftentimes does not reflect commonly shared understandings but is part of the endeavour that consists in settling normative disagreement. Moreover, since positions, interests, values, communication strategies and, as a result, discernible approaches to legal norms vary, we should also consider the perhaps not only symbolic value of speaking of *discourses* in the plural.

The still-prevalent emphasis on existing international law that is seen as imposing rigid standards and a certain conduct from "above" should be supplanted by the view that law can also facilitate, offer guidance, reflect mutual commitments and serve to stabilize expectations.[370] As it will be argued in the following chapters, recognizing the norm creative capacity of the actors involved in peace negotiations is one avenue to use legal norms more constructively and effectively in the context of the negotiated resolution of internal

---

[367] "Colombia's Santos Says FARC Must Be Allowed to Participate in Politics," *CNN* (28 September 2012), online: CNN <http://amanpour.blogs.cnn.com/2012/09/28/colombias-president-on-negotiating-with-farc/?iref=allsearch>.

[368] "FARC Santos Govt Peace Talks, Who and What?," *Colombia Politics* (16 October 2012), online: Colombia Politics <http://www.colombia-politics.com/farc-santos-govt-negotiating-team-and-agenda/>.

[369] For the argument that no normative order is totally imposed or entirely spontaneous and autonomous, see Macdonald, "Here, There ... and Everywhere," *supra* note 1.

[370] According to Niklas Luhmann, law serves primarily to stabilize expectations. Niklas Luhmann, *Das Recht der Gesellschaft* (Frankfurt: Suhrkamp, 1995), 131. As Frédéric Mégret has summarized the view of what he calls "apologists" with respect to international law: "in this view, international law provides an indispensable tool of communication that enables social life by limiting misunderstandings, stabilising expectations, and increasing transparency". Frédéric Mégret, "International Law as Law," in James Crawford & Martti Koskenniemi, eds., *The Cambridge Companion to International Law* (Cambridge: Cambridge University Press, 2012), 64, 78.

armed conflicts. We will see that a pluralistic and socio-legal understanding of law is therefore more valuable than an orthodox advocacy claiming to uphold the international rule of law. Law is indeed not simply a social artefact; norms are not scientifically objective.[371] According to such a view, legal norms have a genuine potential to facilitate the interaction between the actors involved in peace negotiations.

---

[371] Macdonald & Sandomierski, *supra* note 81 at 611.

3

The Normative Dimensions of Peace Mediation

Mediators, in addition to states and nonstate actors as direct parties concerned, are regularly involved and assist in the negotiated resolution of internal armed conflicts. Quantitatively speaking, states are still the most important mediators, followed by the United Nations, most importantly the secretary-general and his special representatives or envoys, and regional organizations and non-governmental organizations.[372] It should be borne in mind that because of the complexity of a mediation process, one sole mediator can hardly cover every role necessary to carry out and complete a process.[373] As a result, most processes are mediated by several actors, either subsequently or concurrently.[374]

So far, there has been little discussion in the literature on the legitimacy and, more generally, on the normative involvement of third parties in peace negotiations.[375] The literature has rather focused on possible legal obligations of third parties following the conclusion of an agreement.[376] In particular, the status of

---

[372] Damiano Sguaitamatti & Simon J. A. Mason, "Vermittler im Vergleich: Bedeutung für die Schweiz als Mediatorin" (2011) 83 *Zürcher Beiträge zur Sicherheitspolitik* 69 at 84.

[373] Ibid., 69.

[374] For an analysis of numbers retrieved from the Uppsala Conflict Data Program (published by Lotta Harbom & Peter Wallensteen, "Armed Conflicts, 1946–2009" (2010) 47:4 *Journal of Peace Research* 501), see ibid., 83.

[375] Kirchhoff similarly notes that "the procedural role of third party interventions is significantly underdeveloped." Lars Kirchhoff, *Constructive Interventions: Paradigms, Process and Practice of International Mediation* (Alphen aan den Rijn: Kluwer Law International, 2008), 330.

[376] Bell, "Peace Agreements: Their Nature and Legal Status", *supra* note 57 at 395. As Bell argues, "The limits and deficits of legal form may be compensated for by how an agreement's obligations are crafted, to some extent" (ibid.). For an earlier analysis of third-party involvement in classic state-to-state negotiations and applicable treaty law, see Farooq Hassan on the legal status of the United States' involvement in the 1978 Camp David peace process and its legal consequences, such as possible obligations and rights under international law accruing to the United States and arising out of the agreements concluded between Egypt and Israel. Farooq Hassan, "The Legal Status of United States Involvement in the Camp David Peace Process" (1983) 16 *Vand J Transnat'l L* 75.

third parties and the legal value of their signature on peace agreements as witnesses or guarantors have been examined. Christine Bell provides an overview of the possible roles and functions of third parties with respect to the conclusion of peace agreements: "at the top end of the spectrum, third-party delegation is legally binding; at the bottom end, it amounts to little more than a forum for purely political bargaining".[377] In a nutshell, third parties can be "external guarantors" and commit themselves to play a role in the implementation of the agreement;[378] "self-guarantors" or "second parties", which concerns their own involvement in the conflict, such as a commitment to nonintervention;[379] or, beyond a particular commitment to the agreement and as an expression of a more general normative ambition, "norm promoters" or "fourth parties".[380]

In the post-agreement period, third parties can thus be entrusted with the interpretation and authorization of peace agreements.[381] The involvement of international third parties can also be viewed as a delegation of rule making, as exemplified in the role of the United Nations High Commissioner for Refugees with respect to implementing provisions on refugees and displaced persons and the ICRC with respect to the release of prisoners.[382] In the Dayton Peace Agreement, for instance, "the Parties call upon the United Nations High Commissioner for Refugees ... to develop in close consultation with asylum countries and the Parties a repatriation plan that will allow for an early, peaceful, orderly and phased return of refugees and displaced persons ... The Parties agree to implement such a plan and to conform their international agreements and their laws to it".[383]

In this context, Bell has identified a normative framework in order to hold third-party enforcers accountable for their transitional actions, drawing on overlapping legal regimes produced by international humanitarian law, human rights law and domestic constitutional principles.[384] In short, the role

---

[377] Bell, "Peace Agreements: Their Nature and Legal Status", *supra* note 57 at 400.

[378] Bell, *Law of Peace*, *supra* note 28 at 177–178. The Special Court for Sierra Leone uses similar language in *Kallon*, arguing that the signature of third parties on the Lomé Peace Agreement evidences that these parties were "moral guarantors" and "assumed no legal obligation". See *Prosecutor v. Kallon & Kamara*, *supra* note 63 at para 41.

[379] Bell, *Law of Peace*, *supra* note 28 at 178–179.

[380] Ibid., 179–180.

[381] Ibid., 181–187.

[382] Ibid., 185.

[383] *Dayton Peace Agreement*, *supra* note 205, Annex 7, art II.5. See also the *General Peace Agreement for Mozambique*, *supra* note 55, Protocol VI, art III.B: "The International Committee of the Red Cross [...] shall agree on the arrangements for and the verification of the prisoner release process". On the role that was given to the "facilitator" Blaise Compaoré in the Accord de Ouagadougou, see Section 3.1.3.

[384] Bell, *Law of Peace*, *supra* note 28 at 260, 268–278.

of third parties with respect to the enforcement of peace agreements is highly complex and can take various forms, and it is often difficult to draw a clear line between delegation of implementation or interpretation and continuing mediation.[385]

Besides the multitude of possible functions following the conclusion of a peace agreement, it should be recalled that getting involved as a mediator is only one strategy among several others to address an internal armed conflict of concern to an external actor and potential intermediary. Depending on the political will, diplomatic calculations, resources and opportunities, third parties may, for instance, intervene actively as an ally of one of the belligerents, support one of them more passively or discreetly or remain a member of an interested audience.[386] As will be argued in Section 3.1.2, external actors may, however, not always be entirely free to choose whether and in which way to intervene: under certain circumstances they may have a duty to get involved by making offers of mediation.

In sum, the question of possible obligations of third parties following the conclusion of a peace agreement has not yet been fully explored. Furthermore, as we will see in this chapter, exploring the normative dimensions of the involvement of external actors during the negotiations presents even more and different kinds of challenges. Yet without recognizing the existence and without an analysis of process-related norms and associated obligations, the conduct of mediators is neither legitimate nor illegitimate and can therefore not be assessed from a normative perspective; conformity with legal obligations, moreover, confers legitimacy.[387] A consideration of the normative role of mediators also has wider implications for the theory and practice of peace negotiations. Recognizing and adequately conceiving the normative basis of the conduct of mediators and their normative impact on the negotiations are essential to grasp the normative framework of peace negotiations. The role of mediators is, indeed, highly illustrative of these normative dynamics. Mediators take part in the negotiations; as normative actors, they influence and are influenced by the normative framework constructed in this specific context. At the same time, they are, at least to some extent, outsiders who

---

[385] Ibid., 188.

[386] For a further discussion on possible roles of third parties, see Christopher R. Mitchell, "The Motives for Mediation," in Christopher R. Mitchell & Keith Webb, eds., *New Approaches to International Mediation* (New York: Greenwood Press, 1988), 29, 48 [henceforth Mitchell, "Motives for Mediation"].

[387] For a similar argument, see Michelle Gallant, "Law and Legal Process in Resolving International Conflicts," in Dennis J. D. Sandole et al., eds., *Handbook of Conflict Analysis and Resolution* (London: Routledge, 2009), 396, 397.

introduce into the negotiations preconceived norms and normative beliefs. In other words, mediators cannot be concerned exclusively with the specific context of negotiations in which they are involved and rely solely on the respective norms generated in interaction with the negotiating parties. They also operate within a larger normative framework where international legal norms are highly influential, with respect to both their own behaviour and, more generally, the manner in which the negotiations are conducted. One of the results is that peace mediators increasingly bear a normative ambition vis-à-vis the negotiators and are committed to norm-promotion.

In this sense, the peace mediator symbolizes the archetypical normative actor: actively and constantly involved in the process of norm-creation and norm-application, in interaction with the negotiating parties and other stakeholders in a specific context of negotiations; yet inevitably inspired and directed by largely external normative influences, such as international legal norms and related obligations, that are consciously or unconsciously internalized and assumed. The concept of "epistemic communities" elucidates the role of and especially the interaction among peace mediators. The term, coined in international relations theory, refers to knowledge-based transnational networks, often in relation to technical or scientific matters, through which shared interpretations, understandings and normative beliefs and commitment are constructed and transmitted in the absence of a hegemonic world order.[388] Despite the typically confidential or even secret nature of mediation efforts, peace mediators cooperate with and learn from each other. While some of these exchanges might only have an indirect impact, it is remarkable that several actors, including the United Nations, regional organizations and some nongovernmental organizations, actively and intentionally provide mediation support to other actors, notably by sharing experiences and knowledge. HD Centre, for instance, aspires to "further the debate on the challenges facing the mediation community" and "develops practical information resources, including training material, which it makes available to the wider mediation community".[389] Through the language used, HD Centre clearly underlines

---

[388] For the concept of epistemic communities in international relations, see, in particular, the 1992 special issue of *International Organization*. Peter M. Haas refers to epistemic communities as "a network of professionals with recognized expertise and competence in a particular domain and an authoritative claim to policy-relevant knowledge within that domain or issue-area". Peter M Haas, "Introduction: Epistemic Communities and International Policy Coordination" (1992) 46:2 *International Organization* 1 at 2. On shared normative commitments of epistemic communities, see ibid., 19.

[389] HD Centre, "Mediation Support," online: Centre for Humanitarian Dialogue <http://www.hdcentre.org/support>.

its conviction that such a "mediation community" exists. The formal status of mediation organizations within this community appears secondary; nongovernmental organizations work with, support and are supported by states and international and regional organizations.[390] The community experienced a certain institutionalization with the establishment, in 2008, of the Mediation Support Network,[391] a global network of primarily nongovernmental organizations intended to support mediation in peace negotiations and share information among peace organizations. Hence peace mediators not only draw on experiences shared by other actors but also contribute to building a shared set of knowledge about peace mediation and to generating, both individually and collectively, the legal-normative framework of peace negotiations.

The place and role of mediators in the normative framework of peace negotiations will be analysed along two aspects. The first relates to the subtle yet increasingly noticeable normative basis of the conduct of peace mediators. In the absence of formal rules authorizing and governing their involvement, these actors, in interaction with the negotiating parties and other stakeholders, must find ways to ascertain their own legitimacy. The morality and the motives of mediators as well as the principles of mediator neutrality and impartiality are central to this endeavour. The second aspect concerns the significant normative impact mediators have on negotiations, regardless of their various possible functions and roles. This impact may be fairly manifest when mediators consciously and explicitly vindicate their normative ambition; it may also be more latent and unrelated to a deliberate strategy pursued by the mediator, as in the case of facilitative mediators concerned with encouraging party self-determination and upholding their own neutrality and impartiality throughout the process. Though rarely recognized, this normative impact is, nonetheless, omnipresent.

3.1. A NORMATIVE BASIS FOR THE INVOLVEMENT OF PEACE MEDIATORS

In judicial systems, whether at the domestic, regional or international level, a judge can be expected to conduct his or her work within a well-developed legal

---

[390] By way of example, the Crisis Management Initiative supports the European Union in peace mediation. Crisis Management Initiative, "CMI Closely Supports the EU in Peace Mediation" (26 October 2012), online: Crisis Management Initiative <http://www.cmi.fi/media-2/news/europe/657-cmi-closely-supports-the-eu-in-peace-mediation>; similarly, HD Centre collaborates with regional organizations, such as the African Union and ECOWAS. "Support to Regional Organizations," online: HD Centre <http://www.hdcentre.org/en/our-work/mediation-support/current-activities/support-to-regional-organisations/>.

[391] See <http://www.mediationsupportnetwork.net>.

framework and to enjoy a certain legitimacy grounded in the system itself. In contrast, peace mediators cannot be considered premandated or preapproved by an authoritative institution. This would have, at least initially, an innate legitimizing effect. In the absence of an existing framework where peace mediators are legitimated similar to judges in a functioning justice system, consensual acceptance[392] by the main parties to the conflict is, therefore, one of the most fundamental requirements to legitimize the involvement of a mediator.

Generally, the field of mediation has experienced increasing attempts at regulation, either by the state or through professional organizations.[393] There seems to be an inclination to try to guarantee a legitimate involvement of a third party, be it a judge, arbitrator or mediator, and to ground this involvement on general principles that are established independently from a specific situation and independently from the approval of the disputing or negotiating parties. Moreover, few organizations that are active in the field of peace mediation operate according to well-determined standards and principles. The ICRC stands out as a norm-based, neutral, impartial and independent organization having a well-defined mandate focused on humanitarian action that is laid out in the Geneva Conventions and the ICRC's Statutes. Because of this mandate, however, the possibilities for the ICRC to become involved as a peace mediator in the context of internal armed conflicts are also limited, with its focus again on humanitarian matters.[394]

The normative framework of peace negotiations thus eschews straightforward claims with respect to the legitimacy of mediators. Some aspects that are explicitly identified in definitions of mediation can provide guidance as to what appear to be legitimate ways for peace mediators to get involved.

---

[392] As it has been argued more generally with respect to consensuality, "consensual decision-making by the parties" is a "core attribute of mediation". Hilary Astor, "Mediator Neutrality: Making Sense of Theory and Practice" (2007) 16:2 *Soc & Leg Stud* 221 at 229.

[393] On the regulation of mediation and concerns regarding state-controlled mediation, see Spencer & Brogan, *supra* note 187 at 379–387. With respect to international mediation, it has been suggested that it is "necessary to *codify* the basic procedural approach and the central ethical code of conduct for the intermediary ... in order to better communicate the specific character and potential of interest-based, facilitative mediation". Kirchhoff, *supra* note 375 at 338 (emphasis added).

[394] As it has been argued by an ICRC delegate in the Colombian context, "Mediation [in humanitarian matters] by the ICRC has a good chance of success where the crisis is limited in both time and space, and the players are clearly identifiable." Thomas Jenatsch, "The ICRC as a Humanitarian Mediator in the Colombian Conflict: Possibilities and Limits" (1998) 38:323 *Int'l Rev Red Cross* 303. The ICRC typically proposes its good offices in order to increase respect for international humanitarian law and functions as "amiable compositeur", for instance, to secure the release of prisoners. See François Bugnion, *Le Comité international de la Croix-Rouge et la protection des victimes de la guerre* (Geneva: Comité international de la Croix-Rouge, 1994), 468, 803–808.

Furthermore, more implicit, underlying principles about the motives, the morality and the ethics of peace mediators may have given or may give rise to certain norms regarding the involvement of mediators and their legitimacy. Little consensus appears to have emerged, with the legitimacy of mediators constantly being reassessed and renegotiated, notably with respect to the neutrality/impartiality rule.

3.1.1. *Defining Mediation – Formal Criteria*

The different ways in which mediation has been defined are revealing about the key characteristics generally associated with this endeavour and to assumptions about a legitimate involvement. Numerous attempts have been made to define mediation comprehensively, without leading to one established definition. Mediation has been described by Ronald Fisher as "a pacific, noncoercive and non-binding approach to conflict management that is entered into freely by the concerned parties, who at the same time maintain control over the substance of the agreement".[395] Oran R. Young has defined third-party intervention, which includes mediation, as "any action taken by an actor that is not a direct party to the crisis, that is designed to reduce or remove one or more of the problems of the bargaining relationship and, therefore, to facilitate the termination of the crisis".[396] Most definitions[397] emphasize the will of the parties to voluntarily reach an agreement, the mediator's neutrality and/or impartiality, as well as a certain structure of the process. The European Code of Conduct for Mediators, for instance, a nonbinding document[398] developed by stakeholders with the assistance of the European Commission, stipulates:

> For the purposes of the code of conduct, mediation means any structured process, however named or referred to, whereby two or more parties to a

---

[395] Ronald J. Fisher, "Methods of Third Party Intervention," in *Berghof Handbook for Conflict Transformation* (Berlin: Berghof Conflict Research, 2001), online: Berghof Conflict Research <http://www.berghof-handbook.net/documents/publications/fisher_hb.pdf> at 4.

[396] Oran R. Young, *The Intermediaries: Third Parties in International Crises* (Princeton, NJ: Princeton University Press, 1968), 34.

[397] For an overview of academic definitions, see Susan Nauss Exon, "The Effect that Mediator Styles Impose on Neutrality and Impartiality Requirements of Mediation" (2008) 42 *USF L Rev* 577 at 579–80.

[398] While the code is not formally binding on mediators, the latter may, as the code stipulates, "voluntarily decide to commit themselves, under their own responsibility" to these principles. See preamble of the *European Code of Conduct for Mediators*, online: European Commission <http://ec.europa.eu/civiljustice/adr/adr_ec_code_conduct_en.pdf>. Such codes of ethics have been widely criticized for contradicting themselves and for failing to recognize the existence of different mediation models; see e.g. Ellen A. Waldman, "Identifying the Role of Social Norms in Mediation: A Multiple Model Approach" (1997) 48 *Hastings LJ* 703 at 765.

dispute attempt by themselves, on a voluntary basis, to reach an agreement on the settlement of their dispute with the assistance of a third person – hereinafter "the mediator".[399]

Similarly, the Model Standards of Conduct for Mediators, an initiative of the American Arbitration Association, the American Bar Association and the Society of Professionals in Dispute Resolution, "establishing a standard of care for mediators",[400] define mediation as "a process in which an impartial third party facilitates communication and negotiation and promotes voluntary decision making by the parties to the dispute".[401] To mention another example, the Massachusetts Uniform Rules on Dispute Resolution define mediation as "a voluntary, confidential process in which a neutral is invited or accepted by disputing parties to assist them in identifying and discussing issues of mutual concern, exploring various solutions, and developing a settlement mutually acceptable to the disputing parties".[402]

Although education requirements and the conduct of mediators are not regulated comprehensively by national, and even less so by international, standards, various codes of ethics share common elements and increasingly attempt to outline the mediator's role, above all through an emphasis on facilitative, neutral and impartial mediation. The European Code of Conduct for Mediators requires a mediator to be independent and impartial. Regarding impartiality, the Code provides that "mediators must at all times act, and endeavour to be seen to act, with impartiality towards the parties and be committed to serve all parties equally with respect to the process of mediation".[403] With respect to his or her independence, the mediator must inform

---

[399] *European Code of Conduct for Mediators, supra* note 398, preamble. The importance of structure should, however, not be overrated, especially when mediation is compared with other forms of social ordering, such as legislation and adjudication. As Fuller argued, "For of mediation, one is tempted to say that it is all process and no structure.... It is the mediational process that produces the structure." Lon L. Fuller, "Mediation – Its Forms and Functions" (1971) 44 *S Cal L Rev* 305 at 307–308 [henceforth Fuller, "Mediation"].

[400] *Model Standards of Conduct for Mediators* (August 2005), online: American Bar Association <http://www.abanet.org/dispute/news/ModelStandardsofConductforMediatorsfinalo5.pdf>, Note on Construction.

[401] Ibid., preamble.

[402] Commonwealth of Massachusetts, *Supreme Judicial Court Rule 1:18, The Uniform Rules on Dispute Resolution* (June 2005), online: Commonwealth of Massachusetts <http://www.mass.gov/courts/admin/legal/newadrbook.pdf>, rule 2.

[403] *European Code of Conduct for Mediators, supra* note 398, preamble. Similarly, the Model Code of Conduct for Mediators of the ADR Institute of Canada stipulates that "the Mediator shall be and remain wholly impartial and shall not act as an advocate to any party to the Mediation." ADR Institute of Canada Inc., *Model Code of Conduct for Mediators of the ADR Institute of Canada*, online: ADR Institute of Canada <http://www.adrcanada.ca/rules/documents/code_of_conduct2008.pdf> at IV.2.

the parties of "any financial or other interest, direct or indirect, in the outcome of the mediation".[404] The United States Model Standards of Conduct for Mediators similarly stipulate that "[a] mediator shall conduct a mediation based on the principle of party self-determination. Self-determination is the act of coming to a voluntary, uncoerced decision in which each party makes free and informed choices as to process and outcome".[405] Moreover, offering advice to the parties is proscribed by most codes of ethics for mediators. As the Massachusetts Uniform Rules on Dispute Resolution state, "A neutral may use his or her knowledge to inform the parties' deliberations, but shall not provide legal advice, counselling, or other professional services in connection with the dispute resolution process".[406]

Relating to the more specific context of armed conflicts, it is worth highlighting that the importance of the principles of neutrality, impartiality and confidentiality of an intermediary has been confirmed in the field of international criminal law, in particular by the ICTY. In *Simic*, the ICRC argued that its officials should and could not testify before the Tribunal, among other things because such a testimony would put at risk the future work of the ICRC, which was acknowledged by the Trial Chamber:

> the ICRC has a right to insist on such non-disclosure by parties to the Geneva Conventions and the Protocols. In that regard, the parties must be taken as having accepted the fundamental principles on which the ICRC operates, that is *impartiality, neutrality and confidentiality*, and in particular as having accepted that confidentiality is necessary for the effective performance by the ICRC of its functions.[407]

This reasoning cannot easily be extended to any intermediary, with the status and role of the ICRC being quite different from most peace mediation organizations.[408] However, the ICTY decision, along with the Rules of Procedure and Evidence of the ICC,[409] which point in the same direction, can be seen

---

[404] *European Code of Conduct for Mediators, supra* note 398, art 2.1.

[405] *Model Standards of Conduct for Mediators, supra* note 400, Standard I.A.

[406] Commonwealth of Massachusetts, *supra* note 402, rule 9(c)(iv).

[407] *Prosecutor v. Blagoje Simic et al*, IT-95-9, Decision on the Prosecution Motion under Rule 73 for a Ruling Concerning the Testimony of a Witness (27 July 1999) (International Criminal Tribunal for the Former Yugoslavia, Trial Chamber) at para 73 (emphasis added). On the ICRC's understanding of neutrality and impartiality, see also *infra* note 414.

[408] See also above, Section 3.1.

[409] The Rules of Procedure and Evidence of the ICC also recognize the particular status of the ICRC and prevent the Court from using privileged information obtained by the ICRC while performing its official functions. *Rules of Procedure and Evidence of the International Criminal Court*, 9 September 2002, Assembly of States Parties, 1st sess, Official Records ICC-ASP/1/3, rule 73.4.

as reflecting a widespread understanding with respect to the necessity of upholding the principles of neutrality, impartiality and confidentiality of an intermediary.

Neutrality and impartiality are clearly interconnected concepts, with one often being used to help define the other. By way of example, the term "a neutral" is employed by the Massachusetts Uniform Rules on Dispute Resolution to speak of "an impartial third party", which includes in this case "a mediator, an arbitrator, a case evaluator, and a conciliator".[410] In the mediation literature, the two terms appear to be used interchangeably, or at least without much precision, by most authors.[411] While a careful distinction does, therefore, seldom appear necessary in mediation theory and practice, with neutrality functioning "like a folk concept, talked, practiced, and researched on the basis of tacit and local understandings",[412] the two concepts do relate to different ideas. Neutrality, on the one hand, can be associated with the more general condition and stance of the mediator vis-à-vis the conflict. Enquiring into a mediator's neutrality means asking what he or she brings to the table, such as particular interests, prior relationships with the parties or potential benefits to be gained from the outcome of the mediation. Impartiality, on the other hand, relates more to the process and the way a mediator behaves towards the parties in the course of that process than to the background of the mediator. An impartial mediator, in other words, does not take sides or favor one of the parties and seeks to avoid creating the perception of bias.[413] When exploring particular examples in the following discussion, neutrality and impartiality

---

[410] Commonwealth of Massachusetts, *supra* note 402, rule 2.

[411] For an overview, see Christine Morris, "The Trusted Mediator: Ethics and Interaction in Mediation," in Julie Macfarlane, ed., *Rethinking Disputes: The Mediation Alternative* (Toronto: Edmond Montgomery Publications, 1997), 301, 318–320. As Morris summarizes, "The terms are not always defined. Existing definitions are inconsistent. Concepts are entangled. The result is considerable confusion" (ibid., 319). Morris also points out the general limitation of codes of ethics, which can only "provide a rather narrow answer" (ibid., 318). See also Cobb & Rifkin, *supra* note 187.

[412] Cobb & Rifkin, *supra* note 187 at 37.

[413] The salient criteria of "impartiality" are well explained in a paper containing draft guidelines for ethical mediation in armed conflict: "the best way to help the parties to elicit and reach a mutually determined and peaceful solution is to remain a genuinely disinterested third party and not favour one side over the other. In all their considerations and actions, mediators should be free from bias or prejudice regarding any party. At all times, the mediator should make decisions that are based on the *best interests of the process* and not the interests of one or other party or of one or other particular solution." Hugo Slim, "Towards Some Ethical Guidelines for Good Practice in Third Party Mediation in Armed Conflict" (2006), online: Oslo forum <http://www.osloforum.org/sites/default/files/TowardssomeEthicalGuidelinesforGoodPracticein3rdPartyMediationinArmedConflict.pdf> at 79.

will be referred to along these meanings,[414] although, in many instances, the negotiating parties, mediators and analysts will refer to a general sense expressed through terms including "neutrality", "impartiality", "objectivity", "independence", "fairness" and "nonpartisanship". It is worth highlighting that the UN secretary-general has characterized impartiality in a similar way, associating it with a mediator's ability to "run a balanced process that treats all actors fairly".[415] The secretary-general clearly distinguishes impartiality, "a cornerstone of mediation"[416] from neutrality; the latter is implicitly denied as a fundamental principle, since "a mediator, especially a United Nations mediator, is typically mandated to uphold certain universal principles and values".[417] The United Nations, quite contrary to its earlier approach in officially adopting the principles of both neutrality and impartiality for its role in peacekeeping,[418] thus sees itself as an impartial but, owing to its normative approach to mediation that will be discussed in more detail in Section 3.2.3, nonneutral mediator.

Although not too much emphasis should be given to this requirement, some process or structure must be ascertainable to be able to speak of mediation. In addition to neutrality and impartiality of the mediator, facilitation, empowerment of and voluntary decision making by the parties to the dispute

---

[414] Some documents, such as the Guidelines of the Law Society of New South Wales, do explicitly distinguish the two terms along these lines. Law Society of New South Wales, *The Law Society Guidelines for Those Involved in Mediation* (1993), online: The Law Society of NSW <http://www.lawsociety.com.au/idc/groups/public/documents/internetcontent/026506.pdf> at 5.1. and 5.2. It is interesting to note that in the context of humanitarian action, neutrality is associated with abstention, in other words, with refraining from participating in a conflict, while impartiality is rather a principle of action meaning that humanitarian action ought to be performed "in accordance with an objective standard applied equally to all parties". Marc Weller, "The Relativity of Humanitarian Neutrality and Impartiality" (1997) 91 *Proceedings of the Annual Meeting of the American Society of International Law* 441 at 443. For Hans Haug from the ICRC, "The relationship between neutrality and impartiality is evident. A neutral movement, which refrains from participating in conflicts and controversies, is ready and in a position to give its whole attention to suffering individuals and help them in proportion to their suffering, without a secondary purpose and without discrimination. Active, all round and impartial readiness to help, taking true needs into account, stems from renunciation and abstention." Hans Haug, "Neutrality as a Fundamental Principle of the Red Cross" (1996) 36:315 *Int'l Rev Red Cross* 627, online: ICRC <http://www.icrc.org/eng/resources/documents/misc/57jncv.htm>.

[415] *Strengthening the Role of Mediation*, *supra* note 328, Annex I, Guidance for Effective Mediation at para 26.

[416] Ibid.

[417] *Ibid* at para 27.

[418] For this discussion and criticism of this position, arguing that the UN is never neutral, see Steven R. Ratner, *The New Peacekeeping: Building Peace in Lands of Conflict after the Cold War* (New York: St. Martin's Press, 1995), 52–53.

are considered central definitional criteria, to which some peace mediation organizations explicitly commit themselves. One of the principles guiding the Carter Center, for instance, is to be "nonpartisan" and to act "as a neutral in dispute resolution activities".[419] It would seem that contrary to an adversarial approach associated with adjudication, a language of compromise and relationship is typically privileged over a discourse of legal rights and principles.[420] Corresponding to this common assumption, the notion of normative mediation and the idea that mediators can be norm advocates or even norm entrepreneurs appear underdeveloped. As I argue, mediators are normative actors who do exercise a highly normative influence on the negotiating parties not only regarding the perception of the legality and legitimacy of a peace agreement but also on the creation and respect of legal norms by the negotiating parties throughout the peace process.

As it has been stated above, the consent of the main parties to the conflict is a fundamental requirement for a mediator's involvement. However, the definitions quoted above do appropriately not include a requirement that the parties actually choose the mediator, which means that the mediator may not be either party's first choice. In the absence of better alternatives, the mediator might nevertheless be accepted by all the parties, although showing goodwill in this regard might be used at the negotiating table in exchange for other concessions.

Regarding the acceptance of mediation offers, it can be argued that Article 33 of the Charter of the United Nations, which requires all parties to any interstate dispute to "seek a solution by negotiation, enquiry, mediation, conciliation" or other means, is, if not binding for the parties in the context of an internal armed conflict, at least relevant. Article 33 certainly reflects a widely shared commitment to seek a peaceful resolution to any conflict and can therefore be seen as a normative proposition for parties to a conflict to negotiate and, if necessary, request the assistance of a mediator. Yet there can be no obligation to accept a particular mediation offer, since the precise means to resolve any conflict, whether interstate[421] or intrastate, cannot be imposed on the parties. In extreme situations, mediation offers by a third party to resolve

---

[419] See online: Carter Center <http://cartercenter.org/about/index.html>.

[420] As Trina Grillo summarizes, "The informal law of mediation settings requires that discussion of principles, blame, and rights, as these terms are used in the adversarial context, be deemphasized or avoided. Mediators use informal sanctions to encourage the parties to replace the rhetoric of fault, principles and values with the rhetoric of compromise and relationship". Trina Grillo, "The Mediation Alternative: Process Dangers for Women" (1991) 100 *Yale LJ* 1545 at 1560.

[421] Even under Article 33.2 of the UN Charter, the Security Council can only "*call upon* the parties to settle their dispute by such means" (emphasis added).

internal armed conflicts may even be viewed as an illegitimate intervention violating state sovereignty. The politically and militarily more powerful party – usually the state – may also reject such offers to prevent nonstate actors from gaining recognition on the international scene.[422]

Numerous examples illustrate this dilemma faced by potential mediators, which is amplified in situations of asymmetrical internal armed conflicts. The unwillingness of the Sri Lankan government to engage in internationally mediated peace negotiations with the Liberation Tigers of Tamil Eelam (LTTE) is linked to the concern that such negotiations confer certain legitimacy to the LTTE and increase the possibility of separation.[423] The proscription of the LTTE in India, the regional power, as a terrorist organization also created a "legal restriction" that prevented India from officially interacting with LTTE leaders.[424] Israel, in the negotiations in the early 1990s, fearing that direct negotiations with Palestinian representatives would imply recognition of Palestinian independence, only accepted the PLO as part of a Jordanian-Palestinian team.[425] Similarly, the Sudanese government has been reluctant to accept mediation offers, in particular from non-Arab or non-African states, intended to facilitate the negotiations with the rebel groups from Darfur. Finally, it was a former foreign minister of Burkina Faso, Djibril Bassolé, who was appointed chief mediator of the United Nations and the African Union and who succeeded in making the Sudanese government sign in Doha in February 2010 a promising cease-fire agreement with the Justice and Equality Movement (JEM),[426] a rebel group that had not signed the 2006 Abuja Agreement. The difficulty faced by a mediator in such situations of asymmetrical conflict to attempt to balance to a certain extent the power of the parties, while gaining the confidence of the more powerful party in order to be entrusted with the role of a mediator, will be discussed in more detail in Section 3.2.1.

---

[422] Similarly, powerful third-party states may be reluctant to "foreign" mediation in their sphere of influence. One of the many examples is India with respect to the Sri Lankan peace process. See Höglund & Svensson, *supra* note 114 at 345.

[423] See ibid., 349; S. I. Keethaponcalan, "The Indian Factor in the Peace Process and Conflict Resolution in Sri Lanka," in Jonathan Goodhand, Jonathan Spencer & Benedikt Korf, eds., *Conflict and Peacebuilding in Sri Lanka: Caught in the Peace Trap?* (London: Routledge, 2011), 39, 41, 43.

[424] Keethaponcalan, *supra* note 423 at 43, 52.

[425] William J. Bien, "The Oslo Channel," in Melanie C. Greenberg, John H. Barton & Margaret E. McGuinness, eds., *Words over War: Mediation and Arbitration to Prevent Deadly Conflict* (Lanham, MD: Rowman & Littlefield, 2000), 109, 117.

[426] *Framework Agreement to Resolve the Conflict in Darfur between the Government of Sudan (GoS) and the Justice and Equality Movement Sudan (JEM)*, 23 February 2010, UN Doc. S/2010/118.

Despite the parties' freedom to ignore mediation offers, justifying the repeated rejection of sincere and reasonable offers might be difficult, in the light of Article 33 of the UN Charter and in particular when several external actors voice a shared commitment to assist the belligerents in negotiating an end to their conflict. Such a policy could even be considered a threat to international peace and security and trigger Security Council action under chapter VII of the UN Charter. This means that, in extremis, mediation offers could be mandated by the Security Council, thus bearing a somewhat forceful legitimization vis-à-vis the negotiating parties, above all the state actor. Its usefulness being doubtful, such a measure, which would represent a radical departure from the largely voluntary nature of mediation, is likely to remain a theoretical option. Without an external authoritative, or even coercive, validation, the initial challenge for a third party consists, therefore, in getting involved as a peace mediator and in gaining legitimacy among the parties.[427] This question, in the quasi absence of formal definitional criteria, is shaped by several underlying principles.

3.1.2. Motives, Morality, Ethics – Underlying Principles

The legitimacy of a mediator, as perceived and constructed by the negotiating parties and other stakeholders, such as civil society actors, is intrinsically linked to his or her moral integrity, ethical behaviour and the motives that underlie the mediator's involvement. The kind and degree of normative impact on the peace negotiations also depend considerably on these factors.

External actors may have various motives for getting involved as mediators in a peace process. Of the five categories suggested by Christopher R. Mitchell, security rewards – in other words, the achievement of local and/ or regional peace and stability (and status or reputational awards), which can be of particular importance to third states and international or regional organizations – reflect well the public and private gains that may be generated by successful mediation.[428] Such rewards might serve the institution that is represented by the mediator or be of particular importance to the individual acting as a mediator. Hence, personal motives related to respect and self-esteem of a leading mediator can be an important factor and even outweigh geopolitical considerations. How the negotiating parties perceive such motives is, in fact, more significant for the legitimization of the involvement and of the conduct of a mediator than a presumably more objective assessment of his or

[427] For more information on this discussion, see Aggestam, *supra* note 105 at 72.
[428] Mitchell, "Motives for Mediation," *supra* note 386 at 44–45.

her motives. Indeed, a possible norm with respect to appropriate motives is, to a great extent, contingent on the subjective understanding of the parties and on mutual expectations, resulting from the interaction between potential mediators and negotiators. By way of example, while the United States has always been an interested party in the Israeli-Palestinian conflict, the significance of personal motives, as perceived by the negotiating parties, can be considered to have prevailed, at least at some points in the peace process. As recalled by a member of the Palestinian delegation in the 2000 Camp David negotiations, emphasizing personal over institutional or ideological motives, President Clinton simply "wanted success".[429] According to this line of analysis, "he was also defending his personal ambition to secure a prominent place in history.... The last thing he needed was yet another failure, especially so close to the end of his presidency".[430]

The involvement of the United States in the Balkan peace negotiations in the mid-1990s illustrates another set of motives as well as the fact that national interests may shape the mediation strategy and, therefore, affect the course of the negotiations. While Washington's primary objective was certainly to end the war, other factors relevant for the United States also played an important role. It was clear from the outset that the Balkan peace process would affect the influence of the United States in Europe and the role of NATO in the post–Cold War era. In this regard, the chief mediator, Richard Holbrooke, even affirmed explicitly in his account of the negotiations that "our responsibility was to implement the American national interest".[431]

Various motives can be attributed to Blaise Compaoré, who has played a key role as mediator in several West African countries, including in Côte d'Ivoire, Guinea, Togo and Mali. Compaoré himself has underlined the stabilization of the region as the major motive for his involvement.[432] At the same time, his mediation efforts also allowed him to develop his personal image as a reliable elder statesman and peacemaker, a considerable asset for instance for the 2010 presidential elections. As the International Crisis Group stated,

---

[429] Akram Hanieh, "The Camp David Papers" (2001) 30:2 *Journal of Palestine Studies* 75 at 89.

[430] Ibid., 90.

[431] Richard Holbrooke, *To End a War* (New York: Random House, 1998), 166. On the particularly delicate involvement of the president of the United States in the negotiations, whose "failure or error can hurt the national interests", see ibid., 301.

[432] "Nous avons des responsabilités à assumer dans le cadre de la stabilisation du continent. C'est pour nous-mêmes un devoir. Nous pensons qu'il est essentiel d'aller à la paix pour aller au développement. Mais il est aussi essentiel pour nous que l'Afrique prenne ses responsabilités face à ces crises". "Blaise Compaoré sur France Ô: 'L'Afrique doit assumer ses responsabilités'" (16 July 2010), online: Congrès pour la Démocratie et le Progrès <http://www.cdp-burkina.org/index.php?option=com_content&view=article&id=454&catid=30>.

Compaoré "est soucieux de soigner une image de leader sage, pondéré et moderne. S'il devient l'artisan de la paix au Togo et en Côte d'Ivoire, il peut espérer faire oublier son ancienne réputation de déstabilisateur discret de la région".[433] While a detailed analysis would go beyond the scope of this section, it is warranted to claim that in addition to concerns about his personal image, the pursuit of certain policy objectives, such as protecting the interests of the millions of Burkinabe citizens residing in Côte d'Ivoire and stabilizing Burkina Faso's relations with Côte d'Ivoire,[434] were among Compaoré's main motives to get involved as a mediator in various crises in West Africa.

Some of the motives outlined above may also represent reasons not to get involved as a mediator in peace negotiations. Besides factual constraints, such as the lack of expertise to function professionally as a mediator, the reputational risks might be perceived as being too high. A failure of a mediation endeavour can indeed hurt the image of a government or head of state involved in the process. The risks are even higher if the negotiations take place in the direct sphere of influence of the mediator. For instance, the political costs that could have been engendered by a failed negotiation effort made Washington very reluctant to hold the Bosnian peace talks on the territory of the United States.[435] If assuming the role of a mediator may be risky and costly in various ways for governmental actors, nongovernmental organizations may be more ready to get involved in a mediation process; political calculations and reputational risks are usually less important concerns for non-governmental organizations than for governmental actors. They can "swallow" a failed mediation effort more easily than a politically accountable government.[436] Moreover, because of their relative insusceptibility to public opinion, nongovernmental actors may be more flexible, inter alia with respect to the time frame of the negotiations.[437] An instructive example is the so-called Oslo channel that led

---

[433] International Crisis Group, "Côte d'Ivoire: faut-il croire à l'accord de Ouagadougou?" (27 June 2007), online: International Crisis Group <http://www.crisisgroup.org/~/media/Files/ africa/west-africa/cote-divoire/French%20translations/Cote%20dIvoire%20Can%20the%20 Ouagadougou%20Agreement%20Bring%20Peace%20French.ashx> at 6. Compaoré was also considered a supporter of Charles Taylor, convicted for war crimes and crimes against humanity by the Special Court for Sierra Leone. See ibid.

[434] Ibid.

[435] See Holbrooke, *supra* note 431 at 192. More generally, according to Holbrooke, the US government had "put American prestige on the line in 1995 to end the war" (ibid., 368).

[436] Chung-Chian Teng, "Introduction: Security, Conflict Management and Resolution in East Asia," in Jacob Bercovitch, Kwei-Bo Huang & Chung-Chian Teng, eds., *Conflict Management, Security and Intervention in East Asia: Third-Party Mediation in Regional Conflict* (New York: Routledge, 2008), 1, 11.

[437] Aggestam, *supra* note 105 at 11. Similarly, Oliver P. Richmond has argued that NGOs "provide a way of bypassing sovereignty and gaining internal access into societies, economies,

to the 1993 Israeli-Palestinian Declaration of Principles. To ensure maximum confidentiality and avoid undesired media attention, the meetings, although largely facilitated by the Norwegian government, were held under the cover of academic activities related to non-governmental organizations, such as the Norwegian FAFO (Institute for Applied Social Sciences).[438]

While an external actor, similar to the largely voluntary nature that a mediation process has for the parties, cannot be obliged to assume the role of a mediator, an involvement may be required under certain circumstances. In the light of the concept of the responsibility to protect (R2P) and informed by its principles, the high stakes that come along with deficient or not initiated peace negotiations suggest a possible duty of those third parties who have a reasonable chance of being accepted as mediators to get involved and attempt to assist the parties in finding a negotiated solution to an internal armed conflict. A detailed analysis of the still heavily debated concept of the responsibility to protect and the question as to whether it has given rise to specific rights and obligations would go beyond the scope of this book. However, it is not necessary to determine the precise ramifications of what Jutta Brunnée and Stephen Toope have called a "candidate norm".[439] What can be maintained is that, with military intervention being an option of last resort and the declared necessity to explore other avenues first,[440] the concept confirms a widely shared consensus towards the peaceful resolution of armed conflicts. In simple terms, this consensus reflects itself in a commitment to "do something" if a population suffers serious harm, as in the case of internal armed conflicts. While the concept of R2P has mostly been concerned with state sovereignty and its relationship to military intervention, in other words, with the responsibilities of states and the international community of states,[441] it can be argued that this commitment does not only engage states anymore. Against

and polities, with a high degree of legitimacy and flexibility". Oliver P. Richmond, "The Dilemmas of Subcontracting the Liberal Peace," in Oliver P. Richmond & Henry F. Carey, eds., *Subcontracting Peace: The Challenges of NGO Peacebuilding* (Aldershot: Ashgate, 2005), 19, 23. It should be noted that NGOs have been criticized for various reasons. For a comprehensive summary of critiques of NGOs, including issues of independence and accountability, see Kim D. Reimann, "Up to No Good? Recent Critics and Critiques of NGOs," in Oliver P. Richmond & Henry F. Carey, eds., *Subcontracting Peace: The Challenges of NGO Peacebuilding* (Aldershot: Ashgate, 2005), 37. See also the discussion in Chapter 4, Section 4.4.

[438] Aggestam, *supra* note 105 at 76.

[439] Brunnée & Toope, *supra* note 79 at 324.

[440] As the 2001 landmark document states, "Every diplomatic and non-military avenue for the prevention or peaceful resolution of the humanitarian crisis must have been explored." International Commission on Intervention and State Sovereignty, *The Responsibility to Protect* (Ottawa: International Development Research Center, 2001), UN Doc. A/RES/60/1 at 36.

[441] See the core principles in *ibid* at XI.

the backdrop of this responsibility to protect, states, international and regional organizations and nongovernmental organizations with mediation experience or significant knowledge of the respective conflict are therefore increasingly expected to get involved and may even be under an emerging obligation to do so. A serious mediation offer might be one strategy to fulfill this obligation, and a growing awareness that the reluctance to become involved can contravene, or at least breach the spirit of, the responsibility to protect might be developing. This awareness and associated commitments manifest themselves in the substantial efforts of the United Nations to render the field of peace mediation more effective and to provide a normative basis for the involvement and conduct of mediators,[442] as well as in the call of eminent peace brokers, such as Richard Holbrooke, for a stronger involvement of influential states in peace negotiations.[443]

Linked to the more specific motives for getting involved as a mediator and his or her legitimacy is the underlying morality of mediators. Despite the increasing adoption of codes of ethics in the field of mediation,[444] the morality of mediation is still marked by the absence of universally accepted rules.[445] We will see, moreover, that even some concepts that used to be considered fundamental, such as mediator neutrality and impartiality, have been discarded. Prescriptive norms, as in the form of codes of ethics, can only provide scant guidance in an assessment of the morality of mediation. The distinction of three domains of ethics made by Robert Van Es is more helpful to elucidate the different moral values and norms that underlie a mediator's approach and strategy. As Van Es shows, a successful outcome of the mediation effort is dependent on the appropriate ethical focus. He distinguishes personal ethics, which reflect the moral values and norms applied primarily in the private sphere; professional ethics, which relate to the moral values and norms used at work; and public ethics, which are linked to societal moral values and norms related to political questions.[446] Analysing the moral notions present in the Bosnian negotiations, Van Es concludes that personal and professional ethics outweighed public ethics in this context. According to him, a comparison

---

[442] See, in particular, the normative guidance provided through *Strengthening the Role of Mediation*, *supra* note 328, Annex I, Guidance for Effective Mediation.

[443] Holbrooke, *supra* note 431 at 369.

[444] It should be kept in mind that owing to the fundamentally different nature of peace negotiations as compared with mediation in domestic settings, the pertinence of these codes and their normative value are somewhat limited for a discussion on peace mediation.

[445] Keith Webb, "The Morality of Mediation," in Christopher R. Mitchell & Keith Webb, eds., *New Approaches to International Mediation* (New York: Greenwood Press, 1988), 16, 27.

[446] Robert Van Es, "Moral Compromise: Owen and Holbrooke Mediating the Bosnia Conflict" (2002) 7 *International Negotiation* 169 at 174–175.

of the two main mediation attempts confirms the assumption that restraining personal ethics and emphasizing professional ethics is more successful.[447] The first mediation attempt in the early 1990s, spearheaded by the European Community and the United Nations, was largely shaped by personal ethics.[448] The account of the European Community's representative David Owen is evocative. He describes, for instance, that he and his co-mediator Cyrus Vance "both felt throughout a deep sense of outrage" vis-à-vis the Balkan negotiators' behaviour,[449] who were all "masters of disinformation, propaganda and deceit".[450] Furthermore, Owen's objective was to achieve a compromise of integration through cooperative negotiations.[451] He "tried to be impartial" and aimed to achieve a "just and peaceful settlement".[452] Encountering a very different approach pursued by the Balkan negotiators, Owen was "offended" and complained about the other negotiators' behaviour; yet he did not adjust his own approach accordingly.[453]

Richard Holbrooke, on the other hand, the chief mediator of a subsequent mediation attempt made by the United States, restrained his personal ethics, focused on professional ethics and also expressed his views in terms of professional experiences.[454] According to Van Es, "Holbrooke's underlying emotions were always directly linked to his work".[455] Compared with the clear commitments and loyalties of Holbrooke, who emphasized that his team would "take orders only from President Clinton",[456] Owen tried to serve the interests of the twelve member states of the European Community, thus creating a more complex set of loyalties.[457] Moreover, Holbrooke had apparently learned from the preceding – failed – mediation attempt and adjusted his style to the conception of most negotiators in the Bosnian context: the "warrior conception".[458]

---

[447] Ibid., 176–177.

[448] Ibid., 177.

[449] David Owen, *Balkan Odyssey* (London: Indigo, 1995), 116.

[450] Ibid., 93.

[451] Van Es, *supra* note 446 at 172, 181. Van Es calls this approach the "*civil* conception", where "the other is assumed to be an equal, free civilian, and the right way to deal with the other is through soft, but argumentative negotiating" (ibid., 172).

[452] Owen, *supra* note 449 at 1.

[453] Van Es, *supra* note 446 at 173.

[454] Ibid., 177.

[455] Ibid., 176.

[456] Holbrooke, *supra* note 431 at 150.

[457] Van Es, *supra* note 446 at 176–177.

[458] Ibid., 173. In Van Es's "*warrior* conception", "self-interests are promoted according to opportunism.... The 'other' is an enemy, and the right way to deal with him is through hard, confrontational negotiating" (ibid., 172). Holbrooke also referred in the negotiations to his own past wartime experiences in Vietnam (see Holbrooke, *supra* note 431 at 217) and, as Van Es argues, exploited fighting as a "catalyst or obstacle" to the negotiations (ibid., 176).

This can also explain to some extent why Holbrooke's objective was not a compromise of *integration* but a compromise of *settlement*, to be achieved through confrontational negotiations.[459] It should be noted that the ethical focus associated with the different style of the mediation effort preceding the negotiations orchestrated by Holbrooke was certainly not the only factor that led to their failure. Other factors included disregarding the concept of ripeness of the conflict, with the mediators failing to wait for a window of opportunity and reacting to public pressure rather than to the demands of the parties,[460] as well as the lack of credible military-political backing of a mediated agreement.[461] The two examples of mediation attempts taken from the Bosnian context show that the conduct of mediators, in particular at the international level, is not only not formally regulated but also fairly undertheorized, which may be seen as obstructing a positive development of the field of peace mediation. Some commentators have even lamented the fact that "international mediation has not been conducted and developed in a systematic and professional manner."[462] This may be aggravated by the fact that it is not always the professional expertise of a mediator that accounts for his or her selection but other factors, such as status as a public figure.[463]

Clearly, peace mediation efforts should be made competently. A few general requirements for mediators have been identified, which include "sufficient knowledge to allow for an understanding of the phenomena encountered ... as well as of the practice undertaken ... a commitment to continuously improve understanding and competence, and a sense of integrity and standards for ethical conduct which will govern interactions with those who are served".[464] While professionalism seems essential for successful mediation efforts,[465]

---

[459] Ibid., 172, 181.

[460] Greenberg, Barton & McGuinness, "From Lisbon to Dayton," *supra* note 45 at 39.

[461] Ibid., 40.

[462] Nathan, *supra* note 214 at 1. The United Nations also expressed its preoccupation in this regard and identified a great need for professionalization of peace mediation. The *Guidance for Effective Mediation*, annexed to the 2012 secretary-general report on *Strengthening the Role of Mediation* (*supra* note 328), is part of the United Nations' efforts to address this need.

[463] This is pointed out in a technical brief drafted by the Public International Law & Policy Group for USAID: US Agency for International Development, "Technical Brief: Key Considerations when Supporting Peace Processes" (March 2013), online: USAID <http://www.usaid.gov/sites/default/files/documents/1866/Peace%20Processes%20Technical%20Brief%20FINAL.pdf> at 2.

[464] Fisher, *supra* note 395 at 23.

[465] The increasing move towards professionalization of mediation bears, however, certain dangers. Morris, for instance, argues that "there is a steady development of ethical standards which promote North American dominant culture values of individual autonomy and objectivity, without acknowledgement of the diversity of cultures and practices in the field of dispute resolution." Furthermore, "to what extent should a 'profession' composed of powerful

the freedom of mediators to adopt what they consider the most effective strategy and style to steer the negotiations is fundamental. Van Es has even argued that "in reaching agreements, negotiators do not need comprehensive, substantial moral theories.... If the parties believe the deal to be fair, it gives them in itself a motive for upholding it".[466]

In short, it appears that the normative disagreement on the necessity of regulating the conduct of peace mediators and, more specifically, of determining acceptable reasons that motivate their involvement has not been settled, at least not at the moment. Such attempts would, in any event, bear the danger of taking prescriptivist forms and thus run the risk of being counterproductive and of removing the essence of the mediator's role. The current situation does not preclude the negotiators or external actors to argue and conclude that the motives of a primarily self-interested mediator infringe certain principles and are in contradiction to the notion of mediation. In other words, there is no absolute necessity to identify and further develop such normative principles in the abstract, that is, removed from a specific context of peace negotiations, and to posit them explicitly in the form of "hard" criteria.

3.1.3. *Legitimacy in Motion – Reshaping the Neutrality/Impartiality Rule*

While an exclusively positivistic and prescriptive understanding of law would lead to the assumption that the conduct of peace mediators is virtually unregulated, a socio-legal and pluralistic approach, which does not focus on written, enforceable rules but takes into account and values the creation of legal norms – whether written or unwritten, formal or informal – by each and every actor, reveals a more nuanced portrait and is more truthful to the normative content of a mediation enterprise. In particular, as will be explored in Chapters 4 and 5, certain emerging obligations of international mediators have been identified by human rights activists and academics and have also been acknowledged by mediating organizations themselves. Regarding which mediators may get involved in peace negotiations, states, regional organizations and nongovernmental organizations do not follow a comprehensive set of rules or comply with well-defined or standardized ethical principles when getting involved as peace mediators. The United Nations can be considered as the only exception. While far from explicitly regulating the conduct of mediators, its attempts made in recent years, in particular through its *Guidance for Effective Mediation*, annexed

organisations of mediators decide what are the goals, values and ethics of mediation?" (Morris, *supra* note 411 at 344).
[466] Van Es, *supra* note 446 at 177.

to a 2012 report of the secretary-general on peace mediation, have paved the way for an increasingly norm-based conduct of mediators.[467]

Moreover, certain rules that were assumed to be generally valid are increasingly being rejected, both by commentators and in international mediation practice. By way of example, the traditional view that mediators must necessarily be strictly neutral and impartial to carry out their task successfully, with nonneutral and biased mediation bearing a supposedly inherent contradiction, has been refuted by conflict researchers. A number of studies carried out in the context of international negotiations have shown that mediator bias is not necessarily an obstacle and may, in fact, increase the efficiency of the mediation effort.[468] The mediator's special relationship with one of the parties might, for instance, be key to persuading this party to come to the negotiating table and to consent to an agreement.[469] An insider who is familiar with the conflict, knows the parties and might also have an interest in and benefit from a sustainable solution, might be a more credible and successful mediator than an outsider.[470] The neutrality of a mediator can, in other words, be considered a frequent but certainly not a necessary element to establish his or her legitimacy.

Several situations of peace mediation attempts confirm this assumption and convey a shared consensus on the nonexistence of a dogmatic rule on neutrality. The president of Burkina Faso, Blaise Compaoré, acted as a mediator in the negotiations that took place in Ouagadougou between the government of Côte d'Ivoire, represented by President Laurent Gbagbo, and the rebellious "Forces nouvelles", represented by Guillaume Soro, and that led to the 2007 Accord politique de Ouagadougou. Because of the open support of his government for the former rebels during the Ivorian crisis,[471] and Burkina Faso's traditionally strong relations with Côte d'Ivoire pertaining to trade, employment

---

[467] *Strengthening the Role of Mediation, supra* note 328, Annex I, Guidance for Effective Mediation. See also Chapter 5, Section 5.2.

[468] For an overview of such studies, see Christophe Dupont & Guy-Olivier Faure, "The Negotiation Process," in Victor A. Kremenyuk, ed., *International Negotiation: Analysis, Approaches, Issues,* 2nd ed. (San Francisco: Jossey-Bass, 2002), 39, 58–59; Jeffrey Z. Rubin, "Psychological Approach" in ibid., 256 at 260.

[469] Albin, *Justice and Fairness, supra* note 115 at 29.

[470] For this argument and examples, including Sierra Leone and Nicaragua, see Jacob Bercovitch & S. Ayse Kadayifci-Orellana, "Religion and Mediation: The Role of Faith-Based Actors in International Conflict Resolution" (2009) 14 *International Negotiation* 175 at 186–187.

[471] Ouagadougou supported the rebels logistically, financially and militarily; see International Crisis Group, "The War Is Not Yet Over" (28 November 2003), online: International Crisis Group <http://www.crisisgroup.org/~/media/Files/africa/west-africa/cote-divoire/Cote%20dIvoire%20The%20War%20Is%20Not%20Yet%20Over.ashx> at 10. For more information on the role of Burkina Faso in the Ivorian crisis, see Richard Banégas & René Otayek, "Le Burkina Faso dans la crise ivoirienne: effets d'aubaine et incertitudes politiques" (2003) 89 *Politique Africaine* 71 at 72.

and remittances,[472] Compaoré was never perceived as a perfectly neutral mediator. Furthermore, Ouagadougou had a particular interest in resolving the conflict because of the numerous Burkinabés who had lived in Côte d'Ivoire and massively returned to Burkina Faso after the start of the crisis in 2002.[473] Compaoré was nevertheless accepted by both sides, with the Ivorian government presumably taking into account his capacity to establish and maintain useful channels of communication with the Forces nouvelles. In the Accord politique de Ouagadougou, the parties even added to his facilitative role during the negotiations and conferred on him the function of an arbitrator to be assumed in the implementation phase of the agreement: "les Parties s'engagent à s'en remettre à l'arbitrage du Facilitateur [Blaise Compaoré] en cas de litige sur l'interprétation ou la mise en œuvre du présent Accord".[474] This means that an at least earlier predisposition of Compaoré regarding the Forces nouvelles did not hurt his image; it seems that he did not even have to publicly affirm his neutrality. Rather, he was, as an important and influential regional player, especially within the Economic Community of West African States (ECOWAS), deemed a legitimate and authoritative peace mediator.[475]

While difficult to summarize because of its complexity and varying nature over time, the role played by the United States in the Israeli-Palestinian peace process is also instructive. Far from being a strictly neutral facilitator without its own interests,[476] the United States was nevertheless considered a decisive player having the ability to broker a peace agreement. Personal qualities of key actors relating to a certain impartiality or perception thereof were an important factor, which, at times, raised increased expectations. Akram Hanieh, a member of the Palestinian team in the 2000 Camp David negotiations, recalls in his account of the negotiations that the Palestinians saw in President Clinton "a person who could listen and understand".[477] In the words of Hanieh, because the Palestinians suffered "from the total pro-Israeli bias

---

[472] United Nations Development Programme, "Issue Brief: The Conflict in Côte d'Ivoire and Its Effect on West African Countries: A Perspective from the Ground" (July 2011), online: UNDP <http://web.undp.org/africa/knowledge/issue-cotedivoire.pdf> at 5.

[473] Ibid.

[474] *Accord politique de Ouagadougou, supra* note 237, art 8.1.

[475] ECOWAS itself has also been characterized as an "insider-partial" mediator. For this argument in the context of Liberia and Sierra Leone, see Elgström, Bercovitch & Skau, *supra* note 327 at 18–24.

[476] In the words of a member of the US delegation, Robert Malley, "The United States had several different roles in the negotiations, complex and often contradictory: as principal broker of the putative peace deal; as guardian of the peace process; as Israel's strategic ally; and as its cultural and political partner". Malley & Agha, *supra* note 318.

[477] Hanieh, *supra* note 429 at 78.

of the US peace team, they were betting on – or had convinced themselves of – Clinton's objectivity".[478] If, according to Hanieh, the Americans, including their president, turned out to be incapable of being a reliable mediator at Camp David,[479] it is evident that the Palestinians had not expected to obtain a disinterested, perfectly neutral mediator but one who would be, thanks to his personal qualities, reasonably objective and impartial in the proceedings. Here, expectations that the mediator's personal qualities could ensure fair proceedings appear to have been more significant than the institutional background of the mediator, notably the United States' national interests.

If a universal rule on the neutrality and impartiality of peace mediators cannot be identified, a more subtle relationship between the two attributes appears to exist. Such an interplay between neutrality and impartiality can hardly be resolved in the abstract, but it can be argued that a nonneutral mediator might have to make stronger claims regarding his or her impartiality, while a neutral mediator might be able to balance in a more explicit manner the parties' power in a situation of an asymmetrical conflict. Connected to this notion are the style a mediator pursues and the degree of his or her intervention. We will see that the approach of nongovernmental actors to mediation resembles the one of smaller, neutral states but is different from the strategy usually pursued by more powerful states. How the principles of neutrality and impartiality are interpreted, valued and applied reflects the possible functions and scope of action of mediators and gives rise to different mediation styles: facilitative, formulative – or even manipulative – mediation.

3.2. POSSIBLE FUNCTIONS AND SCOPE OF ACTION OF MEDIATORS – SEIZING THE NORMATIVE IMPACT

Peace mediators may assume various functions and pursue very different styles. In this regard, the large literature on mediation in the domestic context[480] and its theorization of different mediation styles is helpful to some extent. While mediation has spread to various fields since the 1980s, including to business and commerce, the mediation styles described – notably facilitative,

---

[478] Ibid.

[479] Ibid., 92.

[480] It should be noted that what is called "domestic mediation" here is not necessarily limited to a national context. International business and commercial mediation can be considered an expansion of domestic mediation to the transnational level. However, the very concept of mediation, the different styles of mediators, proposed standards of ethics and other attributes characterizing the domestic mediation process, hardly change. Moreover, contrary to the context of peace mediation, litigation and arbitration usually remain genuine alternatives.

evaluative and transformative mediation[481] – are shaped by concepts that have been developed in well-defined and rather limited fields, such as family, employment and community disputes. Moreover, mediation in the domestic context is one form of so-called alternative dispute resolution, which can replace or precede litigation. Mediation is, therefore, usually considered an alternative to court proceedings, which is why the literature often focuses on comparing its benefits and shortcomings with judicial mechanisms. It is worth noting that contrary to the determinedly voluntary nature of mediation, the fairly recent popularity of so-called *alternative* dispute resolution mechanisms in domestic systems has led, somewhat paradoxically, to mandatory mediation. In some jurisdictions, certain cases must now undergo a mediation procedure as a prerequisite for litigation.[482]

Mediation in the context of the resolution of internal armed conflicts distinguishes itself from these more common forms of mediation in several ways. In the absence of a state-like legal system embracing and enforcing judicial decisions, adjudication is not an alternative. As a result, peace negotiations are never conducted against the backdrop of a possible decision made by a judge, which would be binding on the parties. It is also impossible to conceive the dispute in question as primarily private because of the very public nature of armed conflicts, which affect large portions of or the whole population of a state or region and regularly threaten regional or even global peace and security. A mediator, as will be explored in more detail in Sections 3.2.1 and 4.4, will often have to address related questions, such as representation of the belligerents and participation of stakeholders, such as civil society actors, at the negotiations. Furthermore, internal armed conflicts are usually highly asymmetrical in several aspects, which creates specific challenges for a mediator and his or impartiality.

In spite of these differences, the two main styles that characterize mediation more generally are also present in the context of the resolution of internal armed conflicts, and the subsequent analysis is pursued along these two styles. The conceptualization of these styles is borrowed from the mediation literature and can easily be applied to the more specific situation of peace mediation. The first style is facilitative mediation, which is sometimes also called pure mediation. This approach focuses on party self-determination and

---

[481] See e.g. Leonard L Riskin, "Mediator Orientation, Strategies and Techniques" (1994) 12 *Alternatives to the High Cost of Litigation* 111. For a thorough overview, see also Exon, *supra* note 397 at 589–594.

[482] For more information, see John W. Cooley, *The Mediator's Handbook: Advanced Practice Guide for Civil Litigation*, 2nd ed. (Louisville, CO: National Institute for Trial Advocacy, 2006), 21.

mediator impartiality. It can be formulative to a certain extent and include elements of norm-promotion. Nongovernmental actors and smaller, neutral states typically pursue this mediation style. The second style, sometimes called principal mediation, is more interventionist, generally also more formulative and at times even coercive. The normative impact of powerful states, which characteristically pursue this second style and can make use of their leverage on the negotiating parties as mediators, may be more visible than in the case of primarily facilitative mediation; in reality, as it will be argued, this impact is not necessarily more significant. While vindicating a more neutral and disinterested image, facilitative mediators may also bear an important normative ambition and influence peace negotiations in a significant way.

Distinguishing these two styles in their ideal forms should only be seen as serving to facilitate the analysis of the possible functions and the normative impact of mediators. In fact, these mediators always act along a continuum. Everything is a question of degree: clear boundaries neither should nor can be drawn, and one specific negotiation context can rarely be associated exclusively with one mediation style. As Christopher R. Mitchell has noted, too many factors are relevant, including "different levels of interaction, degrees of influence on the parties, interest in the outcome, coercive potential, dependence upon the adversaries, commitment to salient values for the conflict".[483] A mediator may as well pursue several styles subsequently or even simultaneously – with respect to different issues – in the same situation. Facilitative and interventionist mediation styles are therefore not fixed categories but reflect tendencies in mediation theory and practice.

3.2.1. *Facilitative Mediation – Beyond Neutrality and Impartiality?*

The most basic purpose of facilitative mediation is to bring the parties to the negotiating table and to enable communication between them. The mediator focuses on procedural issues to ensure that the parties meet and talk to each other but plays otherwise a rather passive role. The negotiating parties themselves have the main responsibility to initiate substantive discussions about agenda items and possible compromises on substantive matters. Respect for party autonomy and the parties' own personal evaluations, and even the application of the parties' own benchmarks and standards of fairness shape the mediator's role.[484]

---

[483] Mitchell, "Motives for Mediation," *supra* note 386 at 49–50.
[484] David A. Hoffman, "Paradoxes of Mediation," in Daniel Bowling & David A. Hoffman, eds., *Bringing Peace into the Room: How the Personal Qualities of the Mediator Impact the Process of Conflict Resolution* (San Francisco: Jossey-Bass, 2003), 167, 178; Exon, *supra* note 397 at 591.

Model examples of this kind of mediation in the context of peace negotiations include the mediation by the Community of Sant'Egidio of the 1992 Mozambican peace agreement and the 1993 Oslo Peace Accords between Israel and the PLO, facilitated by the Norwegian government and a nongovernmental organization. The mediators' reputation for neutrality has been highlighted as one of the key factors of successful mediation in these cases. The Norwegian mediators also had clear procedural rules on how to maintain their neutrality, throughout the negotiations, as "active facilitators" and not as "interested mediators".[485] Perfectly equal treatment of the parties on all procedural matters, including in providing equivalent rooms and meals, was a major concern.[486] Moreover, the main goal of the intervention was not to alter the negotiation structure or the extant power dynamics but to help the parties improve their communication.[487]

This type of mediation resembles most forms of mediation in the domestic context, where the mediator usually remains in the sphere of facilitation and is committed, as generally expected by the parties, to strictly maintaining his or her neutrality. In this context, the mediator does not assume an interventionist role by actively proposing solutions to the parties. Smaller states and nongovernmental organizations usually pursue such a facilitative mediation style. Surprisingly, the academic literature on international negotiations[488] reflects an apparently still common assumption that nongovernmental organizations play an important role as advocates but not as actors that are directly involved and participate in the negotiations, either as negotiators[489] or mediators. However, in recent years, several nongovernmental organizations have become specialized in the peaceful resolution of armed conflicts, such as the HD Centre,[490] Conciliation Resources,[491] the Centre for Conflict Resolution,[492] the Crisis

---

[485] Bien, *supra* note 425 at 129–130. See also Aggestam, *supra* note 105 at 77.

[486] Bien, *supra* note 425 at 130.

[487] Aggestam, *supra* note 105 at 77.

[488] See e.g. Brigid Starkey, Mark A. Boyer & Jonathan Wilkenfeld, *Negotiating a Complex World: An Introduction to International Negotiation*, 2nd ed. (Oxford: Rowman & Littlefield, 2005).

[489] For the involvement of civil society actors in peace negotiations, see Chapter 4. It has been pointed out that the direct influence of local nongovernmental organizations on peace negotiations is understudied. Susan Burgerman, "Voices from the Parallel Table: The Role of Civil Sectors in the Guatemalan Peace Process," in Oliver P. Richmond & Henry F. Carey, eds., *Subcontracting Peace: The Challenges of NGO Peacebuilding* (Aldershot: Ashgate, 2005), 85.

[490] See <http://www.hdcentre.org>.

[491] See <http://www.c-r.org>.

[492] See <http://ccrweb.ccr.uct.ac.za>.

Management Initiative,[493] International Alert[494] and the Carter Center.[495] It should be noted that individuals may as well play a pivotal role as mediators, although they usually represent a government, an international organization or a nongovernmental organization. A good example is the role of Martti Ahtisaari, a former president of Finland, and his nongovernmental organization, Crisis Management Initiative, in mediating a peace agreement for the Indonesian province of Aceh.[496]

It has rightly been pointed out that much attention has been given to religion as a source of conflict but not to religion as a source of peacemaking.[497] Yet faith-based nongovernmental organizations may also become involved as mediators in peace negotiations. This does not necessarily result in religion itself turning into the main framework for the negotiations, but, as it is argued here, such mediators certainly introduce principles and concepts rooted in their religion. The Catholic Church, for instance, has played a key role in the peace negotiations in Mozambique and Colombia. Widely respected in the country, the Catholic Church has been a moral guide for the process in the case of Colombia.[498] In Mozambique, the Catholic Church had already assisted in the negotiations of the Front for the Liberation of Mozambique (FRELIMO) with Portugal, which resulted in Mozambique's independence in 1975.[499] Having started to provide humanitarian aid to Mozambique in the 1980s,[500] the Roman Catholic Community of Sant'Egidio became actively involved in 1990 as a mediator in the peace negotiations between the FRELIMO government and its rival RENAMO (Mozambican National Resistance) in the civil war. These negotiations culminated in the conclusion

---

[493] See <http://www.cmi.fi>.

[494] See <http://www.international-alert.org>.

[495] See <http://www.cartercenter.org/peace/conflict_resolution/index.html>.

[496] For an overview, see Eric Teo Chu Cheow, "The 'Track 2' Process within ASEAN and Its Application in Resolving the Aceh Conflict in Indonesia," in Jacob Bercovitch, Kwei-Bo Huang & Chung-Chian Teng, eds., *Conflict Management, Security and Intervention in East Asia: Third-Party Mediation in Regional Conflict* (New York: Routledge, 2008), 165.

[497] David Smock, "Divine Intervention, Regional Reconciliation through Faith" (2004) 25 *Harvard International Review* 46 at 46. The Pope has traditionally played an important role as an intermediary. For examples of the involvement of the Holy See as peace mediator, see Janne Haaland Matlary, "The Just Peace: The Public and Classical Diplomacy of the Holy See" (2001) 14:2 *Cambridge Review of International Affairs* 80 at 89–91.

[498] For more information on the peace process, see Arvelo, *supra* note 347.

[499] For more information, see Pierre Anouilh, "Sant'Egidio au Mozambique: de la charité à la fabrique de la paix" (2005) 59 *Revue internationale et stratégique* 9 at 13.

[500] Ibid., 15.

of the Rome Accords in 1992.[501] While the Community of Sant'Egidio benefits from its location in Rome and its ties to the Vatican and Italian diplomacy, it remains, as a nongovernmental actor, independent in its policy decisions.[502] The mediation strategy of the Community of Sant'Egidio tries to combine the official, or "institutional", with the flexibility of the "informal".[503] However, as a member of the Community has noted, "The real factor behind the success of this formula is the fact that St. Egidio is interested solely in putting an end to the conflict; it has no other interests to defend and considers any contribution that can work to this end useful and welcome".[504] Compared with the typical motives of third parties getting involved in a peace process, a "low" agenda, besides altruism and humanitarian interests, stands out in this case. The triggering cause for the Community was the realization that its humanitarian aid to Mozambique would not be effective without reaching a lasting peace agreement, which meant for the Community, "leaving the field of simple solidarity and development work and entering the conflictual world of politics and war".[505]

Smaller, peaceful states that are driven by humanitarian interests but do not have other major interests in the respective conflict region may assume a similar role. Comparative advantages of Switzerland as a mediator, for instance, have been described as lying in its credibility, proficiency and reliability.[506] Regarding internal armed conflicts in Africa, Switzerland has the additional intrinsic assets of not having a colonial past or particular economic interests. Similarly, Norway's approach to mediation has been portrayed as benefiting from "impartiality, consistency, and confidentiality with the resources of an industrialized state".[507] Oslo's close collaboration with

---

[501] *General Peace Agreement for Mozambique*, supra note 55. For a more general analysis of the Mozambique negotiations, see Ibrahim Msabaha, "Negotiating an End to Mozambique's Murderous Rebellion," in I. William Zartman, ed., *Elusive Peace: Negotiating an End to Civil Wars* (Washington, DC: Brookings Institution, 1995), 204.

[502] Mario Giro, "The Community of Saint Egidio and Its Peace-Making Activities" (1998) 33:3 *International Spectator* 85 at 87.

[503] Ibid., 89.

[504] Ibid. Giro also notes that "the Community's approach to peace-making is based on [a] fundamental social commitment to the poor and the dispossessed" (ibid., 86).

[505] Ibid., 89.

[506] Sguaitamatti & Mason, supra note 372 at 100. The fact that Switzerland is not part of a strong regional organization, the missing cultural proximity to most conflict regions and an underdeveloped tradition of leadership because of Switzerland's consensus-based political system are cited as comparative disadvantages (ibid., 101).

[507] Daniel Lieberfeld, "Small Is Credible: Norway's Niche in International Dispute Settlement" (1995) 11:3 *Negotiation Journal* 201 at 201. Norway has been involved, inter alia, in the peace processes in Israel-Palestine, Guatemala and Sri Lanka.

nongovernmental organizations to conduct peace talks, as, for instance, in Sri Lanka and Sudan,[508] also confirms the assumption that a clear and generalized distinction between the role and mediation approach between state actors and nonstate actors cannot be made. Although the coercive potential of nongovernmental actors and smaller states may be limited, we will see that their normative ambition, combined with their legitimacy and credibility, may have an equally or even more significant and long-lasting normative impact on the negotiations than power-based and more interventionist mediation.

Even a somewhat minimalist view on the role and impact that a facilitative mediator has or might have bears two important caveats. First, the mere presence of mediators inevitably influences the negotiating parties.[509] The behaviour of the negotiating parties changes with the presence of an intermediary, even if he or she does not have a clear normative ambition regarding, for instance, fair and equal representation at the negotiating table or the inclusion of human rights and transitional justice elements on the agenda. A certain procedure, which may be suggested explicitly or implicitly by the mediator, may nevertheless have to be followed by the parties, and their style of communication and negotiation strategies may change simply because of the presence of a mediator.

Second, neutrality itself cannot be taken for granted, even if the mediator is perceived as neutral or impartial by the parties and actively tries to preserve this perception. As already mentioned, the neutrality and impartiality of a mediator have often been cited as crucial elements of successful peace negotiations. With respect to the mediator's role in the negotiations leading to the 1992 Mozambican peace agreement, for instance, a member of the Community of Sant'Egidio emphasized the importance of "the [mediator's] ability to convince the parties to the conflict of one's impartiality, an essential premise for mediation".[510] Maintaining an image of impartiality represents a particular challenge for mediators in the case of internal armed conflicts, which are characterized

[508] See Ann Kelleher & James Larry Taulbee, "Building Peace Norwegian Style: Studies in Track 1½ Diplomacy," in Oliver P. Richmond & Henry F. Carey, eds., *Subcontracting Peace: The Challenges of NGO Peacebuilding* (Aldershot: Ashgate, 2005), 69, 78.

[509] Daniel Bowling & David A. Hoffman, "Bringing Peace into the Room: The Personal Qualities of the Mediator and Their Impact on the Mediation," in Daniel Bowling & David A. Hoffman, eds., *Bringing Peace into the Room: How the Personal Qualities of the Mediator Impact the Process of Conflict Resolution* (San Francisco: Jossey-Bass, 2003), 13, 21. Bowling and Hoffman draw an interesting parallel between the mediation context and the discovery of the physicist Werner Heisenberg that the observation of particles influences their behaviour (ibid., 20).

[510] Giro, *supra* note 503 at 100 (emphasis omitted).

by a multidimensional asymmetry.[511] These asymmetries include the legal status of the parties, with nonstate actors seeking international recognition through the negotiation process and uneven military and material capabilities, as well as negotiation capacities.[512] Mediators can accept an imbalance between the parties and pursue a strategy of "even-handedness", or they can try to empower the weaker party through an "equalizing strategy" based on the assumption that strictly facilitative mediation in situations of important power imbalances only allows the stronger party to dominate the weaker party and is, therefore, ineffective.[513] While mediation researchers disagree on whether equal power is a necessary prerequisite for effective and fair mediation,[514] the mediator must take a stance in an uneven situation and make a decision between maintaining or attempting to equalize the imbalance. A legal asymmetry can be levelled by conferring some legitimacy to nonstate actors,[515] who may be regarded as mere "insurgents" or "criminals" by the state actor. This may turn out to be a challenging endeavour for the mediator. As it has been argued, in situations of asymmetrical conflicts, "maintaining a perception of neutrality becomes, over time, close to impossible".[516] Describing the involvement of the Norwegian government as a mediator in the Sri Lankan peace process and the contribution of the Nordic countries (Norway, Sweden, Denmark, Finland and Iceland) to the Sri Lanka Monitoring Mission in the early 2000s, Höglund and Svensson provide a good account of the challenges that an a priori neutral third party might experience. Despite the clear objective of remaining neutral and being continuously perceived as neutral, the Nordic mission faced harsh criticism of bias, for instance, after making a proposal to the Sri Lankan government to recognize the Sea Tigers, the naval unit of the LTTE, as a de facto naval unit.[517]

---

[511] Höglund & Svensson, *supra* note 114 at 343. On the resolution of asymmetrical conflicts, see generally Christopher R. Mitchell, "Asymmetry and Strategies of Regional Conflict Resolution," in I. William Zartman & Victor A. Kremenyuk, eds., *Cooperative Security: Reducing Third World Wars* (Syracuse: Syracuse University Press, 1995), 25. On the asymmetrical nature of internal armed conflicts and its implications for the reciprocal nature of international humanitarian law, revealing "the emptiness of a purely positivistic grounding of these norms", see René Provost, "Asymmetrical Reciprocity and Compliance with the Laws of War," in Benjamin Perrin, ed., *Modern Warfare: Armed Groups, Private Militaries, Humanitarian Organizations, and the Law* (Vancouver: UBC Press, 2012), 17, 37.

[512] Höglund & Svensson, *supra* note 114 at 344.

[513] Ibid., 345. Exon points out that such a more directive mediation style "may infringe on the parties' rights of self-determination, which in turn may affect the mediator's neutrality and impartiality" (Exon, *supra* note 397 at 595).

[514] See Höglund & Svensson, *supra* note 114 at 345, n 6.

[515] See ibid., 346.

[516] Ibid., 359.

[517] Ibid., 351–353.

In addition to the difficulties of maintaining an image of neutrality and impartiality that a mediator might experience in practice, it should be highlighted that the involvement of a human being, whether in a more personal capacity or as a representative of an institution, is based on assumptions, values and norms that might differ from those of the negotiating parties. In other words, a mediator will always have to manage some tensions between the parties' objectives and his or her own normative beliefs and principles.[518] These beliefs and principles may be evident; more often, however, they are latent, albeit not necessarily less powerful. In the context of a discussion on the morality of mediators, it has been argued that "the act of mediation is not a neutral act…. The mediator may claim to be neutral with respect to the values and claims of the combatants, but the activity of mediating is still a declaration of values held by the mediator".[519] A commitment to neutrality, impartiality and objectivity, in line with prevalent Western dispute resolution practice and evoking a Rawlsian "veil of ignorance",[520] can certainly not hide cultural assumptions.[521] Morris argues convincingly that

> people who are enculturated within a given social system often consider the prevailing norms, however unfair, to be "objective".… Everybody has values and biases. It is not possible for mediators to park them at the door of the hearing-room. The ideal of autonomous objectivity does not recognise the fact that mediators are influenced far more than they may realise by the culture and social setting in which they live, and the political, social and power structures within which they operate.[522]

Good examples are faith-based organizations, such as the Community of Sant'Egidio, which may claim to be strictly neutral in mediating peace negotiations. Yet they certainly stand for and introduce certain values into the negotiations and shape, at least to a certain extent, both the procedure and the substance of the negotiations accordingly. In the words of Morris, the "'objective' mediator is a mythical creature removed from the realities of interaction among human beings who live in communities".[523]

Furthermore, and related to the degree of intervention, mediation practice has shown that mere facilitation is not always constructive. An explicit

---

[518] Bowling & Hoffman, *supra* note 510 at 23.
[519] Webb, *supra* note 445 at 16. This is also recognized by practitioners involved in peace negotiations. See, for instance, the document prepared by the Public International Law & Policy Group for USAID: US Agency for International Development, *supra* note 463 at 2.
[520] John Rawls, *A Theory of Justice* (Cambridge, MA: Harvard University Press, 1971), 136–142.
[521] For this argument, see Morris, *supra* note 411 at 313, 329–330.
[522] Ibid., 330.
[523] Ibid.

acknowledgement that a strictly noninterventionist approach may lead to an impasse can be found in the 2005 version of the Model Standards of Conduct for Mediators, a revision of the 1994 Standards: "although party self-determination for process design is a fundamental principle of mediation practice, a mediator may need to balance such party self-determination with a mediator's duty to conduct a quality process".[524] In the context of peace mediation, more powerful states are often more ready to go beyond facilitation. They may have a considerable coercive potential and may even use their leverage to pursue a proactive "carrots and sticks" – mediation style, which may lead to more tangible results than merely facilitative mediation.

3.2.2. Interventionist Mediation and Its Limits

Compared with nongovernmental organizations and smaller, neutral states not having particular interests in the respective conflict region, the mediation style and strategy as well as the normative ambition of more powerful third states is more frequently linked to their political, military and economic influence on the negotiating parties. Moreover, since noncompliance with projected norms may be sanctioned by an interventionist powerful mediator, the normative impact on the negotiations is regularly more visible than in the case of nongovernmental organizations, whose normative ambition must be voiced and implemented through more subtle means.

It should be recalled that "power" and "influence" are, of course, contextual. A state that is generally seen as powerful may not necessarily be able to channel its influence towards the negotiating parties in any situation. The negotiations in Bosnia and Northern Ireland, which both took place in the mid-1990s and in which the United States was involved, are a good example. Senator George Mitchell could not use much of the "power" of the United States in Northern Ireland and pursued a largely facilitative mediation style in this context, while Richard Holbrooke, relying on the great influence of the United States, pursued a highly interventionist approach to mediation in Bosnia.[525] The potential of powerful states to pursue a highly interventionist mediation style may as well be constrained by internal factors. In contrast to nongovernmental organizations being able to assume the role of peace mediators with more flexibility, the mediation strategy of a state is affected by the mediator's greater public exposure and by the fact that a mediator who represents a government is – directly or indirectly – accountable to its electorate.

---

[524] *Model Standards of Conduct for Mediators, supra* note 400, Standard I.A.1.
[525] Peter Wallensteen, *Understanding Conflict Resolution*, 3rd ed. (London: Sage, 2012), 292–293.

This may not only influence significantly the mediation strategy but also introduce certain views and concepts that a government represents and that may, as a result, be normative for the negotiations. The internal decision-making process within larger administrations regarding the role to be played by the mediation team and steps to be proposed to the negotiating parties tends to be lengthier and more complex. Robert D. Benjamin uses the metaphor of a trickster to explain why independent mediators, who may employ various imaginative techniques, are often more successful than mediators representing larger institutions:

> The mythological trickster figure offers a metaphor and a better model of mediation practice. Tricksters are not experts; they are collaborators and sometimes coconspirators with the parties in effecting settlement of conflict. This is perhaps why the institutionalization of mediation can be so problematic. Mediators working within an agency or organization may be constrained and stifled.[526]

The importance that a mediation team maintains a relatively large *marge de manoeuvre* and flexibility in the negotiations was also underlined by Richard Holbrooke. In his words, the "unprecedented degree of flexibility and autonomy" that the Balkan mediation team had been granted by the US government, was vital for a successful outcome. "We were concerned that if ... we were subjected to the normal Washington decision-making process, the negotiations would become bogged down".[527] In other words, requiring a mediator to conduct his or her work according to strict rules of the institution he or she acts on behalf of would represent an undesired and unconstructive overregulation of mediation.

Internal armed conflicts, owing to their typically asymmetrical nature, may arguably not be prone to strictly facilitative mediation but may warrant a more interventionist approach. Besides the traditional concepts of party self-determination, consensuality and mediator neutrality and impartiality, newer ethical standards reflect a trend towards fair results and related concepts of fairness, such as balancing the parties' power.[528] In situations of asymmetrical conflict, the weaker party may be more willing to accept a mediation style that

---

[526] Robert D. Benjamin, "Managing the Natural Energy of Conflict: Mediators, Tricksters, and the Constructive Use of Deception," in Daniel Bowling & David A. Hoffman, eds., *Bringing Peace into the Room: How the Personal Qualities of the Mediator Impact the Process of Conflict Resolution* (San Francisco: Jossey-Bass, 2003), 79, 129.

[527] Holbrooke, *supra* note 431 at 170.

[528] Exon, *supra* note 397 at 613. Exon shows that embracing fairness concepts leads to tensions with the impartiality requirement.

goes beyond facilitation. While some critics have called such a more evaluative mediation style, because it jeopardizes mediator neutrality, an oxymoron,[529]
other mediation scholars argue that certain elements of evaluation – and not
only facilitation – can, or even must, be part of a mediation.[530]

This consideration, for instance, can explain why the Palestinian negotiators have accepted the United States, despite its general backing of Israel and
support of Israel's interests, as a mediator. Washington's potential leverage over
Israel, combined with a more directive and evaluative mediation style that goes
far beyond mere facilitation, certainly reduces the parties' self-determination
and discards mediator neutrality as a central attribute.[531] It may also contribute
to balancing asymmetry between the parties, which can be considered vital
for the Palestinian side. The mediation efforts made by the United States in
the situation of Bosnia, resulting in the 1995 Dayton Peace Agreement, illustrate these aspects related to such an evaluative and formulative, and at times
also coercive and manipulative, mediation style.[532] Contrary to the earlier
Vance-Owen attempt, which has been characterized as "an exercise in classical mediation", with the mediators having "no leverage or power other than
the parties' goodwill",[533] Dayton went far beyond facilitative mediation. As
Holbrooke noted, "'Dayton' has entered the language as shorthand for a certain type of diplomacy – the Big Bang approach to negotiations: lock everyone
up until they reach agreement".[534] Formulative mediation may be particularly
important if the negotiating parties lack or have asymmetrical diplomatic and
legal drafting skills. In Dayton, the mediation team not only shuttled between
the parties and tried to facilitate communication between them but assumed

[529] Kimberlee K. Kovach & Lela P. Love, "'Evaluative' Mediation Is an Oxymoron" (1996) 14:3
Alternatives to the High Cost of Litigation 31. According to Maureen E. Laflin, "Mediators
who approach the process as 'advocates of a good solution' are necessarily adopting an attitude of power and control over the outcome, an attitude which cannot but compromise the
principles of self-determination and impartiality." Maureen E. Laflin, "Preserving the Integrity
of Mediation through the Adoption of Ethical Rules for Lawyer-Mediators" (2000) 14 *Notre
Dame JL Ethics & Pub Pol'y* 479 at 498.

[530] For more details, see Exon, *supra* note 397 at 604.

[531] For more information on this debate, see ibid., 603.

[532] For a more thorough discussion of formulative and manipulative mediation styles, see Starkey,
Boyer & Wilkenfeld, *supra* note 489 at 38.

[533] Greenberg, Barton & McGuinness, "From Lisbon to Dayton," *supra* note 45 at 47. According
to these authors, the subsequent Owen-Stoltenberg plan similarly "expose[d] the true failure
of classical mediation" (ibid., 54).

[534] Holbrooke, *supra* note 431 at 232. For a more general analysis of US approaches to negotiation,
see Richard H. Solomon & Nigel Quinney, *American Negotiating Behavior: Wheeler-Dealers,
Legal Eagles, Bullies, and Preachers* (Washington, DC: United States Institute of Peace, 2010).
Solomon and Quinney identify, for instance, four mindsets – businesslike, legalistic, moralis-
tic and superpower negotiation – that shape US negotiating behaviour (ibid., 19–45).

the responsibility to draft the texts to be negotiated. In one of the key moments at Dayton, it was the mediation team that handed each delegation the draft annexes pertaining to the constitution, the electoral system and the NATO-led implementation force (IFOR).[535] Regarding the coercive-manipulative component, Holbrooke recalled this power approach to mediation repeatedly in his account of the negotiations. For instance, he recalls threatening the Bosnian foreign minister that Washington would hold him publicly responsible if the conclusion of a pre-agreement to Dayton failed.[536] At a later meeting, US Secretary of State Warren Christopher warned that "the situation would have to be cleared up right away if Sarajevo wanted to avoid serious consequences to its relations with the United States".[537] The Bosnian context also shows that the negotiating parties might willingly acknowledge the leverage that a powerful mediator has on the other parties, or even contribute to building a common perception of this leverage. Dismissing concerns that the Bosnians might not agree to a US proposal, President Milosevic expressed his perception of the leverage of the United States to Holbrooke in the following way: "you are the United States. You can't let the Bosnians push you around this way. *Just tell them what to do*".[538]

Such a highly interventionist involvement of a mediator can reach an extreme level, pushing the limits of an acceptable mediation environment and challenging the very notion of mediation. Moreover, the policy of the US mediation team to support the continuation of some fighting, such as a Croatian offensive "valuable for the negotiating process",[539] and to press for a military intervention by NATO and, subsequently, for an extension of the bombing campaign,[540] which supposedly created "ripeness" for a negotiated solution of the conflict,[541] appears hardly compatible with the notion of a peace mediator who is committed to avoiding more violence.

In line with the mediation literature focusing on domestic contexts, an "overly zealous" peace mediator who exercises excessive influence or coercion should be viewed critically[542] and remain an exception. Not only are agreements concluded under external pressure often breached as soon as this pressure lessens;[543] there simply does not seem to exist a widely shared consensus as

---

[535] Holbrooke, *supra* note 431 at 240.
[536] Ibid., 139.
[537] As cited by Holbrooke in ibid., 183.
[538] As cited in ibid., 306 (emphasis added).
[539] Ibid., 68.
[540] In Holbrooke's words, "Give us bombs for peace" (ibid., 132).
[541] Greenberg, Barton & McGuinness, "From Lisbon to Dayton", *supra* note 45 at 63.
[542] See Exon, *supra* note 397 at 608.
[543] Sguaitamatti & Mason, *supra* note 372 at 74.

to the compatibility of such conduct with the very notion of peace mediation. Exploring the principles of justice and fairness in international negotiation and emphasizing the "voluntary acceptance by parties of whatever arrangements are proposed" as a core criterion,[544] Cecile Albin has maintained that negotiations should never take place in a coercive or manipulative context.[545] According to her, "Agreements held in place by force are clearly seen as illegitimate".[546] While Albin argues convincingly that upholding justice and fairness improves the chances of reaching a widely respected agreement, some flexibility might be required in balancing these principles. Coercion is certainly antithetical to mediation. Although the conduct of the US mediation team in the Bosnian situation must therefore be considered incompatible with the traditional notion of requiring a mediator to remain impartial and to honour party self-determination, Dayton has nevertheless shown that some coercion may be constructive to make the parties engage in serious negotiations and accept certain compromises. Dayton thus pushed the limits of the notional concept of mediation in a rather exceptional manner that was, however, consented to both by the negotiating parties and the international community. In this sense, this process contributed to transforming the normative framework of peace negotiations by diluting, in a fairly unequivocal way, a widely shared commitment to neutral, impartial, noncoercive and nonmanipulative peace mediation.

In sum, the boundaries of legitimate peace mediation styles certainly are malleable, and grey zones remain. What can be concluded is that a forceful imposition of the text of a peace agreement on the parties would certainly go beyond the acceptable scope of action of a mediator and would be considered manifestly illegitimate conduct. In addition, the foregoing analysis along facilitative and interventionist mediation styles has not only shown that different actors mediate in different manners but that, depending on the status and the style pursued, the legitimacy of a mediator and compliance of the negotiating parties with projected norms may be more or less difficult to ascertain. Yet peace mediation is always a normative enterprise. From powerful states or strong regional organizations to small nongovernmental organizations, mediators never act in a legal vacuum and may also assume an active norm-promoting role.

---

[544] Albin, *Justice and Fairness, supra* note 115 at 12. For an example of the debate on how mediators should deal with justice and fairness, see Jonathan M. Hyman, "Swimming in the Deep End: Dealing with Justice in Mediation?" (2004) 6:19 *Cardozo Journal of Conflict Resolution* 19.

[545] Albin, *Justice and Fairness, supra* note 115 at 12. See also Avishai Margalit, who argues more generally that "an agreement based on coercion is not a compromise." Avishai Margalit, *On Compromise and Rotten Compromises* (Princeton, NJ: Princeton University Press, 2010), 92–93.

[546] Albin, *Justice and Fairness, supra* note 115 at 12.

3.2.3. *The Normative Ambition of Peace Mediators*

As mentioned above, because of fundamental differences in the nature of the respective disputes, the literature on domestic mediation is only partly helpful for the analysis of peace negotiations aiming to end internal armed conflicts. The three mediation models as conceived by Ellen A. Waldman, however, are useful for going beyond the general discussion on mediation styles; they elicit more specifically the normative ambition of peace mediators vis-à-vis the negotiating parties. Instead of focusing on the traditional distinction made by mediation researchers between pure and principal mediation or facilitative, evaluative and transformative styles, Waldman frames her models – norm generating, norm educating and norm advocating – by conceptualizing the mediator's approach towards excluding or including existing legal and social norms in the process. In Waldman's words,

> the model characterized as "norm generating" corresponds to traditional notions of mediation, in which disputants are encouraged to generate the norms that will guide the resolution to their dispute. In this model, disputants negotiate without recourse to existing social norms. The models characterized as "norm educating" and "norm advocating" constitute more recently evolved paradigms, in which societal norms occupy a significant role in the disputants' negotiations.[547]

In a norm generating mediation process,[548] the mediator therefore assists the parties in identifying the main issues but is otherwise mostly concerned with facilitating communication and guiding the parties through the process. Since norms external to the process are irrelevant in this model, with the ultimate authority belonging to the parties themselves,[549] the parties largely build their own normative framework and identify themselves the parameters of the negotiations and the criteria for an acceptable solution of the dispute. "Empowerment" of the parties and "relational concerns"[550] are central. Waldman identifies several areas where applying this model seems appropriate, including disputes of little public concern, such as neighbourhood quarrels, and in situations of conflicting legal or social norms where

---

[547] Waldman, *supra* note 398 at 708 (footnote omitted).
[548] See generally ibid., 713–723. It is worth emphasizing that Waldman does not conceive the mediator as norm generator.
[549] Ibid., 718.
[550] Ibid., 720. Or, as Fuller argues, "the central quality of mediation ... [is] its capacity to reorient the parties toward each other, not by imposing rules on them, but by helping them to achieve a new and shared perception of their relationship" (Fuller, "Mediation", *supra* note 399 at 325).

neither norm has achieved consensus status in society.[551] In a nutshell, norm generating mediation works best between relative equals in the private sphere.

Norm-based mediation, with its varieties norm education and norm advocacy, was, according to Waldman, a response from the mediation field to concerns that strictly private, norm generating mediation could endanger the application of widely accepted societal norms and, in particular, disregard protective norms.[552] In the norm education model, the mediator educates the parties about existing legal and social norms relevant to the dispute, without seeking their implementation by the parties.[553] While the parties are free to waive their rights with full knowledge of the underlying norms, such a waiver is unproblematic for the specific dispute and society at large.[554] This model is now regularly applied in divorce contexts, although other fields are also mediated "in the thick shadow of the law".[555]

Waldman convincingly argues that norm education may be insufficient in protecting the interests of the parties as well as societal concerns, in particular in situations of extreme power imbalance between the parties or when the dispute involves fundamental public values.[556] For these cases, one has to go beyond traditional views on mediation. Waldman proposes the norm advocating model, where the mediator not only educates the parties about legal and social norms but insists on their incorporation into the agreement and becomes, to some extent, a "safeguarder" of these norms.[557] As an example, environmental disputes are usually mediated within a framework defined by environmental regulations.[558]

The three models are not mutually exclusive and can be applied simultaneously; depending on the nature of the dispute, a mediator might combine two or even all three models.[559] Similarly, any mediation attempt in the context of the resolution of internal armed conflicts can hardly be subsumed under one single model. As argued above, in the absence of a hierarchical legal

---

[551] Waldman, *supra* note 398 at 721.

[552] Ibid., 724–727, 730.

[553] Ibid., 730.

[554] Ibid., 741.

[555] Ibid., 733. For a discussion on an appropriate use of the norm education model, see ibid., 738–742.

[556] Ibid., 742.

[557] Ibid., 745. See also Exon, *supra* note 397 at 599. Norm advocacy shares some features with the notion of norm entrepreneurship put forward in international relations theory. See e.g. Ann Florini, "The Evolution of International Norms" (1996) 40:3 *International Studies Quarterly* 363 at 375.

[558] Waldman, *supra* note 398 at 747.

[559] For an example taken from a divorce context, see ibid., 756.

order readily available, the legal-normative framework of peace negotiations is primarily generated by the negotiating parties, with a mediator guiding them through the process and influencing the negotiations more or less directly and intentionally. It is evident, however, that an armed conflict, which affects the population at large and possibly threatens regional and international peace and security, is not a private dispute between relative equals. Moreover, protective norms and fundamental values of concern to the global community as a whole may be at stake. As a result, mediators increasingly – and appropriately – acknowledge that existing norms, and notably international legal norms, are relevant in peace negotiations. Mediators have therefore started to exercise more consciously a highly normative influence on the negotiating parties not only regarding the perception of the legality and legitimacy of peace negotiations but also on the respect of legal norms by the parties throughout the process. Two groups of actors, namely, international organizations and nongovernmental organizations, illustrate well this normative consciousness and ambition of mediating organizations.

Because of the high number of peace processes it has been involved in, the United Nations plays a pivotal role with respect to mediation in the context of internal armed conflicts.[560] Furthermore, the conduct of its representatives must correspond to standards the organization itself stands for. By way of example, the signature of a UN representative, such as a special representative of the secretary-general, on a peace agreement signals "some type of UN endorsement, meaning that the UN should have audited the agreement in terms of the normative requirements which it promulgates and claims to uphold".[561]

In the 2000s, the mediation strategy of the UN has experienced an increasing normatization, with the field of transitional justice and the trend towards individual accountability for core crimes being the most visible element. While the UN had participated in several peace negotiations with amnesties on the agenda, thus giving such amnesties "a kind of international legitimacy",[562]

---

[560] A list of recent situations in which the United Nations led or supported mediation is included in the report of the secretary-general, *Strengthening the Role of Mediation, supra* note 328 at para 22. To render its mediation activities more effective, the United Nations established in 2006 the Mediation Support Unit in the Department of Political Affairs. See <http://www.un.org/wcm/content/site/undpa/main/issues/peacemaking/mediation_support>.

[561] Bell, "Peace Agreements and Human Rights: Implications for the UN," *supra* note 185 at 250.

[562] Kai Ambos, "The Legal Framework of Transitional Justice," in Kai Ambos, Judith Large & Marieke Wierda, eds., *Building a Future on Peace and Justice: Studies on Transitional Justice, Peace and Development, The Nuremberg Declaration on Peace and Justice* (Berlin: Springer, 2009), 9, 57, n 240. For an overview of the UN policy with respect to amnesties and peace building in the 1990s, see Stahn, "United Nations Peace-Building," *supra* note 249.

the organization now regularly assumes transitional justice obligations with respect to its role as a mediator in peace negotiations, as confirmed in several documents. Most notably, in 1999, following the signing of the Lomé Peace Agreement and the famous disclaimer of the special representative of the secretary-general with respect to amnesties for grave crimes committed in the conflict in Sierra Leone,[563] the secretary-general issued guidelines to his envoys and representatives regarding the respect of human rights in peace negotiations.

> During the course of the year, I issued guidelines to my envoys and representatives involved in peace negotiations to assist them in tackling human rights issues that may arise during their efforts. These guidelines address the tensions between the urgency of stopping fighting, on the one hand, and the need to address punishable human rights violations on the other. *The guidelines do not attempt to provide sweeping answers* to these questions. However, they are, I believe, a *useful tool* with which the United Nations can assist in brokering agreements in conformity with law and in a manner which may provide the basis for lasting peace.[564]

Although these guidelines were not published, they represented a first step in addressing the assumed dilemma of a mediator between aspiring to honour the necessity of punishing perpetrators of core crimes and seeking to end the hostilities. They also reflect the UN's appreciation of the obligations of an international mediator to bear a normative ambition vis-à-vis the negotiating parties. In line with one of the main arguments of this book, the importance of these guidelines does not lie in determining a specific outcome but in providing a normative tool that shapes the process and contributes to the development of a legal-normative framework for peace negotiations, in this case with UN participation.

The 2008 Nuremberg Declaration on Peace and Justice, a document elaborated by a group of international experts and adopted by the UN General Assembly, points in the same direction and illustrates the growing awareness that mediators have obligations regarding their own conduct during peace negotiations and that they fulfill a norm-promoting role vis-à-vis the negotiating parties:

> Mediators bear a *responsibility* to contribute creatively to the immediate ending of violence and hostilities while promoting sustainable solutions. Their *commitment* to the core principles of the international legal order has to be

---

[563] See Chapter 2, Section 2.3.2. (in particular *supra* note 248 and accompanying text).
[564] UN, "Secretary-General Comments on Guidelines," *supra* note 329 (emphasis added).

beyond doubt. They *should promote* knowledge among the parties about the normative framework, including international human rights standards and humanitarian law, and available options for its implementation, so that the parties can make informed choices.[565]

The role of the UN as a peace mediator can, therefore, be conceived as norm promoting, which embraces Waldman's notions of norm education and norm advocacy. The mandate of the UN consists not only in raising awareness about fundamental human rights norms but also in supporting their respect throughout the process as well as in seeking to construe them, at least partly, as the normative basis of a peace agreement. Because of this involvement, the negotiating parties are continuously encouraged to consider, internalize and eventually comply with the respective norms projected. The secretary-general's 2012 report on the mediation activities of the United Nations evokes a successful example of the implementation of this norm-promotional approach: the secretary-general's special adviser for Yemen is said to have "explained United Nations principles and standards relating to women and peace and security to government officials and stressed that a transition process must include the participation of women. As a result of those efforts, the 2011 Yemen Transition Agreement called for women to be represented in key institutions".[566] In the same report, the secretary-general underlines as well that the participation of women must be further promoted and that the "United Nations will continue to do its part to push for the adequate representation of women and availability of gender expertise in peace process".[567] The *Guidance for Effective Mediation*, annexed to this report, is remarkable for its ambition to guide not only UN mediators but also other mediators involved in peace negotiations. In a norm entrepreneurial manner, the United Nations thus underlines the need for a more professional approach to mediation – "mediation is a specialized activity"[568] – and advises peace mediators that they, among others, "ensure and seek to demonstrate that the process and the treatment of the parties is fair and

---

[565] *The Nuremberg Declaration on Peace and Justice*, UN Doc. A/62/885 (2008) at IV, 1.2 (emphasis added).

[566] *Strengthening the Role of Mediation*, *supra* note 328 at para 25.

[567] Ibid., para 77(b).

[568] Ibid., Annex I, Guidance for Effective Mediation at para 12. Regarding the professional approach to mediation, the guidelines also state that "[a] good mediator promotes exchange through listening and dialogue, engenders a spirit of collaboration through problem solving, ensures that negotiating parties have sufficient knowledge, information and skills to negotiate with confidence and broadens the process to include relevant stakeholders from different segments of a society. Mediators are most successful in assisting negotiating parties to forge agreements when they are well informed, patient, balanced in their approach and discreet" (ibid.).

balanced",[569] and "ensure that the parties understand the demands and limits of applicable conventions and international laws".[570]

The mediation approach of the United Nations is probably the most visible example of the normatization of a peace mediator's strategy that aspires to have a normative impact on the negotiating parties. However, other mediators, as exemplified by the norm promoting role of the Catholic Church in the Colombian peace process,[571] also bear a similar normative ambition. Indeed, several nongovernmental mediation organizations have outspokenly acknowledged that a willingness to educate the negotiating parties about their legal obligations and to advocate for their respect – for instance, in the field of justice and accountability – may determine the negotiations significantly. As it has been noted in a report of the Centre for Humanitarian Dialogue, "of course the positions of the parties are key, but even where negotiators are ambivalent or initially resistant, much can be achieved through a proactive mediator ... The mediator should be clear in advising on the demands and limits of international law, and use expert input where necessary".[572]

Similarly, International Alert, a peace-building nongovernmental organization, expresses at greater length in its code of conduct its commitment to advocate for the inclusion of human rights standards in peace agreements and the establishment of accountability mechanisms:

> *We are committed to* pressing for international human rights standards to be recognised and incorporated in settlement agreements and for the establishment and development of effective institutions for the protection, promotion and implementation of civil, political, economic, social and cultural rights. *We are also committed to* supporting measures which address the problems of impunity and injustice, historical truth and compensation for victims.[573] ...
> The question of impunity in protracted violent conflicts can be particularly problematic. The strengthening of the judiciary as well as the establishment of effective institutions such as independent human rights commissions, truth commissions or independent tribunals are possible measures that can

---

[569] Ibid., para 28.

[570] Ibid., para 42.

[571] The 1990 agreement characterizes the Catholic Church as "moral and spiritual guide". *Acuerdo político entre el gobierno nacional, los partidos políticos, el M-19, y la iglesia católica en calidad de tutora moral y espiritual del proceso*, supra note 233. See also Bell, "Peace Agreements: Their Nature and Legal Status," *supra* note 57 at 401.

[572] Priscilla Hayner, "Negotiating Justice: Guidelines for Mediators," *Centre for Humanitarian Dialogue & International Centre for Transitional Justice* (February 2009), online: Centre for Humanitarian Dialogue <http://www.hdcentre.org/files/negotiating%20justice%20report.pdf> at 20–21 [henceforth Hayner, "Negotiating Justice"].

[573] International Alert, *supra* note 336 at 5 (emphasis added).

be taken to ensure that violations in the past do not recur in the future. Where appropriate, *promoting awareness* of the International Criminal Court and related institutions and mechanisms should also be encouraged.[574]

These examples illustrate that the models of norm education and norm advocacy are applied in practice by mediating organizations. A strong normative element is introduced into the negotiations through the mediator's assertion of certain values and principles, for instance, regarding the respect of norms projected by international human rights law and international criminal law. The normative bearing on the negotiations is not necessarily directed at a specific outcome but primarily at the process. It is a process-related norm that provides the parties and the mediator with a legitimate zone of possible agreement. The use of the necessary leverage by a powerful mediator might, however, shift the focus from the process to the outcome and lead to a result-based normatization of the negotiations. Mediating the Bosnian negotiations, the United States, for instance, had a rather well-defined policy and openly stood for certain principles. The mediation team took a hard stance on justice and insisted on individual accountability for the crimes committed by the Bosnian Serbs. In the words of Holbrooke, "I am not going to cut a deal that absolves the people responsible for this ... It would be better to risk failure in the negotiations than let the Serbs get away with another criminal act".[575] It was also clear that Washington would not support a separation of the Bosnian territory,[576] which would have meant to "legitimize Serb aggression or encourage Croat annexation".[577] In other words, the *marge de manoeuvre* of the negotiating parties might be thin if an influential mediator has a clear normative ambition and, additionally, shifts the focus from process to outcome.

3.3. CONCLUSION

This chapter has shown that the normative dimensions of peace mediation manifest themselves at all stages of the involvement of mediators. The way in which a mediator appears, both before and when getting involved as a mediator, is related to his or her motives, underlying morality and ethics and determines perceptions of his or her legitimacy. In certain cases, potential

---

[574] Ibid., 10 (emphasis added). Similarly, HD Centre proclaims that "the HD Centre's operational work suggests that justice and the rule of law play a central role in sustainable conflict resolution." See <http://www.hdcentre.org/projects/justice-peacemaking>.

[575] Holbrooke, *supra* note 431 at 90, 92. See also Van Es, *supra* note 446 at 176.

[576] See e.g. Holbrooke, *supra* note 431 at 117.

[577] Ibid., 233.

mediators may also be under an emerging obligation to intervene, in other words, to make serious mediation offers and use their expertise to convince the belligerents that a peaceful resolution of the conflict is both possible and valuable. These aspects as well as additional concerns such as a mediator's impartiality – and his or her understanding thereof – have a normative bearing on the conduct of a mediator during the negotiations, regardless of the mediation style pursed. Both facilitative and more interventionist mediators shape the process of the negotiations and may influence the substance of a peace agreement significantly. It is at this stage that the mediators' normative ambition, which may be latent or openly proclaimed, reveals itself most forcefully.

This chapter has also argued that the involvement of mediators in peace negotiations and ways to legitimize this involvement are creative, and norm creative, endeavours. Generalized, universally applicable norms are rare; even principles like mediator neutrality and impartiality cannot be taken for granted. They have to be dealt with by the mediators, who are normative actors, in interaction with other normative actors involved in every context of peace negotiations. At the same time, the actors do not have to reinvent the normative wheel every time. By forming an influential epistemic community, it is above all the mediators themselves who ensure interaction and exchange of normative knowledge between different contexts. If the right balance between facilitative and interventionist mediation cannot be reached in the abstract, some normative trends are developing, such as with respect to the necessity of going beyond strictly facilitative mediation in certain situations, especially in the context of asymmetrical conflicts, and to a not clearly delineated yet nevertheless existing boundary as to the acceptable behaviour of an interventionist peace mediator.

The examples analysed in this chapter, taken from various contexts and including states, the United Nations and nongovernmental organizations as peace mediators, show that these mediators not only assist the negotiating parties in generating their proper normative framework but are also norm promoters and norm creators who may introduce predominantly external norms into the negotiations. Fundamental requirements for the open pursuit of such normative mediation are the acknowledgement by the mediator of his or her potential to have a normative impact on the negotiations, her aspiration to go beyond mere facilitation, and a commitment to put into practice this normative ambition. Moreover, latent forms of normative commitments and effects are omnipresent and not necessarily less influential in the context of peace negotiations, a point that will be explored in more detail in the discussion of civil society actors in Chapter 4.

While it is difficult to measure the direct effects of a mediator's normative commitment to include, for instance, issues of justice and accountability into the negotiations and raise awareness about the ICC, such a commitment shapes the normative framework of peace negotiations and can be highly influential for the conduct of the negotiating parties. Clearly, the respect of legal norms introduced into the negotiations can usually not be enforced by a normpromoting mediator in the absence of a coercive sanction-based system. These norms, nonetheless, may shape the negotiations significantly and may provide considerable guidance with a view to rendering them more legitimate. Furthermore, mediators do not operate in isolation but always interact, in some way or another, with other mediation actors. The direct and indirect sharing of experiences, knowledge and normative beliefs within the epistemic community of peace mediators thus contributes to the development of shared norms and facilitates their promotion.

Shifting our lens to the process and to an aspirational view, and beyond static requirements like "neutrality" and "impartiality", may again be helpful. Such requirements should not be considered according to a binary "either-or" logic but as something that a mediator should, self-reflectively[578] and in interaction with the parties, strive for throughout the process;[579] being satisfied with the fulfillment of pre-established standards is simply insufficient. Similarly, party self-determination and their control over the process are relative variables that do not predetermine the process. Because a mediator should generally not impose his or her views against the will of the parties, one of the objectives of a mediator should be the maximization of party self-determination.[580] Yet a mediator should also make conscious decisions as to his or her intervention that may be required, such as to balance the typically unequal capacities of the negotiating parties in the context of an asymmetrical internal armed conflict.

Especially when emphasizing process over outcome, it is apparent that mediators increasingly assume an internalized commitment to play a norm-promotional role, most notably regarding the respect of international human rights and humanitarian law. This shapes the behaviour of the negotiating parties, can have a significant effect on their compliance with the respective norm projected and contributes to identifying the contours of a legal framework that can be used as a parameter to assess the conduct both

---

[578] For a discussion of self-awareness and self-reflectivity in mediation, see Astor, *supra* note 392 at 230.

[579] For this perspective and associated difficulties, see ibid., 227–228.

[580] Ibid., 234–235.

of mediators and the negotiating parties, as well as the legitimacy of peace negotiations more generally, thus increasing their effectiveness. This framework manifests itself in more specific emerging legal obligations, such as those relating to the participation of civil society actors and to addressing justice and accountability, that are introduced, deliberated and increasingly internalized by the negotiating parties and peace mediators.

4

Civil Society Actors – Legal Agency and Emancipatory Obligations

The increasing normative consciousness and ambition of peace mediators instantiate a tendency towards norm-based peace negotiations as well as a growing emphasis on process-related norms over specific outcomes. If peace mediators may have, as an epistemic community consisting of a loose network of more or less professional organizations, a fairly visible and congruent impact on the legal-normative framework of peace negotiations, they are, of course, not the only actors involved in this norm creative enterprise. In addition to the main negotiating parties and peace mediators, civil society actors play an increasingly important role, not only in the implementation phase of a peace agreement but also while an agreement is being negotiated. As we will see, they may perform a variety of roles but are, in comparison to peace mediators, even less tangible as a "community". Despite the heterogeneous nature of civil society, it is important to adequately seize the diverse roles that these actors play in different contexts and to reveal their location in and contribution to the normative dynamics of peace negotiations.

This chapter argues that civil society actors do not only have significant norm ascertaining and norm creative capacities; their involvement also manifests the interrelatedness of legal obligations of some of the actors involved in peace negotiations and the norm creative capacities of others. These obligations and capacities can be seen as relational and, in fact, mutually enhancing: while the norm creative capacities of civil society actors add to the obligation of negotiators and mediators to render the negotiations more inclusive, the same obligations recognize and facilitate the development of the capacities of civil society actors to shape the legal-normative framework of peace negotiations. At the same time as peace negotiators and mediators increasingly recognize and respect their obligations vis-à-vis the participation of civil society actors in the negotiations, civil society actors not only ask for such participation but contribute to the normative dynamics of peace negotiations in various ways.

4.1. CONTEXTUALIZING THE INVOLVEMENT OF CIVIL SOCIETY ACTORS

Since the term "civil society" does not refer to the same kind of actors or organizations in every context, with the notion of civil society being inherently dynamic, a fixed definition appears futile.[581] Nonetheless, several useful elements that have been identified in the literature can be discerned: civil society thus refers to a "diversity of spaces, actors and institutional forms" that are, at least in theory, "distinct from those of the state, family and market" and that are characterized by "uncoerced collective action around shared interests, purposes and values".[582]

An analysis of the role of civil society actors in peace processes has been virtually absent in the legal literature. Since the peace and conflict studies literature, which is much richer in this regard, can provide important insights, the arguments made in this chapter also rely on this body of literature. Generally, it can be said that from a conflict-resolution perspective, emphasizing the role of civil society actors is part of the idealist-inspired conflict-resolution and the conflict-transformation schools. Contrary to the realist-inspired conflict management school, these schools focus on the root causes of conflicts and on the relationships among the parties.[583] The idea that every conflict and every conflict-resolution process bears the potential to make all the actors involved reconsider and possibly transform their relationship is reflected in the concept of transformative mediation. As Bush and Folger have argued,

> the central feature of human nature, when perceived from the starting point of transformation value, is neither individuality nor connectedness (and their associated qualities) but the element that relates the two in an integrated, whole human consciousness – the relational capacity. Human beings are thus simultaneously separate and connected, autonomous and linked,

[581] For a similar approach, see Maria Jessop, Diana Aljets & Betsie Chacko, "The Ripe Moment for Civil Society" (2008) 13 *International Negotiation* 93 at 94.

[582] These elements are part of the useful working definition used by the London School of Economics' Centre for Civil Society (last updated 23 April 2009), online: British Library <http://www.webarchive.org.uk/wayback/archive/20100820110531/http://www.lse.ac.uk/collections/CCS/introduction/what_is_civil_society.htm>.

[583] Thania Pfaffenholz, "Civil Society beyond the Liberal Peace and Its Critique," in Susanna Campbell, David Chandler & Meera Sabaratnam, eds., *A Liberal Peace?* (London: Zed Books, 2011), 138, 142.

self-interested and self-transcending. Furthermore, they are capable of relating these dualities in an integrated wholeness that makes them capable of genuine goodness of conduct.[584]

Such an approach resonates strongly with a pluralistic and socio-legal understanding of legal normativity and its focus on human interaction. This pluralistic conception allows us, again, to recognize the norm creative capacity of all the actors involved in peace negotiations and to appreciate the continuous creation and adjustment of legal norms as well as their organizing and guiding role.[585] In this sense, law is not a one-way projection of authority[586] but a process itself that is continuously negotiated by legal actors. These actors, moreover, "possess a transformative capacity that enables them to produce legal knowledge and to fashion the very structures of law that contribute to constituting their legal subjectivity".[587] It is not the formal origin of the norms that matters, but the relevance accorded to them by the legal actors, their "lived interaction" with the norms.[588]

Constructivist approaches developed in the field of political science and international relations are also insightful here. As Emanuel Adler has summarized, "Constructivism is the view that the manner in which the material world shapes and is shaped by human action and interaction depends on dynamic normative and epistemic interpretations of the material world".[589] For constructivist scholars, identities and interests are not given but socially constructed,[590] and norms and normative considerations are central to the

---

[584] Bush & Folger, *supra* note 7 at 243.

[585] For the argument that law assumes an "organizing, reminding and guiding role in providing part of the communication structure" of post-conflict societies, see Zumbansen, *supra* note 29 at 9.

[586] This is drawn on Fuller's understanding of law. Fuller, *The Morality of Law, supra* note 1 at 192.

[587] Martha-Marie Kleinhans & Roderick A. Macdonald, "What Is a *Critical* Legal Pluralism?" (1997) 12 *CJLS* 25 at 38.

[588] Macdonald & Sandomierski, *supra* note 81 at 618–619. Macdonald & Sandomierski argue that "legal norms, in whatever site of law, are imagined by human beings, given expression by human beings, lived by human beings, followed by human beings, modified by human beings, rejected by human beings – in a word, constituted by human beings not primarily as passive legal subjects, but above all as active legal agents. The obligational force of legal rules derives not from the normative status with which they are vested when ultimately wielded by officials, but from the normative status human beings afford them in their everyday lives" (ibid., 614–615).

[589] Emanuel Adler, "Seizing the Middle Ground: Constructivism in World Politics" (1997) 3:3 *European Journal of International Relations* 319 at 322 (emphasis omitted).

[590] John Gerard Ruggie, "What Makes the World Hang Together? Neo-Utilitarianism and the Social Constructivist Challenge" (1998) 52:4 *International Organization* 855 at 856, 862–864.

analysis of international politics and international relations.[591] Law is not a given either that is conceptually separate from legal subjects and detached from its social context.[592]

While the direct or indirect participation of such civil society actors in peace negotiations is emphasized in this chapter, it should be borne in mind that numerous other activities of these actors may further the objective of concluding a lasting peace agreement, for instance, through the promotion of popular support for peace.[593] As is shown throughout the chapter by means of several examples, civil society actors may play different and changing roles during the negotiations themselves. A good example worth explaining at some length here is the Inter-Religious Council of Sierra Leone (IRCSL). The IRCSL, established by Sierra Leone's religious leaders in 1997,[594] not only called on the warring parties to end the violence and organize campaigns to sensitize the whole population about the impact of the conflict on Sierra Leoneans;[595] through its activities, it also laid the groundwork for and facilitated formal negotiations between the main belligerents, namely, the government of Sierra Leone and the leaders of the RUF, to end the decadelong conflict. While condemning the intense atrocities, in particular those committed by the RUF, the IRCSL also listened to the grievances of the rebels and provided them with other ways of expression than violence.[596] As Maria Jessop, Diana Aljets and Betsie Chacko have argued by drawing on language coined by Saadia Touval and I. William Zartman, the IRCSL helped the parties overcome a mutually

---

[591] See the overview in Finnemore & Sikkink, *supra* note 56 at 889–891. As Ruggie nuances, "Constructivists do not claim to understand the extraordinarily complex processes regarding constitutive rules fully (or even mostly). But neorealists and neoliberal institutionalists lack even a place for them in their ontology. The scope of their theories, as a result, is confined to regulative rules that coordinate behaviour in a preconstituted world" (Ruggie, *supra* note 591 at 874).

[592] See also Chapter 5, Section 5.3.

[593] Walton provides an overview of the main objectives related to civil society peace activities: complementing track one negotiations; creating a peaceful and prosperous society; building a democratic polity; and fostering popular support for peace (Walton, *supra* note 189 at 187).

[594] The IRCSL included, among others, the Supreme Islamic Council, the Sierra Leone Muslim Congress, the Federation of Muslim Women Associations in Sierra Leone, the Council of Imams, the Roman Catholic Church and the Pentecostal Churches Council. Thomas Mark Turay, "Civil Society and Peacebuilding: The Role of the Inter-Religious Council of Sierra Leone" (2000) 9 *Accord* 50, online: Conciliation Resources <http://www.c-r.org/sites/c-r.org/files/Accord%2009_10Civil%20society%20and%20peacebuilding_2000_ENG.pdf> at 51.

[595] Jessop, Aljets & Chacko, *supra* note 582 at 99–100. The IRCSL was in part inspired by the Liberian Inter-Religious Council, which had openly condemned human rights violations during and after the conflict in Liberia. Turay, *supra* note 595 at 51.

[596] Jessop, Aljets & Chacko, *supra* note 582 at 101.

hurting stalemate and "created what might be termed 'psychosocial' MEOs [mutually enticing opportunities] that ripened the conditions for formal peace negotiations".[597]

At the beginning, the IRCSL thus assumed primarily a rather typical role for a faith-based civil society movement – peace advocacy – quite similar, for instance, to the role of the Acholi Religious Leaders's Peace Initiative in northern Uganda.[598] In early 1999, however, the IRCSL started to act as an intermediary and began to meet directly with President Kabbah and the RUF leaders, and later also with the Liberian president Charles Taylor in order to address the regional dimensions of the conflict.[599] Finally, members of the IRCSL, respected by the government and the RUF, broader civil society as well as the relevant external actors, facilitated the negotiations culminating in the conclusion of the Lomé Peace Agreement in July 1999.[600] It is worth highlighting that while the IRCSL was perceived as a fundamentally "neutral" actor, it is obvious that the IRCSL – just like any other civil society actor – stood for certain convictions[601] and introduced certain norms and values into the peace process, such as forgiveness and reconciliation.[602] In this sense, the involvement of the IRCSL contributed to building a shared normative foundation of the negotiations.

In Sierra Leone, faith-based civil society organizations were thus able to unite and to become actively involved in the peace process. Even if the RUF resumed the fighting the year after the conclusion of the Lomé

---

[597] Ibid., 100–101.

[598] The Acholi Religious Leaders Peace Initiative was the driving force behind the adoption of the 1999 Amnesty Act. Refugee Law Project, "Behind the Violence: Causes, Consequences and the Search for Solutions to the War in Northern Uganda" (February 2004), online: Refugee Law Project <http://www.refugeelawproject.org/working_papers/RLP.WP11.pdf> at 44. In an interview on the armed conflict between the government and the LRA in northern Uganda, Archbishop Odama recalled the peace advocacy of the religious leaders. He argued that "military responses have always been destructive and do not solve anything. They multiply problems.... We have advocated for a peaceful way of resolving this conflict." Elizabeth Drew, "Regional Community Peacebuilding and the LRA Conflict: A Conversation with John Baptist Odoma, Archbishop of Gulu, Uganda" (2011) 22 Accord 54, online: Conciliation Resources <http://www.c-r.org/sites/c-r.org/files/Accord%2022_14Regional%20communiy%20peacebuilding%20and%20the%20LRA%20conflict_2011_ENG.pdf> at 56.

[599] Turay, *supra* note 595 at 52. Interestingly, the special envoy of the United Nations secretary-general, Francis Okelo, also relied on the IRCSL and its capacity to initiative a dialogue between the government and the RUF (ibid.).

[600] Jessop, Aljets & Chacko, *supra* note 582 at 104–105.

[601] As mentioned, the IRCSL did speak out against the violence and condemned in particular the brutality of the RUF, which made the RUF abduct religious leaders, kill missionaries and attack religious institutions. Turay, *supra* note 595 at 50.

[602] Jessop, Aljets & Chacko, *supra* note 582 at 105.

Peace Agreement and attacked members of the UN peacekeeping mission UNAMSIL, which led to a strong military response and ultimately to the capture of the RUF leader, Foday Sankoh,[603] the IRCSL played an important role in the effort to bring about a peaceful resolution of the conflict. The involvement of the IRCSL also underlines that civil society actors may not only be valuable as observers or secondary negotiators, possibly reminding the primary negotiating parties and mediators to deal with the underlying causes of an armed conflict, transitional justice, the situation of minorities, the return of refugees and internally displaced persons and other issues of concern to a society emerging from a violent conflict. Civil society actors may also introduce normative elements in the negotiations and be effective as confidence builders and facilitators of the actual negotiations. In the Lomé Peace Agreement, the signing parties formally recognized this important role played by the IRCSL by entrusting members of the Council with the interpretation of agreement provisions in the case of conflicting views of the parties.[604] The following section will explore whether the normative basis for an involvement of civil society actors in peace negotiations, as in the case of the IRCSL, must be built in every context or whether international law can provide a more generalized normative basis for this involvement.

4.2. FILLING A NORMATIVE GAP – THE LIMITED GUIDANCE OF FORMAL LAW

Peace negotiations are not founded on generally accepted, democratic rules of representation and participation, and, therefore, tend to be undemocratic per se. Unlike interstate negotiations, where negotiators can be expected to be equipped with an official and well-defined mandate and where diplomatic calculi put forward by elites prevail,[605] intrastate peace negotiations cannot build on clear mandates and a finite number of actors. While these negotiations will have a direct impact on the whole population, especially when taking place in the context of a major political transition, effective representation of the

---

[603] For more information, see Arthur Abraham, "Dancing with the Chameleon: Sierra Leone and the Elusive Quest for Peace" (2001) 19:2 *Journal of Contemporary African Studies* 205 at 223–225.

[604] *Lomé Peace Agreement*, *supra* note 40, Part Two, art VIII. Two of the five members of the proposed Council of Elders and Religious Leaders were to be appointed by the IRCSL. While a powerful signal, this Council was, however, never set up. See Turay, *supra* note 595 at 53.

[605] For a critical account of the current system governing diplomatic relations, see Carne Ross, *Independent Diplomat: Dispatches from an Unaccountable Elite* (Ithaca, NY: Cornell University Press, 2007).

population concerned cannot be taken for granted, even if representatives of the main belligerent parties in the conflict are present. Pre-negotiations regarding which groups will participate in the negotiations and how they will be represented determine the outcome of the whole process. Moreover, the important creation of ownership of a process, which is ideally supported by the society at large, will in most instances only be reached through extended participation. As a result, just and equal representation, the participation of marginalized groups and, more generally, the involvement of civil society actors are increasingly recognized as major concerns that must be taken into account by negotiators and mediators.

A related line of reasoning concerns the difficulty that the legitimation of a peace agreement entails. The "prelegitimate" moment,[606] in which a small number of negotiators without clear, democratically validated mandates make far-reaching decisions by concluding a peace agreement, is most visible in the case of those agreements that go beyond the conclusion of a mere ceasefire and contain constitution-like provisions. Many peace agreements providing for some form of power sharing or seeking to alter the constitutional order are, therefore, particularly concerned with elections and the electoral process.[607] Some agreement provisions are explicitly transitional in nature.[608] In other words, being a representative of one of the warring parties who contributes to ending an armed conflict by negotiating and signing a peace agreement might be seen as conferring some legitimacy; this legitimacy is, however, insufficient to generate and validate, on its own and automatically, any provisions that go beyond transitional arrangements. An agreement concluded among elites after exclusive, possibly even secret, negotiations will always be built on a thin legitimate foundation and call for a broader process of legitimation. Moreover, from a practical conflict-resolution respective, and although democratic consent is admittedly still an underappreciated factor in assessing the success or failure of a peace agreement,[609] it can be assumed that comprehensive peace agreements will rarely last without some form of democratic validation.

---

[606] For a discussion of the notion of a prelegitimate moment, see Chapter 1, Section 1.1.

[607] See e.g. the *Accord politique de Ouagadougou*, *supra* note 237, sections I and II. The transitional character of the period starting with the ceasefire and ending with the holding of elections is also recognized explicitly in the *General Peace Agreement for Mozambique*, *supra* note 55, Protocol V, art III.

[608] *Lomé Peace Agreement*, *supra* note 40, Part Two. See also Chapter 1.

[609] Little research has been carried out in this regard, which means that this argument must remain somewhat speculative. See Ben Reilly, "Democratic Validation," in John Darby & Roger Mac Ginty, eds., *Contemporary Peacemaking: Conflict, Violence and Peace Processes* (New York: Palgrave Macmillan, 2003), 174. The study of peace agreement provisions on civil society involvement is similarly inconclusive. A significant number of intrastate peace

External actors, such as third states and international and regional organizations, and their shared normative expectations also contribute to the constructed necessity that agreements be democratically validated. Particularly in the absence of readily available or recognized means of domestic validation, international legal norms of political participation and democratic governance are often invoked. Based on what, already in the early 1990s, Thomas Franck called "emerging international rules and processes by which the governance of nations is increasingly being monitored and validated",[610] external actors may indeed have an important normative influence in post-conflict situations and can also extend, at least to some degree, legitimacy to a negotiated solution.[611]

An approach anchored in international human rights law arguably reinforces the need to reach beyond political and military elites as sole negotiators and ensure increased participation of civil society actors.[612] The obligation to open up negotiations and attempt to democratize them cannot, however, be rooted directly in existing formal international law. As a matter of fact, a conventional human rights–based approach that emphasizes the right to vote and the right to take part in the conduct of public affairs only provides limited guidance. As the ICCPR, the most relevant instrument in this regard, states in its article 25:

> Every citizen shall have the right and the opportunity ...
>
> (a) To take part in the conduct of public affairs, directly or through freely chosen representatives;
> (b) To vote and to be elected at genuine periodic elections which shall be by universal and equal suffrage and shall be held by secret ballot, guaranteeing the free expression of the will of the electors.[613]

agreements include provisions on civil society, for instance, on its role in transitional governance, in monitoring of the agreement or in the delivery of humanitarian relief. See Christine Bell & Catherine O'Rourke, "The People's Peace? Peace Agreements, Civil Society, and Participatory Democracy" (2007) 28:3 *International Political Science Review* 293 at 298–302. However, it is not possible, because of multiple other variables and definitional difficulties, to attempt a genuine evaluation of the relationship between such provisions and the success or failure of peace agreements. For this argument, see ibid., 306. For an overview of peace agreement provisions on civil society according to its function (humanitarian relief; agreement monitoring; legitimization and promotion; transitional governance and institutional development) in the period from 1990 to 2006, see ibid., 307–320.

610 Franck, "The Emerging Right," *supra* note 79 at 50.
611 Franck speaks of the "capacity of the international community to extend legitimacy to national governments" (ibid., 51).
612 For this argument, see e.g. International Council on Human Rights Policy, *supra* note 132 at 112.
613 This provision was largely inspired by Article 21 of the Universal Declaration of Human Rights. It should be noted that in case of a public emergency, Article 25 may be derogated from

Hence, while the right to vote in elections is relatively specific and violations of this right assessable without too much difficulty, the scope and elements of the broader right to take part in the conduct of public affairs are vague and its applicability is controversial.[614] It seems that the drafters of the ICCPR were mostly concerned with the proviso on *elections* but did not deliberate much on the right to *take part*.[615] The resulting focus in practice and in the academic literature on the right to vote, a fairly well-defined and channelled expression of democratic participation,[616] is therefore not surprising, and it has been arduous to give proper meaning to the right to take part in the conduct of public affairs. The Human Rights Committee's General Comment on Article 25 has not added much clarity to this right. In this document, the conduct of public affairs is defined as a

> broad concept which relates to the exercise of political power, in particular the exercise of legislative, executive and administrative powers.... The allocation of powers and the means by which individual citizens exercise the right to participate in the conduct of public affairs protected by article 25 should be established by the constitution and other laws.[617]

It can be concluded that the scope of the right to take part has not been specified in a general manner; rather, as the Human Rights Committee also stated in *Marshall v. Canada*, "It is for the legal and constitutional system of the State party to provide for the modalities of such participation".[618] With peace

---

according to Article 4 of the ICCPR. However, since there is no reason to conclude that this right is necessarily or entirely suspended during an armed conflict or during negotiations seeking to end it, Article 25 remains a relevant normative source.

[614] Henry Steiner, "Political Participation as a Human Right" (1988) 1 *Harv Hum Rts YB* 77 at 78. Thomas Franck has argued that a "normative requirement of a participatory *electoral* process" has emerged and has demonstrated its increasing determinacy, which bestows legitimacy. Franck, "The Emerging Right," *supra* note 79 at 63–77. See also the discussion in Gaëlle Missire, *Women's Right to Political Participation in Post-Conflict Transformation* (LLM Thesis, McGill University, Faculty of Law, 2008) [unpublished] at 43–47.

[615] Steiner, *supra* note 615 at 85. Steiner argues that the provisions of Article 25 do not only declare a right but "articulate a political ideal inspiring a right" and emphasizes that they have to be read in the context of other rights, especially those relating to free speech, press, assembly and association, laying the groundwork for the political participation of citizens (ibid., 86, 88).

[616] It should be noted that the ICCPR does not offer much guidance on several issues, including those relating to the electoral system and to the question as to whether freedom for opposition parties is required. For an overview of the drafting history of Article 25 of the ICCPR, see ibid., 89–94.

[617] Human Rights Committee, *General Comment No. 25: The Right to Participate in Public Affairs, Voting Rights and the Right to Equal Access to Public Services (Art. 25)*, UN Doc. CCPR/C/21/Rev.1/Add.7 (1996) at para 5.

[618] *Marshall v. Canada*, Communication No. 205/1986, Human Rights Committee, 43d Sess, UN Doc. CCPR/C/43/D/205/1986 (1991) at para 5.4.

negotiations never being regulated ex ante by national constitutions or other laws, the limited guidance for and applicability to peace negotiations of the right to take part in the conduct of public affairs becomes evident.

With respect to the right to vote, the main problem lies in the fact that this right operates particularly badly in times of crisis. An expeditious process of democratic validation in the form of a referendum or national elections, albeit notionally respecting human rights obligations under Article 25 of the ICCPR, is often not feasible or desirable. First, it may be logistically very challenging, if not impossible, to organize a broad-based referendum to legitimize a peace agreement. Deficient infrastructures may render communication among and movement of electoral officials difficult; electoral boundaries may not yet have been demarcated; and it may prove problematic to register potential voters due to important numbers of refugees and internally displaced persons, with the question as to who should be entitled to vote possibly being contested itself.[619] Second, in the immediate aftermath of an armed conflict, any electoral process is typically determined by the traditional societal fault lines corresponding to those over which the conflict was fought.[620] Divided societies may hence become further divided. The electorate in Burundi in 1993 and in Bosnia in 1996 and 1998, for instance, mobilized along ethnic lines and further entrenched exclusionary and potentially violent policies.[621] Similarly, early elections may not leave enough time for more programmatic political parties to develop, which only helps already established local elites maintain their political influence.[622] In other words, holding elections or a referendum without giving enough time to sincerely discuss the underlying issues may radicalize already extreme positions and result in a new outbreak of violence,[623] and thus undermine the very objectives of such a democratic validation process intended to contribute to building a more peaceful society. In short, insisting on the right to vote, in line with Article 25 of the ICCPR, may be counterproductive. For these reasons, it has been suggested that it may sometimes be wiser to focus first on the local level, to allow local institutions to develop and to build or rebuild democratic institutions from the bottom,

---

[619] By way of example, this has been one of the thorniest questions in the Côte d'Ivoire peace process. As the 2007 Accord de Ouagadougou states, "les Parties signataires du présent Accord ont reconnu que l'identification des populations ivoiriennes et étrangères vivant en Côte d'Ivoire constitue une préoccupation majeure". *Accord politique de Ouagadougou, supra* note 237, art I.

[620] Reilly, *supra* note 610 at 176.

[621] Ibid.

[622] Ibid.

[623] The violence following the 1999 Timor-Leste referendum is an example in point (ibid., 179–180).

and not from the top; concentrating on political participation at the local level should eventually lead to the establishment of functioning institutions at all levels of government.[624] This approach does, of course, not bestow the often desired prompt legitimation of a peace agreement. Moreover, both the external actors involved and the population itself rarely have the patience to sustain such a lengthy process, where none of the actors involved will be able to claim any rapid successes.

The challenges related to an ex post legitimation of a peace agreement make the ex ante legitimacy of a negotiating process even more important. In a nutshell, if peace negotiations and the conclusion of an agreement can be put on a broader and more legitimate basis, there will be less pressure on a subsequent process of democratic validation. Article 25(a) of the ICCPR may, in this sense, provide some guidance, notwithstanding its relative vagueness. Since formal mechanisms, such as national elections, are often not an option, other forms of taking part in the conduct of public affairs must be envisaged. As will be shown by drawing on several examples, Article 25(a) may be seen as inspiring the variable and fluid involvement of civil society actors in peace negotiations. This involvement, in turn, may embody one way to give meaning to this right.

4.3. THE ARGUMENT OF INCREASED EFFECTIVENESS: FROM LEGITIMATE PROCESSES TO DURABLE AGREEMENTS

The warring parties never operate in perfect isolation: their conflict is not a private one but is part of a larger context. The fact that an armed conflict and its resolution can usually not be reduced to the fighting itself provides an important rationale for searching solutions on related issues that often lie at the heart of a conflict, such as access to and distribution of land, resources and power. According to this perspective, not only does the participation of civil society actors as observers bestow some legitimacy to the negotiations and increase the likelihood of their results being accepted by the population; civil society actors may also contribute to bringing certain issues on the negotiating table and facilitate their approval through public advocacy and by liaising with the primary negotiating parties and mediators. Civil society actors are sometimes also directly involved in the negotiations, which may give them the opportunity to voice directly their concerns at the negotiating table and – in an ideal world corresponding to the interests and convictions of the larger

---

[624] This approach was, for instance, taken by the United Nations in Timor-Leste and Kosovo (ibid., 178).

population represented by these actors – to negotiate and insist on certain provisions to be concluded in or removed from the text of an agreement. Akin to the argument that "the more participatory the constitution-making, the higher its legitimacy and acceptance",[625] a productive participation of civil society actors is beneficial both for the process and the content of a peace agreement.

As it has, for instance, been argued in the context of Darfur, where the negotiations leading to the ultimately ineffective 2006 Darfur Peace Agreement were conducted almost exclusively between representatives of the belligerent parties, the involvement of civil society actors

> has the potential to bring excluded ethnic groups into the process, to address social and political issues on which the rebels are not well placed to negotiate, and to generate much needed momentum in what has been a long and difficult process. Civil society as a player in the peace process can no longer be treated as an afterthought. Although integrating it into a larger peace process is a challenge, it is increasingly clear that this is no longer optional – peace cannot be brought without it.[626]

Shifting the legitimacy focus from outcome to process, in other words, from the agreement to the negotiations, is therefore not only a conceptually interesting exercise. The hypothesis that the effectiveness of a peace agreement is directly proportional to the legitimacy of the negotiations leading to the conclusion of an agreement, which, in turn, can be ensured through more inclusive negotiations, finds support in the peace and conflict resolution literature, where a positive correlation between civil society involvement in the negotiations and the durability of peace has been found. The engagement of all stakeholders is necessary to create both vertical and horizontal capacities, which improves relationships and constructive interactions across both the different levels and the traditional lines of divisions of society.[627] As Anthony

---

[625] Klein & Sajó, *supra* note 30 at 424.

[626] Theodore Murphy & Jérôme Tubiana, "Civil Society in Darfur: The Missing Peace" *Special Report of the United States Institute of Peace* (September 2010), online: United States Institute of Peace <http://www.usip.org/files/resources/Civil%20Society%20in%20Darfur%20-%20 Sept.%202010.pdf> at 17. For an overview of the roles of civil society in Darfur, see ibid., 8–9. Or, as Thania Pfaffenholz, Darren Kew and Anthony Wanis-St. John have argued, "It is not whether or not to involve civil society, but how". Thania Pfaffenholz, Darren Kew & Anthony Wanis-St. John, "Civil Society and Peace Negotiations: Why, Whether and How They Could Be Involved" (2006), online: Oslo forum <http://www.osloforum.org/sites/default/ files/CivilSocietyandPeaceNegotiations.pdf> at 74.

[627] The concept of vertical and horizontal capacities was coined by John Paul Lederach, who defines "vertical capacity" as "relationship building across levels of leadership, authority, and responsibility within a society or system, from grassroots to the highest, most visible leaders. This approach requires awareness that each level has different needs and unique contributions to make but

Wanis-St. John and Darren Kew have argued, "The focus on elite interests in peace negotiations often leaves the populace at large without perceived stakes in the agreed peacebuilding frameworks, weakening the ability of governments and transitional authorities to reach a sustainable peace".[628] Numerous conflict resolution specialists, by drawing on various examples,[629] clearly share this presumption that more inclusive and participatory peace negotiations are also more effective, which has led to the conclusion that "the question of whether CSOs [civil society organizations] should have a seat at the table should no longer be a subject of debate. Appropriate civil society actors may be entitled to that seat and can be instrumental in the outcome of a peace process".[630] Successful processes, where civil society actors were actively involved in the negotiations and where sustained peace was the outcome, include those resulting in the 1992 Mozambique Agreement and the 1996 Guatemala Agreement. Negative examples, with low civil society involvement and resumed fighting include the 2006 Darfur Peace Agreement, the 1993 Oslo Accords in the context of the Israeli-Palestinian conflict, the 1993 Arusha Accords that did all but prevent the Rwandan genocide and several Burundi agreements from 1995 onwards.[631] The more recent attempts in the Burundian

---

ultimately they are interdependent, requiring the explicit fostering of constructive interactions across the levels". Horizontal capacities are defined as "the ability to build and sustain relational spaces of constructive interaction across the lines of divisions in systems and societies divided by historic patterns of identity conflict". John Paul Lederach, *The Moral Imagination: The Art and Soul of Building Peace* (New York: Oxford University Press, 2005), 182–183.

[628] Anthony Wanis-St. John & Darren Kew, "Civil Society and Peace Negotiations: Confronting Exclusion" (2008) 13 *International Negotiation* 11 at 13.

[629] By way of example, it has been asserted that the exclusion of civil society from the bargaining table has greatly contributed to the failure of the negotiations to resolve the conflict between Greek and Turkish Cypriots; see A. Marco Turk, "The Negotiation Culture of Lengthy Peace Processes: Cyprus as an Example of Spoiling That Prevents a Final Solution" (2009) 3:31 *Loy LA Int'l & Comp L Rev* 327 at 341–342. For an argument that the inclusion of civil society was part of the success of the peace process in the north of Mali in the 1990s, see Kristine Hauge Storholt, "Lessons Learned from the 1990–1997 Peace Process in the North of Mali" (2001) 6 *International Negotiation* 331 at 338–339, 348–349; see also Katia Papagianni, "Partage de pouvoir et gouvernements en transition: le rôle de la médiation" *Centre for Humanitarian Dialogue* (2008), online: Centre for Humanitarian Dialogue <http://www.hdcentre.org/files/Powersharing%20FR%20final.pdf>.

[630] Jessop, Aljets & Chacko, *supra* note 582 at 107.

[631] Wanis-St. John & Kew, *supra* note 629 at 26–27. Some authors have established a direct link between the internationally mediated Arusha Accords and the genocide that followed. See e.g. Christopher Clapham, "Rwanda: The Perils of Peacemaking" (1998) 35:2 *Journal of Peace Research* 193 at 204. Another example of a process that was considered flawed by parts of the population is the allegedly "non-transparent, non-consultative and elite-driven" drafting process of the 2007 Interim Constitution that was adopted in Nepal. Parlevliet, "Rethinking Conflict Transformation," *supra* note 100 at 10.

context illustrate, however, that the long-term benefits of inclusive processes outweigh the short-term gains of exclusive processes.[632]

While it would, based on an assessment of these situations, be difficult to deny any correlation between the involvement of civil society actors and the effectiveness of peace negotiations, it should be kept in mind that it is never simple to isolate one factor and assess its significance independently from other factors. The examples cited here are therefore not meant to insinuate that it was exclusively the level of participation of civil society actors at the negotiations that determined the success or failure of the respective negotiations. What can be maintained, in the absence of such a clear-cut causal relationship, is that civil society involvement is a substantial factor.

It is also worth noting that in this line of analysis, the character of political participation as instrumental, as a means towards an end, definitely plays a greater role than the notion that participation is an end itself.[633] The underlying assumption is that participation may contribute to making peace negotiations, and hence a resulting agreement, more effective, thus paving the way for a peaceful society. There is, however, also value in recognizing the inherent potential that lies in increased participation, beyond an impact that may be more easily assessable, whether qualitatively or quantitatively, as, for instance, according to variables established in a peace agreements database. Increased participation enhances the feeling of empowerment; in a society emerging from violent conflict, it may indeed be considered particularly important that every actor assume his or her responsibilities and be ready to act, and not only to react. This, as Henry Steiner has argued in the context of the right to political participation, may strengthen "an ethic of civic virtue",[634] which means that participation in peace negotiations can be seen as being part of an important emancipatory process.

Following this argument, each and every actor actually and possibly affected by peace negotiations is and should always be considered a norm applicant and norm creator, and thus an inherent component of the normative dynamics of peace negotiations. Such a view might be deemed to bear some resemblance to the legal empowerment approach,[635] which would mean, in this

---

[632] Elizabeth A. McClintock & Térence Nahimana, "Managing the Tension between Inclusionary and Exclusionary Processes: Building Peace in Burundi" (2008) 13 *International Negotiation* 73 at 75.

[633] For a discussion of these two, certainly interrelated and complementary, conceptions of participation, see Steiner, *supra* note 615 at 100–105.

[634] Ibid., 105.

[635] This approach has become very popular in the field of international development and attempts to reduce poverty based on a human rights-based approach to development. According to the

context, to give a (legal) voice to those who have been affected by a conflict but who will often not be able to play an active role in its resolution. Women and children are, for instance, not only vulnerable and in need of protection; refugees and internally displaced persons are not only helpless victims. Based on Harold H. Koh's model of transnational legal process and his suggestion that more actors should be empowered in order to increase the internalization of international norms, it has, for instance, been argued that Palestinian refugees should be allowed "to participate in the search for their own solutions as recognized under international refugee law".[636] What is important to emphasize is that such "legal empowerment" should not be limited to raising awareness among groups considered vulnerable about their existing rights enshrined in international human rights law and to trying to enable them to use "the law".[637] Rather, the notion of "legal empowerment" should direct our attention to the fact that these legal actors have indeed *power* relating to legal norms – power that does not correspond to perfect freedom and may certainly be limited by presently settled normative assertions,[638] but power that goes beyond using a static body of laws and that includes the capacity to contribute to forming the legal-normative framework of peace negotiations.

United Nations secretary-general, "Legal empowerment of the poor can be understood as the process of systemic change through which the poor are protected and enabled to use the law to advance their rights and their interests as citizens and economic actors". *Legal Empowerment of the Poor and Eradication of Poverty, Report of the Secretary-General*, UN Doc. A/64/133 (13 July 2009) at para 3. The Commission on Legal Empowerment of the Poor, hosted by the United Nations Development Programme and launched by a group of developed and developing countries, bringing together policymakers and practitioners, defined the concept of legal empowerment as "the process through which the poor become protected and are enabled to use the law to advance their rights and their interests, vis-à-vis the state and the market". Commission on Legal Empowerment of the Poor, *Making the Law Work for Everyone*, vol. 1 (New York: Commission on Legal Empowerment of the Poor and United Nations Development Programme, 2008), 26. For a critical assessment, based on empirical work in Sudan, of human rights education workshops meant to empower the poor, see Mark F Massoud, "Do Victims of War Need International Law? Human Rights Education Programs in Authoritative Sudan" (2011) 45:1 *Law & Soc'y Rev* 1.

[636] Terry Rempel & Paul Prettitore, "The Palestinian Refugees: Restitution and Compensation," in Susan M. Akram et al., eds., *International Law and the Israeli-Palestinian Conflict* (New York: Routledge, 2011), 69, 91.

[637] See the definitions of the United Nations secretary-general and the Commission on Legal Empowerment of the Poor, *supra* note 636.

[638] Jeremy Webber argues that "norms always involve a kind of imposition, where parties submit (sometimes by conscious decision, usually by something more like acquiescence) to norms that would not be the ones they would choose if left to their own devices" and that "law, the actual emergence of norms, only occurs when those assertions are settled by some emphatically social, non-individual process". Webber, "Legal Pluralism and Human Agency," *supra* note 139 at 181–182.

The increasing recognition, by the more powerful actors involved in the resolution of an armed conflict, of this contribution made by legal actors who are typically considered less powerful reveals a process of deliberating legal obligations – unquestionably in a context of continuing normative disagreement[639] – with respect to more inclusive negotiations.

4.4. A NORMATIVE COMMITMENT TO INCLUSIVE NEGOTIATIONS

Carefully designing the process, and above all ensuring its legitimacy, is a precondition for a constructive and sustained outcome. Yet the inclusion of civil society actors is not only advisable from a pragmatic conflict resolution perspective; it has rather become part of the normative framework of peace negotiations and, as various situations discussed in this section illustrate, is increasingly being internalized as a legal obligation. This understanding draws on Lon Fuller and relies more particularly on the argument of Jutta Brunnée and Stephen Toope that "legal obligation is therefore best viewed as an internalized commitment and not as an externally imposed duty matched with a sanction for non-performance".[640]

Looking at the discourse on the inclusion of civil society actors in peace negotiations is again telling. Numerous assertions echo the formal call in Security Council Resolution 1325 (2000) for an increased involvement of civil society actors in peace processes.[641] In 2004, for instance, the secretary-general demanded that UN peacemakers ensure "greater consultation with and involvement in peace processes of important voices from civil society, especially those of women, who are often neglected during negotiations".[642] The 2012 secretary-general report on peace mediation explicitly recognizes bottom-up demands and maintains that "civil society actors, such as the youth and women groups, are rightfully demanding a greater voice in political transitions and mediation processes, as seen in the context of the Arab Spring and beyond".[643] Dialogue initiatives can not only "broaden local ownership" but

---

[639] Ibid., 179–182, 187–188, 195. Webber also points out that "it is better to think about law as driven by an aspiration towards order, by a will to live in an ordered community, but where that order has to be made and remade". Webber, "Naturalism and Agency," *supra* note 137 at 214.

[640] Brunnée & Toope, *supra* note 79 at 27. See also Finnemore and Toope, who argue that "to be effective, obligations need to be felt, and not simply imposed through a hierarchy of sources of law". Finnemore & Toope, *supra* note 147 at 755.

[641] SC Res 1325, *supra* note 284.

[642] UN Secretary General's High Level Panel on Threats, Challenges and Change, *A More Secure World: Our Shared Responsibility*, UN Doc. A/59/565 (2004) at 38.

[643] *Strengthening the Role of Mediation*, *supra* note 328 at para 17.

also "complement formal mediation processes" or even, as the national dialogue process did in Tunisia, be used instead of formal mediation processes.[644]
The report also notes that inclusivity "increases the legitimacy and national
ownership of the peace agreement and its implementation" and "reduces
the likelihood of excluded actors undermining the process".[645] Mediators
should therefore "promote understanding among conflict parties of the value
of broader participation and minimize preconditions for participation in the
process".[646] The same report also contains a quite remarkable "guidance" to
peace mediators with respect to addressing international legal norms in the
context of peace negotiations. Regarding "applicable international law and
normative framework", mediators are advised to "facilitate access for partners
and civil society actors to engage directly with conflict parties and other stakeholders regarding applicable norms".[647] Although civil society actors are not
explicitly recognized in this report as having norm creative capacities, they
are certainly seen as normative actors who can and should be part of deliberations, as, for instance, on the relevance and possibly guiding role of legal
norms in the negotiations.

The United Nations has manifestly internalized an obligation vis-à-vis the
participation of civil society actors in peace negotiations that involves normative considerations and that goes beyond merely reaching out and consulting
civil society. Moreover, the United Nations is also unambiguous with respect to
its normative ambition to make other peace mediation organizations recognize
and internalize a similar commitment. Even if such a normative commitment
of other peace mediation organizations may not be observable to the same
degree of explicitness as in the case of the United Nations, it should be kept in
mind that the existence of a commitment and its significance are not contingent on its perceptibility to the outside world. Commitments may be implied
or even internalized unconsciously. It is undeniable that the proposition by
some actors and the possibly resulting internalization of such a commitment
by others is part of the ongoing interaction between the various peace mediation organizations and other actors involved in peace negotiations. The explicit
normative ambition of the United Nations and its proposition regarding the
inclusion of civil society actors cannot be completely ignored by other peace
mediation organizations. These organizations are rather invited to consider and
engage with this proposition regarding the involvement of civil society actors.[648]

---

[644] Ibid.
[645] Ibid., Annex I, Guidance for Effective Mediation at para 29.
[646] Ibid., Annex I, Guidance for Effective Mediation at para 34.
[647] Ibid., Annex I, Guidance for Effective Mediation at para 42.
[648] This is based on the claims made by Macdonald & Sandomierski, *supra* note 81 at 622–623, 631.

Several initiatives illustrate the interactional efforts of civil society organizations to further develop this emerging obligation and their demands that the obligation be respected by negotiators and mediators. In the context of Darfur, these initiatives include the outcome document of the 2008 Heidelberg Darfur Dialogue, which contains Draft Proposals for Consideration in a Future Darfur Peace Agreement, and the so-called Doha Declaration, issued in November 2009.[649] The participants of the Heidelberg Darfur Dialogue, mostly Khartoum-based intellectuals from Darfur,[650] affirm in the outcome document that "a future Final Peace Agreement for Darfur will have to be negotiated not only between the national government of Sudan and the Movements, but also needs to take into account the voices of the Darfurian civil society and of the Darfurian population",[651] with one of the general principles being that "all political forces and civil society organizations [shall be enabled] to play an effective role in achieving a comprehensive peace".[652] The Doha Declaration, issued by approximately 170 Darfur civil society representatives that had met at the first big Darfurian civil society conference,[653] addresses the question of civil society participation even more comprehensively and affirms, inter alia, that "negligence of the civil society role in the peace process is one of the factors that led to [the] failure of the previous peace negotiations".[654] The subsequent mediation attempts made by the African Union High-Level Implementation Panel point in the same direction and also emphasize the importance of incorporating civil society into the formal negotiations.[655]

The significance of the documents drafted by Darfurian civil society actors goes beyond the substantive claims made and any assessable effects on the course of the negotiations; these initiatives are, in fact, significant per se as

---

[649] For a discussion of benefits and shortcoming of these initiatives, see Murphy & Tubiana, *supra* note 627 at 4–5.

[650] Jérôme Tubiana, Victor Tanner & Musa Adam Abdul-Jalil, "Traditional Authorities' Peacemaking Role in Darfur," *Special Report of the United States Institute of Peace* (November 2012), online: United States Institute of Peace <http://www.usip.org/files/resources/PW83.pdf> at 85.

[651] *Heidelberg Darfur Dialogue Outcome Document* (Max Planck Institute for Comparative Public Law and International Law, 2010), online: MPIL <http://www.mpil.de/shared/data/pdf/hdd_outcome_document.pdf>, Preamble and General Principles.

[652] Ibid., para 307(h).

[653] For an overview and discussion of the shortcomings of the so-called Doha 1 (November 2009) and the subsequent Doha 2 (July 2010) civil society conferences, see Murphy & Tubiana, *supra* note 627 at 4–5.

[654] *Doha Declaration*, 20 November 2009 (Darfur). An English version (a "rough translation" [*sic*]) is available online: Darfur Information Center <http://www.darfurinfo.org/doha-english-rough.pdf>.

[655] Murphy & Tubiana, *supra* note 627 at 5.

an expression of the increasing mobilization of civil society actors and their normative contribution to peace processes. Civil society actors are, as underscored by these documents, normative actors aware of their agency. They fulfill functions as norm advocates and even norm entrepreneurs by claiming not only, and more generally, that formal international legal norms and associated obligations ought to be respected but also that the voices of civil society actors must be heard in the negotiations.

One of the earlier examples of the potentially significant impact of civil society actors on the negotiated resolution of an internal armed conflict is Guatemala. In the early 1990s, years during which the peace process faltered, indigenous peoples', women's and other civil society organizations increasingly demanded to be included in the negotiations, a claim that was initially rejected by the primary parties.[656] In 1994, however, a framework agreement was concluded in which the two parties, the government and the UNIDAD Revolucionaria Nacional Guatemalteca (URNG), committed to resuming the negotiations. In the agreement, the parties did not only recognize that civil society organizations "have helped to make possible the start of direct negotiations between the Government and the command of the URNG";[657] they also mandated a civil society assembly to discuss several substantive matters, including constitutional reform and indigenous peoples' rights, and to issue recommendations or guidelines.[658] Moreover, this assembly, presided by Bishop Quezada, was mandated "to consider bilateral agreements concluded by the parties on the substantive issues and endorse such agreements so as to give them the force of national commitments, thereby facilitating their implementation".[659] Civil society actors were thus given much weight in the Guatemalan peace process, with some of their functions being formally institutionalized by the primary negotiating parties. At the same time, this move

---

[656] Enrique Alvarez, "The Civil Society Assembly: Shaping Agreement" (2002) 13 Accord 48, online: Conciliation Resources <http://www.c-r.org/sites/c-r.org/files/Accord%2013_9The%20 civil%20society%20assembly_2002_ENG_0.pdf> at 48. For an overview of the Guatemalan negotiations, see Susan D. Burgerman, "Build the Peace by Mandating Reform: United Nations-Mediated Human Rights Agreements in El Salvador and Guatemala" (2000) 27:3 *Latin American Perspectives* 63 at 72–77. Burgerman also emphasizes the particular role of civil society actors in the process (ibid., 80).

[657] *Framework Agreement for the Resumption of the Negotiating Process between the Government of Guatemala and the UNIDAD Revolucionaria Nacional Guatemalteca*, 10 January 1994, III. The agreement is annexed to the *Letter Dated 17 January 1994 from the Secretary-General to the President of the General Assembly and the President of the Security Council*, UN Doc. A/49/61 and UN Doc. S/1994/53.

[658] Ibid., III.ii.

[659] Ibid., III.iii. Bilateral agreements would, however, be valid even without endorsement by the Assembly. Ibid.

allowed the government and the URNG to keep the civil society assembly separate from the actual bilateral negotiations, which they agreed to "conduct in the strictest secrecy in order to ensure that they are carried on in an atmosphere of trust and in seriousness".[660] The government had therefore managed to prevent a direct involvement of civil society actors, who were largely perceived as pro-URNG, in the negotiations; yet it could not ignore civil society entirely, which would have diminished the legitimacy of the bilateral negotiations.[661] This recognition by the primary parties of the significance of somehow involving civil society actors and its consequences for the negotiations certainly helped identify and address underlying causes of the armed conflict. In the end, despite the fact that Guatemalan civil society had been characterized by deep divisions and mistrust, consensus positions were reached on all substantive issues by the Assembly, and most of its proposals were adopted by the government and the URNG and included in the official 1996 peace agreement.[662]

In contrast to situations like Guatemala and Sierra Leone, religious and other civil society organizations sometimes play only a marginal role in a peace process and do not succeed in shaping its normative framework. In Burundi, for instance, the churches, like most other modern civil society organizations, were so polarized along the dominant ethnic groups that they were effectively excluded from the peace process.[663] As a result, a dialogue process, that was initiated in parallel to the formal negotiations leading to the 2000 Arusha Peace and Reconciliation Agreement for Burundi and that sought to involve "ordinary" citizens in the peace process, did not rely on existing civil society organizations, such as religious communities.[664] What is worth highlighting is that the primary negotiating parties nevertheless put into practice what can be seen as a commitment to reach out to and get input for the formal negotiations from the Burundian population.

As it has been argued above, the emerging legal obligations regarding civil society involvement, unlike those typically referred to under international law, cannot determine a particular outcome. Rather, by creating these norms, the actors involved map out a process that has a higher potential of being considered legitimate and therefore more effective. The example of who participates in which manner in the negotiations illustrates that the legitimacy of peace negotiations may be doubtful, with possibly negative impacts on their

[660] Ibid., V.i.
[661] For this argument, see Alvarez, *supra* note 657 at 50.
[662] Ibid., 52.
[663] McClintock & Nahimana, *supra* note 633 at 87.
[664] Ibid., 88.

effectiveness, if the question of including civil society is left completely unaddressed. A process that does not even attempt to allow for broader participation at certain stages will most likely be considered illegitimate. In the words of Jessop, Aljets and Chacko, "The inclusion of civil society and public participation in peace processes supports a long-term vision of peace-building rather than one predicated on elusive moments of ripeness and short-term goals".[665] In this sense, the involvement of civil society mirrors the shifting relationship of means and ends of legal norms in the context of peace negotiations: while traditionally associated with short-term, measurable outcomes, legal norms can and should be understood according to their process-related and aspirational character.

4.5. FACING A CHALLENGING OBLIGATION

Since different civil society actors may play different roles in different contexts, generalized conclusions with respect to the involvement of these actors in peace negotiations are difficult to make. One of the results is that the question as to how negotiators and mediators can comply with the emerging and increasingly internalized obligation with respect to civil society involvement is not a straightforward matter. Several challenges can be identified with respect to the possible participation of civil society in the negotiations of a peace agreement, notably with respect to the kind of actors to be included.

Successful participation of civil society actors will, first of all, depend on the role that these actors played during the conflict and on their capacity to genuinely represent the interests of the general population.[666] In addition to the dilemma consisting in a general lack of accountability of civil society organizations and an often assumed yet not so simple relationship between a strong civil society and democracy,[667] the inclusion of those civil society actors who only reinforce the voices of the belligerent parties already represented at the negotiating table will most likely miss the objectives of rendering the negotiations more inclusive and representative of the concerns of the population. In some instances, civil society organizations may actually not be representative of the population but rather speak exclusively for certain elites or ethnic groups. Burundi, as already mentioned, is an example in point. Burundian civil society organizations, a relatively new phenomenon, have been described as being "highly ethno-centric,

---

[665] Jessop, Aljets & Chacko, *supra* note 582 at 106.

[666] McClintock & Nahimana, *supra* note 633 at 85. On practical problems regarding the selection of civil society representatives from Darfur, see Murphy & Tubiana, *supra* note 627 at 13–17.

[667] For a critique of this assumption in the context of Bosnia, see David Chandler, *Bosnia: Faking Democracy after Dayton*, 2nd ed. (London: Pluto Press, 2000), especially 135–153.

overwhelmingly dominated by elite Tutsi and *not* representative of the majority population".[668] It should also be kept in mind that not all communities, and within them particular groups such as women, are well represented by their traditional leaders.[669] Nongovernmental organizations may, in fact, stand in opposition to the idea that civil society forms a robust basis of a democratic and peaceful society. As Christine Chinkin has argued, "NGOs are often non-democratic, self-appointed, may consist of only a handful of people, and determine their own agendas and priorities with a missionary-like or elitist zeal".[670]

More inclusive negotiations, whether open or secret, can certainly reduce the risk that influential actors who were excluded from the negotiations try to undermine the implementation of an agreement; central concerns will already have been heard and taken into account during the negotiating phase, when it may also be easier to engage with and moderate initially "hard" positions.[671] At the same time, inclusive negotiations increase the risk of bringing on board potential spoilers. Indeed, peace negotiations almost inevitably create spoilers, since peace is rarely considered beneficial by all actors at every moment. An armed conflict is fought precisely because peaceful means have not proven effective to solve a dispute, at least in the eyes of some actors, and a certain agreement might not be in everybody's interest. As Stephen John Stedman has argued more generally with respect to spoilers in peace processes, a precondition for dealing with this problem successfully consists in the correct identification of spoilers and their motivations.[672] The type of spoiler[673] determines the strategy that may be employed to manage the spoiler. To enable a successful process, such spoilers can be induced, socialized or coerced to change their behaviour.[674] Hence, since there will be no comprehensive agreement without engaging representatives of at least the main belligerent parties, some potential spoilers will likely have to be "managed" during a peace process.

---

[668] McClintock & Nahimana, *supra* note 633 at 86.

[669] United Nations Division for the Advancement of Women, *supra* note 278 at 11.

[670] Christine Chinkin, "Human Rights and Politics of Representation: Is There a Role for International Law?," in Michael Byers, ed., *The Role of Law in International Politics* (Oxford: Oxford University Press, 2000), 131, 143. A broader participation of civil society actors in peace negotiations may also be undesirable for other reasons. The inclusion of Acholi civil society members in the 2007 negotiations with the LRA, for instance, while possibly allowing to deal more comprehensively with the problems in northern Uganda, was also criticized as giving the LRA "undeserved legitimacy". International Crisis Group, "Northern Uganda: Seizing the Opportunity for Peace" (26 April 2007), online: International Crisis Group <http://www.crisisgroup.org/home/index.cfm?id=4791> at 14.

[671] For this argument, see Pfaffenholz, Kew & Wanis-St. John, *supra* note 627 at 69.

[672] Stedman, *supra* note 107 at 7.

[673] Stedman distinguishes three types of spoilers: limited, greedy and total (ibid., 10).

[674] Ibid., 12–14.

Even if these actors may be reluctant to join a peace process or may even try to derail it, they cannot be excluded if genuine negotiations are to be conducted.

Some civil society actors, regardless of their influence on peace negotiations and the general value of including them in negotiations, might act as such spoilers. Since these actors might not be considered absolutely indispensable for successful negotiations, the primary negotiators and mediators might therefore opt for a sequencing strategy of the spoiler problem, conclude a more limited agreement and promote it subsequently to bring recalcitrant actors on board. In contrast to those actors whose participation may be considered a sine qua non to any agreement, potential spoilers originating from civil society may thus simply be sidelined or completely ignored in the negotiations. In short, a selection of possible participants according to their apparent willingness to contribute constructively and in good faith to the negotiations may prevent giving too much influence to those mostly interested in spoiling negotiations.

It should be highlighted that the commitment to render negotiations more inclusive and to appreciate the concerns and interests of usually underrepresented or completely unrepresented groups is all too often built on a simplified concept of civil society.[675] International actors tend to overemphasize and somehow romanticize the democratizing potential of civil society actors who can restrain and counterbalance an "unruly state".[676] However, civil society actors do not necessarily correspond to this image; they are not always preaching nonviolence and striving for peace. By way of example, some civil society groups in Sri Lanka, especially "patriotic organizations" with close links to nationalist political parties, even opposed peace negotiations.[677] Others did not want to be associated with foreign actors to avoid perceptions of an externally imposed agenda.[678] This also illustrates that some civil society actors may actually not want to publicly join a formal process, out of principle or for strategic reasons. Since they may be highly critical of the primary negotiators – and possibly also of the mediators involved – and try to pursue an entirely different discourse, sitting at the "official" negotiating table could convey a confusing message to their constituencies. Intense media coverage might not give the necessary space to build trust and discuss ideas, and cooperation might easily be interpreted as cooption. This means that secret negotiations between

---

[675] For a critique of the dominant prescriptive notion of civil society based on Western models and resulting problems in capturing African associational life, see Nelson Kasfir, "The Conventional Notion of Civil Society: A Critique" (1998) 36:2 *Commonwealth and Comparative Politics* 1.

[676] Walton, *supra* note 189 at 184.

[677] Ibid., 189.

[678] Ibid., 194.

select participants may be more valuable in certain circumstances than an all-inclusive process.[679]

Moreover, civil society organizations are not always clearly separate from the state. As it has been asserted in the context of Sri Lanka, "The liberal approach to civil society has also presented a hard boundary between civil society and the state, which has failed to capture the fluid relationship between the state and civil society arenas that existed in the Sri Lankan context".[680] In some instances, governments even create what appear to be nongovernmental organizations, so-called government-organized NGOs or GONGOs, to increase their influence at this level. The strong ties of the current Sudanese government to some Darfurian civil society organizations have even led some observers to conclude that numerous participants at civil society conferences, like the one in Doha in November 2009, were actually government representatives.[681] A somewhat similar development can be discerned with respect to the relationship between civil society actors and the armed opposition groups in Darfur. At the beginning, the rebel movements were reluctant to include civil society actors, perceived as pro-government, in any negotiations.[682] Yet especially after the 2006 Peace Agreement, the movements began to strengthen their ties with and influence both traditional leaders and spokespersons of refugees and internally displaced persons.[683] At the same time, some prominent civil society figures, above all educated members of the diaspora, attempted to transform themselves into leaders of armed groups.[684] In sum, the independence of civil society actors from the state or from armed groups may be a fiction.

As a result of these dynamics, the involvement of civil society actors is highly context specific and contingent on their constitution, role during the conflict and relationship with the belligerent parties, as well as their objectives

[679] For the benefits of the secret negotiations, held in Rome under the auspices of the Community Sant'Egidio, between the Burundian government and the armed group Conseil National de la Défense de la Démocratie, see McClintock & Nahimana, *supra* note 633 at 80–83.

[680] Walton, *supra* note 189 at 184. For a similar argument, drawing on a case study from Senegal, see Irving Leonard Markovitz, "Uncivil Society, Capitalism and the State in Africa," in Nelson Kasfir, ed., *Civil Society and Democracy in Africa: Critical Perspectives* (London: Frank Cass, 1998), 21.

[681] Murphy & Tubiana, *supra* note 627 at 6. Needless to say, this strategy of state authorities bonding with members of civil society is not new: in Sudan, for instance, the British colonial administration already used traditional leaders in Darfur to implement a system of indirect rule (ibid.).

[682] Ibid., 7.

[683] Ibid.

[684] Ibid., 7–8.

for the negotiations.[685] Rendering peace negotiations inclusive and embracing bottom-up approaches is therefore a challenging enterprise. Despite these obstacles, the notion that peace negotiations are exclusively elite driven and inherently undemocratic is shifting. Secret negotiations between diplomats or politicians and military leaders are no longer the norm but have rather become the exception.[686] The pertinence of including, in some way, civil society actors in the negotiations – as part of official delegations, as separate parties at the negotiations or as intermediaries, at least to keep lines of communication open[687] – is increasingly being recognized, both in theory and in practice.

4.6. TOWARDS EMANCIPATORY OBLIGATIONS

The participation of civil society actors and their norm creative capacity instantiate the normative, and relational, dynamics of peace negotiations and symbolize the legal-normative framework of peace negotiations and emerging legal obligations. Legal norms and associated obligations are made and remade, in constant interaction. Since every situation is different, with some requiring a small negotiating table or even secret negotiations at certain moments, peace negotiators and mediators cannot rely on simple formulae with respect to ensuring effective participation and just and equal representation. To legitimize the negotiations, the legal-normative framework must be built by the actors involved and adapted to the respective circumstances.

As we will also see in the case of transitional justice, an essentialist approach to civil society involvement in peace negotiations is therefore unconstructive. The emerging obligation of negotiators and mediators regarding civil society participation reflects this challenge. This obligation, as it has been argued, is of a general nature, like a skeleton providing a structure, that aspires to render peace negotiations more inclusive and that can alleviate the pressure on the democratic legitimation of an agreement ex post. Yet this obligation does not prescribe specific modes of involvement or participation and does

---

[685] Walton has therefore concluded that a "flexible and adaptive approach towards peacebuilding may provide CSOs [civil society organizations] with the most effective means of exerting political influence in a volatile and antagonistic political environment" (Walton, *supra* note 189 at 198).

[686] Greenberg, Barton & McGuinness, "Introduction," *supra* note 66 at 6.

[687] Wanis-St. John & Kew, *supra* note 629 at 18–21. The authors' more nuanced conclusion with respect to the way civil society actors should participate in the negotiations is that "the ideal parties for durable peace agreements are democratic elites without civil society groups at the table, but with regular civil society influence on those elites. If elites are not democratic representatives, then direct civil society involvement in peace negotiations may increase the durability of agreements reached" (ibid., 14).

not preselect particular actors. Considering the involvement of civil society actors and the precise means of such an involvement in a particular context is, however, not optional, both for the primary negotiators and for mediators. It is above all these two groups of actors who, in interaction with civil society actors, concretize and give life to a general obligation; in this sense, the obligation is emancipatory[688] in nature. At the same, it is demanding, since it is not an easy preset, external command that can be complied with. To the contrary, it is like a shell that every actor, in relation with others, must contribute to filling with content, always pursuing the objective of facilitating human agency – individual, collective and relational.

---

[688] For the argument that anti-prescriptivism has emancipatory power, see Macdonald & Sandomierski, *supra* note 81 at 623–632.

5

Transitional Justice – Internalized Legal Obligations

The complexity of peace negotiations, the external normative pressure exercised on the actors involved as well as the challenges produced for the relationship between law and politics manifest themselves in the highly contentious debate on transitional justice. In this context, different perceptions of law and legal obligations and seemingly incompatible concepts of justice and individual accountability put forward by negotiators, mediators, external actors and various other stakeholders seem to clash.

The concept of "transitional justice" that has developed and is traditionally employed in the context of radical political transformations[689] is also useful to comprehend considerations of justice in peace negotiations. Whether or not the peaceful resolution of an armed conflict implies a radical political transformation, the stakes and possible institutional responses, such as providing accountability for past crimes and offering reparations, revealing the truth and bringing about reconciliation, are similar and can be compared with those in periods of transitions from totalitarian or authoritarian to more democratic regimes.[690] We will see that the dominant discourse puts forward a universalistic conceptualization of transitional justice, in particular with respect to the prosecution of international crimes. Both scholars and mediation practitioners have recognized that international criminal law exercises a particular external pressure on the normative framework of peace negotiations. The language of a report of the HD Centre is evocative. The report grasps well the fact that the negotiating parties and mediators are constantly influenced in making normative choices: "both parties to and mediators of peace talks are

---

[689] By way of example, in her seminal book *Transitional Justice*, Ruti Teitel aims to "explore the role of the law in periods of radical political transformation" (Teitel, *Transitional Justice, supra* note 39 at 4).

[690] For a short discussion of the term transitional justice, see ibid., 5.

now likely to be under considerable pressure to preserve international principles and respect international law in situations of gross abuse by the state or
by non-state actors".[691]

Unfortunately, this debate has often been presented through a somewhat
oversimplifying "peace versus justice" dichotomy, which in the words of
Payam Akhavan has been "embodied in the caricatures of the naïve 'judicial
romantic' who blindly pursues justice and the cynical 'political realist' who
seeks peace by appeasing the powerful".[692] Here, peace and justice appear as
competing, and not as complementary, goods.[693] The debate also mirrors the
dominant perception of law and of the relationship between law and politics
in the context of peace negotiations. According to this logic, law, and in this
case particularly international criminal law, is seen as being imposed en bloc
on the negotiating parties, who must decide according to a binary logic: they
are either within or outside international legality.

Despite the rather recent but escalating influence of international criminal law and international human rights law, which indicates a trend towards
increasingly norm-based peace negotiations, the impact of international treaties and other formal sources of international law on peace negotiations is
still very limited. This legal order is only part of the normative picture and
does not fully describe the legal obligations of negotiators and mediators. It is,
furthermore, not constructive to conceive transitional justice in the context of
peace negotiations by relying exclusively on this fairly well-established legal
order and the premise that the relevant actors have to comply with externally
imposed obligations.

The reach of international criminal law is, of course, enhanced by human
rights standards providing guidelines and examples of best practices. This
so-called soft law can be determinative of transitional legal responses[694] and

---

[691] See Hayner, "Negotiating Justice," *supra* note 573 at 9.

[692] Payam Akhavan, "Are International Criminal Tribunals a Disincentive to Peace?
Reconciling Judicial Romanticism with Political Realism" (2009) 31 *Hum Rts Q* 624 at 625.
As William P. Scharf and Paul R. Williams deplore, "Peace builders often employ the tools
of anti-justice.... While accommodation may be a useful and valuable tool, appeasement
is characterized by an artificial moral equivalence, neutrality in the face of aggression,
active efforts to erode the moral imperative to become involved, and the total exclusion of
the use of force and the norm of justice, with the effect of often encouraging further violence and atrocities". Michael P. Scharf & Paul R. Williams, "The Functions of Justice and
Anti-Justice in the Peace-Building Process" (2003) 35 *Case W Res J Int'l L* 161 at 179, 182.

[693] Margalit argues, for instance, that "to gain peace, we may be forced to pay in justice" (Margalit,
supra note 546 at 8).

[694] Bell, "Peace Agreements and Human Rights: Implications for the UN," *supra* note 185 at 244.
On "hard law" and "soft law", see, for example, Kenneth W. Abbott & Duncan Snidal, "Hard
and Soft Law in International Governance" (2000) 54 *International Organization* 421.

equally or even more compelling than relatively "hard law". However, it is not helpful to conceive the legal norms governing peace negotiations under the dichotomy of "hard law" and "soft law", despite the quite widespread use of these terms. Not only does "soft law" generally not account for unwritten legal norms,[695] which are significant as independent norms and as resources and inspiration for written, explicit norms;[696] it has also been shown in the context of well-established international organizations, such as the Organization for Security and Cooperation in Europe, that the form of law is not necessarily determinative of the degree of norm observance.[697] Most norms actually fall into a grey zone[698] and escape any form of definitive pigeonholing according to pre-established, "hard" criteria. In fact, legal norms are situated and can move along a continuum. By way of example, if a peace process generates fidelity of the parties to seemingly "soft" norms created in the process, it has the potential to lead to "hard" internalized obligations, albeit without taking the form of "hard law" supposedly enforceable in the orthodox sense. With respect to transitional justice, an apparently weak commitment of mediators and negotiators, especially when sustained by a shared understanding as to its legal value, can thus develop into a concrete and potent legal obligation to address such concerns in peace negotiations. The distinction between "hard" and "soft" law is therefore unsatisfactory, and the allusion here to these rather orthodox terms is only meant to help illustrate the fact that peace negotiators, mediators and external actors are, of course, exposed to and rely on existing norms that may take various forms and stem from different sources.

This chapter, in addition to scrutinizing the external normative pressure on negotiators and mediators in the field of transitional justice, claims that an orthodox – in other words, state-centred, formalistic and enforcement-driven – understanding of law cannot fully grasp the normative dynamics relating to transitional justice in the context of peace negotiations and should be supplanted by a focus on legal obligations. It is argued that it is the engagement

---

[695] See e.g. Christine M. Chinkin, "The Challenge of Soft Law: Development and Change in International Law" (1989) 38:4 *ICLQ* 850 at 850, n 1 [henceforth Chinkin, "The Challenge of Soft Law"].

[696] This relies on the argument made by Roderick A. Macdonald, "Custom Made – For a Non-Chirographic Critical Legal Pluralism" (2011) 26:2 *CJLS* 301 at 316.

[697] See, for example, Steven R. Ratner's study on the role of the High Commissioner on National Minorities of the Organization for Security and Cooperation in Europe. Ratner, "Does International Law Matter," *supra* note 327. See also Martha Finnemore, "Are Legal Norms Distinctive?" (2000) 32 *International Law and Politics* 699.

[698] As Christine M. Chinkin has argued in the context of a more general analysis of soft law, "There has always been a blurring of law and non-law in the international arena. The labels have never been precise" (Chinkin, "The Challenge of Soft Law," *supra* note 696 at 865).

with and internalization of such obligations by negotiators and mediators that is determinative of the normative framework of peace negotiations. Moreover, as a manifest instantiation of this internalization, legal obligations with respect to addressing transitional justice issues in the context of peace negotiations have emerged.

5.1. A POST-CONFLICT OBLIGATION TO ADDRESS INTERNATIONAL CRIMES

Peace negotiations take place within an existing legal framework composed notably of international human rights and international humanitarian law, as well as by international criminal law. These overlapping bodies of law, especially through their combined import as a merged regime,[699] assert accountability for grave violations. A specific prohibition has manifestly developed with respect to the granting of blanket amnesties, and a related obligation to establish transitional justice mechanisms is proposed to and is increasingly internalized by peace negotiators and mediators.

5.1.1. *An Outer Limit: The General Prohibition on Blanket Amnesties*

Numerous authors have analysed at length the general prohibition on amnesties for the gravest crimes and the obligation to deal with and ensure accountability for violations of international humanitarian law and international human rights law.[700] In a few words, granting blanket amnesties, especially for genocide, crimes against humanity and war crimes, has become less and less acceptable from a legal perspective, and it can be argued that such amnesties, without providing for any form of individual accountability or truth telling, have largely been outlawed by the international legal community. Although amnesties are, in general, still permissible under international law, the establishment of the ICC and the decisions of regional human rights courts suggest,

---

[699] On "regime merge" in the context of a discussion on the "new law of transitional justice", see Bell, *Law of Peace, supra* note 28 at 249–250.

[700] See e.g. Claus Kress & Leena Grover, "International Criminal Law Restraints in Peace Talks to End Armed Conflicts of a Non-International Character," in Morton Bergsmo & Pablo Kalmanovitz, eds., *Law in Peace Negotiations*, 2nd ed. (Oslo: Torkel Opsahl Academic EPublisher, 2010), 41; Diane Orentlicher, "Settling Accounts: The Duty to Prosecute Human Rights Violations of a Prior Regime" (1990) 100 *Yale LJ* 2537; Michael P. Scharf, "The Letter of the Law: The Scope of the International Obligation to Prosecute Human Rights Crimes" (1996) 59 *Law & Contemp Probs* 41; Darryl Robinson, "Serving the Interests of Justice: Amnesties, Truth Commissions and the International Criminal Court" (2003) 14 *EJIL* 481; Sadat, *supra* note 242; Ambos, *supra* note 563 at 54.

as Leila Nadya Sadat argued in 2006, that "a prohibition against the grant of blanket amnesties for the commission of *jus cogens* crimes may now have crystallized as a matter of general customary international law".[701]

The United Nations has been unequivocal with respect to the meaning of such an obligation in the context of peace negotiations. The secretary-general's 2004 report on the *Rule of Law and Transitional Justice in Conflict and Post-Conflict Settings* insists that

> peace agreements ... [r]eject any endorsement of amnesty for genocide, war crimes, or crimes against humanity, including those relating to ethnic, gender and sexually based international crimes, ensure that no such amnesty previously granted is a bar to prosecution before any United Nations-created or assisted court.[702]

The United Nations' *Updated Set of Principles for the Protection and Promotion of Human Rights through Action to Combat Impunity*, which was established by an independent expert and adopted by the Commission on Human Rights in 2005, confirms this view and indicates the growing shared understanding that impunity in the form of blanket amnesties for grave crimes is not acceptable. Principle 1 affirms the "general obligation of States to take effective action to combat impunity", while principle 24 states that

> even when intended to establish conditions conducive to a peace agreement or to foster national reconciliation, amnesty and other measures of clemency shall be kept within the following bounds:
>
> (a) The perpetrators of serious crimes under international law may not benefit from such measures until such time as the State has met the obligations to which principle 19 [notably "prompt, thorough, independent and impartial investigations of violations of human rights and international humanitarian law"] refers or the perpetrators have been prosecuted before a court with jurisdiction – whether international, internationalized or national – outside the State in question.[703]

The prohibition on amnesties to those most responsible for international crimes is highly relevant for peace negotiators and mediators and can influence the dynamics of peace negotiations in a significant way. In fact, as has been argued, "Decision-makers must take account of an international legal

[701] Sadat, *supra* note 242 at 1022.

[702] *The Rule of Law and Transitional Justice in Conflict and Post-Conflict Settings, Report of the Secretary-General, supra* note 329 at 64 (a) and (b) (emphasis added).

[703] UN Commission on Human Rights, *Updated Set of Principles for the Protection and Promotion of Human Rights through Action to Combat Impunity*, UN ESCOR, 2005, UN Doc. E/CN.4/2005/102/Add.1, principles 1 and 24.

presumption in favour of prosecution that excludes blanket amnesties for those who bear the greatest responsibility for crimes under international law".[704] The situation is unsurprisingly complicated by the fact that those who are regularly most responsible for the worst crimes, namely, the political and military leadership of the belligerent parties, are likely to be among those who are considered indispensable participants at the negotiations. Nevertheless, the recognition that blanket amnesties may not extend to international crimes already finds its manifestation in some peace agreements. The 2003 Accord de Linas-Marcoussis, for instance, provides for an amnesty for crimes committed in the conflict in Côte d'Ivoire but explicitly excludes grave violations of human rights and international humanitarian law: "la loi d'amnistie n'exonérera en aucun cas les auteurs ... de violations graves des droits de l'homme et du droit international humanitaire".[705]

It should be noted that the text of a peace agreement is only one indicator, albeit certainly an important one, of the significance attached to transitional justice issues by negotiators and mediators, with the establishment of a transitional justice mechanism provided for in the formally binding text of an agreement being the most visible manifestation of the commitment to addressing the past and possibly ongoing perpetration of crimes. Indeed, peace agreements may not always represent the most accurate and complete reflection of the extent to which transitional justice is addressed in a peace process. Such issues may be debated during the negotiations but not be included into the text of the agreement and possibly be addressed in a subsequent period of the transition. This means that the obligation to establish transitional justice mechanisms that has been internalized to a certain extent by various actors does not always manifest itself in the immediate inclusion of particular provisions into a peace agreement but can nonetheless be influential for the overall peace process.

5.1.2. *An Implicit Obligation to Set Up Transitional Justice Mechanisms*

As a *pendant* to the prohibition on blanket amnesties for international crimes, an obligation for the negotiating parties and mediators to envisage the establishment of transitional justice mechanisms in order to deal with past crimes has been proposed to negotiators and mediators. As the analysis of the texts of peace agreements has revealed,[706] a growing practice of including references

[704] Kress & Grover, *supra* note 701 at 53.
[705] *Accord de Linas-Marcoussis, supra* note 236, Annexe VII.5.
[706] See Chapter 2, Section 2.3.

to international humanitarian law and human rights law as well as of providing for some sort of accountability can be discerned. At the same time, a significant number of peace agreements are completely silent on individual accountability and transitional justice more generally. If the inclusion of individual accountability mechanisms in peace agreements does therefore not appear to be considered indispensable for any type of violation of human rights law or international humanitarian law, the situation is arguably different when it comes to the most serious crimes, also because some of these crimes are proscribed by the Rome Statute as well as by customary international law allowing third states to assume jurisdiction under the principle of universal jurisdiction. In this case, the *marge de manoeuvre* of the negotiating parties and mediators is significantly smaller owing to the prohibition on amnesties and, as will be argued, because of a related universalized post-conflict obligation to set up transitional justice mechanisms in order to deal with core crimes under international law.

Although only one source among many others possibly inspiring peace negotiations, the Rome Statute stands out as a highly influential one with respect to transitional justice. It can be considered a manifestation and reinforcement of a widely shared commitment to the prosecution of core crimes, which is why this framework merits some further attention. Even though the ICC, on account of its mandate, must be devoted to prosecutions, it can be argued that the acceptance of Truth and Reconciliation Commissions (TRCs) and national amnesty programs by the international community increases the discretion of the ICC prosecutor to defer to non-prosecutorial accountability mechanisms.[707] Indeed, the question as to what degree or precisely through which means individuals must be held accountable in order to satisfy the requirements of the Rome Statute, especially in the context of TRCs, has not been settled. What can be said is that although the delegates at the Diplomatic Conference in Rome could not reach a consensus as to how the ICC should, generally speaking, deal with amnesties or truth commissions, the court could almost certainly never accept blanket amnesties.[708]

Other mechanisms, such as the grant of conditional amnesties by a commission after hearings that come close to judicial proceedings, are not necessarily equivalent to impunity in the sense of the Rome Statute, since they do not threaten the goal of holding individuals accountable and of providing justice to victims. The acceptability of these mechanisms to the ICC is closely

---

[707] I have developed this argument at greater length in Philipp Kastner, *International Criminal Justice in bello? The ICC between Law and Politics in Darfur and Northern Uganda* (Leiden: Martinus Nijhoff, 2012), 133–142.

[708] See also Robinson, *supra* note 701 at 497.

linked to the principle of complementarity and Article 17 of the Rome Statute, which provides, inter alia, that a case is inadmissible when it has been "investigated by a State which has jurisdiction over it and the State has decided not to prosecute the person concerned, unless the decision resulted from the unwillingness or inability of the State to genuinely prosecute".[709] Although it has been argued that only criminal investigations can be subsumed under the term "investigations",[710] the ordinary sense of the word suggests that a commission which systematically and objectively gathers the evidence also meets this criterion.[711] This means that if ordinary criminal investigations and prosecutions have not taken place, the complementarity regime may nevertheless be satisfied if a non-prosecutorial body investigates the crimes.

As an additional requirement of Article 17(1)(b), the state must not be unable or unwilling "genuinely to prosecute", which refers to the provisions stipulated in Article 17(2) and (3). Above all, non-prosecutorial proceedings must not be undertaken with the "intent of shielding the person concerned from criminal responsibility".[712] If the main purpose of a conditional, and not blanket, grant of amnesty is to bring about reconciliation while uncovering the crimes committed, it would not appear to primarily shield the offenders from criminal responsibility. TRCs that share additional attributes with judicial proceedings, such as public hearings, would not appear to be necessarily contradictory to Article 17(2)(c), which states that the proceedings must not be "conducted in a manner which, in the circumstances, is inconsistent with an intent to bring the person concerned to justice".[713] The South African TRC, because of its strong investigatory mandate and the clearly defined conditions for a successful amnesty request,[714] can certainly inspire other democratically

---

[709] *Rome Statute, supra* note 252, preamble, art 17(1)(b).

[710] John T. Holmes, "The Principle of Complementarity," in Roy S. Lee, ed., *The International Criminal Court: The Making of the Rome Statute – Issues, Negotiations, Results* (Leiden: Martinus Nijhoff, 1999), 41, 77. But see Carsten Stahn, "Complementarity, Amnesties and Alternative Forms of Justice: Some Interpretative Guidelines for the International Criminal Court" (2005) 3 *Journal of International Criminal Justice* 695 at 711 [henceforth Stahn, "Complementarity"].

[711] See also Robinson, *supra* note 701 at 500. Similarly, Stahn comes to the conclusion that "any exemption from criminal responsibility must, at least, be accompanied by alternative forms of justice and be open to individualized sanction, including the possibility of criminal punishment" (Stahn, "Complementarity," *supra* note 711 at 710).

[712] *Rome Statute, supra* note 252, art 17(2)(a).

[713] Ibid., art 17(2)(c).

[714] For the "quasi-judicial" legal status of the South African TRC, occupying a "liminal space between state institutions", see Richard A. Wilson, "Reconciliation and Revenge in Post-Apartheid South Africa: Rethinking Legal Pluralism and Human Rights" (2000) 41:1 *Current Anthropology* 75 at 80.

demanded non-prosecutorial mechanisms that aim to fulfil the complementarity requirements of the Rome Statute as well as the more general obligation to deal with crimes committed during an armed conflict.

In sum, in addition to an outer limit that consists in not providing blanket amnesties to those allegedly responsible for the perpetration of international crimes, there is a strong normative claim to provide some form of individual accountability for grave violations of international human rights law and international humanitarian law. This increasingly recognized obligation to combat impunity for violations of international human rights and humanitarian law is, without doubt, still emerging, and quite obvious situations of impunity have been accepted by the international community out of political considerations. By way of example, in 2005, at a time when the Rome Statute had already entered into force and proclaimed in its preamble a global commitment to end a climate of impunity, it seems that the actors involved in the negotiations leading to the Comprehensive Peace Agreement chose to avoid any considerations of transitional justice and individual accountability. As a matter of fact, this agreement, signed in early 2005 between the Sudanese government and the SPLA, was heavily supported by numerous external actors, including neighbouring states, the United Nations, the African Union, the European Union, the League of Arab States and the United States.[715] Yet the agreement, which sought to end the twenty-year conflict between the North and the South and promised the SPLA an important share of political power and oil revenues, was completely silent on accountability for the crimes committed during the conflict. The crimes, including summary executions, rape, abductions and forced recruitment,[716] which had apparently been committed by the Sudanese army and pro-government militias as well as the SPLA, and the question as to how to address them do not seem to have been considered during the negotiations. The virtual ignorance of the crimes committed during the conflict appears to have been regarded as a necessary prerequisite by the numerous external actors to make the belligerent parties, in particular the government in Khartoum, sign the peace agreement.

In other words, the respect for the emerging obligation to address international crimes during peace negotiations has certainly not been consistent. Despite some exceptions like the Sudanese Comprehensive Peace Agreement,

---

[715] See the signatures attached to the Chapeau of the *Comprehensive Peace Agreement, supra* note 217 at xiv–xvi.

[716] For more information on the conflict and the crimes committed, see, for example, Marc Lavergne & Fabrice Weissman, "Sudan, Who Benefits from Humanitarian Aid?," in Fabrice Weissman, ed., *In the Shadow of "Just Wars", Violence Politics and Humanitarian Action* (Ithaca, NY: Cornell University Press, 2004), 137, 147–151.

it can, nevertheless, be argued that the normative disagreement relating to the general existence of an obligation not to ignore the past perpetration of international crimes has been settled and that a widely shared commitment with respect to ensuring accountability for the gravest crimes has emerged. It can also be argued that transitional justice issues have become an intrinsic aspect of peace negotiations and that, in recent years, it has become more and more challenging for negotiators and mediators to justify the ignorance of past crimes during the negotiations. Another Sudanese Comprehensive Peace Agreement, in this form and without the genuine prospect that transitional justice-related issues are addressed, as a minimum, at a later stage in the peace process, would probably be even harder to defend today.

5.2. TRANSITIONAL JUSTICE–RELATED OBLIGATIONS IN ACTION

The above analysis underlines the normative proposition offered to negotiators and mediators to envisage the establishment of some transitional justice mechanism, preferably but not necessarily prosecutorial, to deal with core crimes in a conflict or post-conflict situation. It is particularly the institutionalization of this proposition in the form of the ICC that can be seen as casting a shadow over peace negotiations and the manner in which justice issues are addressed. However, even within this sphere, there is an important *marge de manoeuvre* and space for creative solutions; the ICC Statute does indeed not prescribe a "zero tolerance policy towards amnesties for the core crimes".[717] Furthermore, in line with a legal-pluralistic reading of norms stemming from international criminal law, the "shadow" of the ICC and its underlying norms can be translated into an "invitation" to consider and engage with these "propositions".[718]

A textual analysis of agreements and an analysis of the discourse of the negotiating parties, mediators and influential external actors reveal the relevance of these propositions in practice. As it has been concluded in Chapter 2, international law and international legal obligations in the field of international human rights law and international criminal law are increasingly being referred to during the negotiations, although to a varying degree. The Colombian peace negotiations, and in particular the 2005 Justice and Peace Law,[719] are illustrative of this general development and of the more particular emerging obligations relating to transitional justice. Several negotiators

---

[717] Stahn, "Complementarity," *supra* note 711 at 718.
[718] This is based on Macdonald & Sandomierski, *supra* note 81 at 622–623, 631.
[719] On the Justice and Peace Law, see Arvelo, *supra* note 347 at 414; for a more general discussion of approaches to paramilitary accountability, see ibid., 430.

had argued that the 2003 Santa Fe de Ralito Accord,[720] which envisaged demobilization and reintegration of the paramilitary Self-Defense Forces of Colombia[721] but did not address individual accountability, had to be supplemented by a more robust instrument to avoid an "intervention" of the ICC as well as the prosecution of paramilitaries in other states under the principle of universal jurisdiction.[722] Moreover, numerous international governmental and nongovernmental organizations urged the Colombian government to comply with its international obligations with respect to the prosecution of international crimes.[723] Previous legislative proposals referred to international law, such as a 2004 proposal explicitly mentioning international humanitarian law and human rights treaties ratified by Colombia,[724] but did not go as far as the Justice and Peace Law, which, under the heading "right to justice", explicitly recognizes the duty of the Colombian state to carry out investigations and provide sanctions and remedies:

> De acuerdo con las disposiciones legales vigentes, el Estado tiene el deber de realizar una investigación efectiva que conduzca a la identificación, captura y sanción de las personas responsables por delitos cometidos por los miembros de grupos armados al margen de la ley; asegurar a las víctimas de esas conductas el acceso a recursos eficaces que reparen el daño infligido, y tomar todas las medidas destinadas a evitar la repetición de tales violaciones.[725]

The 2005 Justice and Peace Law, by providing for reduced prison sentences of five to eight years for demobilized members of armed groups having committed serious crimes,[726] can be considered to have been enacted under the continuous impact of international criminal law and the potential of ICC investigations and prosecutions. José E. Arvelo concludes that "as the accountability debate demonstrates, the definition of Colombia's international legal obligations in the context of peace negotiations delineates the contours of

---

[720] *Acuerdo de Santa Fe de Ralito, supra* note 55.

[721] For the origins of the right-wing paramilitary groups, see Arvelo, *supra* note 347 at 419–425.

[722] See Díaz, *supra* note 351 at 476. But see Arvelo, *supra* note 347 at 471, listing several bars to ICC jurisdiction over paramilitaries.

[723] For an overview of the international community's approach to the Justice and Peace Law, see Arvelo, *supra* note 347 at 441. For the increasing use of rights-based language by Colombian civil society actors, see Díaz, *supra* note 351 at 484.

[724] See Arvelo, *supra* note 347 at 435.

[725] *Ley 975 de 2005 [Justice and Peace Law]* (Colombia), 25 July 2005, art 6.

[726] Ibid., art 29. Articles 10–11 outline additional requirements that a demobilized member of an armed group must fulfill in order to benefit from the reduced prison sentence. For shortcomings of the law, see Díaz, *supra* note 351 at 489.

what is considered permissible and legitimate state action on critical issues of war and peace".[727]

It should be noted that the analysis of the influence of international law on a particular peace process, which depends on the role that international law has traditionally played in this state or region, can only benefit from trying to grasp the interpretation and perception of international law by the respective legal community. Regarding Colombia, for instance, some commentators have criticized the fact that only a certain version of international law put forward by its "orthodox proponents"[728] is considered "singularly authoritative"[729] in the country. This version of law is described as "quite unreflective of contemporary international practice; dismissive of legal alternatives; and un-conductive to resolving the conflict".[730] Such a static view of international law, which seems to prevail in most situations, may therefore be seen as significantly limiting the contribution that law can make to the promotion of peace.[731]

Despite this apparent shadow cast by international criminal law, legal obligations assumed by the negotiating parties and mediators in the field of transitional justice do not necessarily have to be considered as normative constraints to reaching a peace agreement. Restraining a certain conduct is, in fact, only one function of legal norms; they also facilitate, empower and guide human behaviour. A first step in the realization of these obligations in the context of peace negotiations may consist in putting the issue of transitional justice on the agenda of negotiations. Deliberating on the precise content of the underlying norms and their implementation in the respective situation may subsequently help delineate the bargaining range, or zone of possible agreement,[732] and provide guidance to find a viable solution.

In this process, some flexibility must be preserved to enable negotiated ends to an armed conflict. The legal obligations operate, again, rather as "framework" obligations whose precise normative content must be specified in every context. As Christine Bell has argued,

> reducing this flexibility further could again lead to normative frameworks being rejected more easily. Any attempts to articulate more clearly within

---

[727] Arvelo, *supra* note 347 at 447.

[728] Esquirol, *supra* note 153 at 70.

[729] Ibid., 24.

[730] Ibid.

[731] Ibid., 70. Arvelo comes to a similar conclusion: "'strict justice' proponents often categorize their conclusions in unqualified legal terms and disregard the fact that the peaceful resolution of disputes is also a long-established goal of international law" (Arvelo, *supra* note 347 at 447).

[732] For the term "zone of possible agreement" (ZOPA) developed in the peace and conflict studies literature, see Kirchhoff, *supra* note 375 at 162.

normative frameworks the permissive scope of exceptions or alternative approaches to accountability, would start to be very prescriptive, and it is unclear that it is a project that has any coherent possibilities at all.[733]

As a matter of fact, mediators and civil society actors have been fairly outspoken with respect to including transitional justice issues in peace negotiation. In the Doha Declaration, civil society actors from Darfur have, for instance, recognized both some outer limits regarding impunity as well as the necessity of a multitiered approach. In this declaration, Darfur civil society thus "stresses the importance of application of transitional justice", emphasizes "that perpetrators of war crimes and crimes against humanity and serious crimes such as rape will not escape with impunity", and recognizes that "different levels of reconciliation must be dealt with in accordance with the appropriate frameworks and mechanisms".[734]

While peace mediators are characteristically cautious with respect to accepting and putting into practice any preset norms that could reduce their and the negotiators' flexibility, one of the functions of peace mediation, as it has been argued above, is norm promotion. Negotiators are hence continuously encouraged to internalize and comply with transitional justice-related norms proposed by mediators.[735] The negotiation strategy of the United Nations is probably the best example, although other mediators also bear a similar normative ambition. Conflict resolution organizations have themselves recognized that the role of the mediator is crucial and that the mediator's perception of the legal obligations to be respected by the mediator and the negotiating parties is highly determinative for the course of the negotiations, in particular in the field of justice and accountability. As it has been noted by Priscilla Hayner in a report of the Centre for Humanitarian Dialogue,

> the inclusion or exclusion of justice elements in an accord does not seem to be determined primarily by political constraints of inflexible positions of the negotiating parties. Of course the positions of the parties are key, but even where negotiators are ambivalent or initially resistant, much can be achieved through a proactive mediator, access to expertise on justice issues, and openness in the process to incorporate expert input.[736]

733 Christine Bell, "The 'New Law' of Transitional Justice," in Kai Ambos, Judith Large & Marieke Wierda, eds., *Building a Future on Peace and Justice: Studies on Transitional Justice, Peace and Development, the Nuremberg Declaration on Peace and Justice* (Berlin: Springer, 2009), 105, 122–123.
734 *Doha Declaration, supra* note 655, art 2.4.4.
735 See similarly Bell, *Law of Peace, supra* note 28 at 179.
736 Hayner, "Negotiating Justice," *supra* note 573 at 20.

Not only human rights activists and academics increasingly argue that mediators have certain obligations regarding justice issues in peace negotiations
mediated by them; mediating organizations themselves also refer to and
acknowledge the normative impact of international developments on their
role and conduct. Hayner argues that

> a mediator today cannot easily ignore justice concerns, even where the parties
> may prefer to. The ascent of the International Criminal Court, the developing
> policy guidelines of international institutions involved in mediation, and the
> expectations created through the increasing use and sophistication of notions
> of "transitional justice" may all create legal and political constraints.[737]

It can therefore be maintained that the credibility and legitimacy of a mediator depend, at least to some extent, on his or her respect of these rather novel
obligations relating to transitional justice. These obligations are, in the civil
law understanding, *obligations de moyens* and not *obligations de résultat*:[738]
if the obligation "to endeavour or to strive to realize a certain result"[739] is
respected, the failure to attain the desired result is not a breach of the obligation and does also not entail specific sanctions. By way of example, a mediator
would not have to withdraw from a peace process and abandon the negotiating parties if justice and accountability issues cannot be put on the agenda or
if the transitional justice mechanism envisaged during the negotiations and
finally established in a peace agreement does not correspond to the requirements established under international law.

In line with an emphasis of process over outcome, it is important to
acknowledge that mediators increasingly assume a conduct-focused internalized commitment – in other words, a legal obligation[740] accepted by the
mediators themselves – regarding fundamental norms, most notably respect
for human rights and humanitarian law principles. The code of conduct of
International Alert is, once more, a good illustration:

> We are committed to pressing for international human rights standards to be
> recognised and incorporated in settlement agreements ... Where appropri-
> ate, promoting awareness of the International Criminal Court and related
> institutions and mechanisms should also be encouraged.[741]

[737] Ibid., 6.
[738] For explanations and a critique of this classification in the context of the International Law
Commission's Draft Articles on State Responsibility, see Pierre-Marie Dupuy, "Reviewing the
Difficulties of Codification: On Ago's Classification of Obligations of Means and Obligations
of Result in Relation to State Responsibility" (1999) 10:2 *EJIL* 371.
[739] Ibid., 375.
[740] This relies on the argument made by Brunnée & Toope, *supra* note 79 at 27.
[741] International Alert, *supra* note 336 at 5, 10.

A commitment to involving the ICC or other transitional justice mechanisms can obviously not be enforced under international law, but, as it has
been argued above, the existence of a legal obligation is not contingent on
its enforcement. An internalized commitment is based on a stronger sense
of obligation and may be more effective than an imposed obligation that can
supposedly be enforced. While it is difficult to measure the direct effects of a
mediator's commitment to including justice and accountability into the negotiations and to raising awareness of the ICC, such a commitment is highly
influential for peace negotiations. It is, moreover, part of the legal framework
of peace negotiations and can be seen as an indicator of the legitimacy of a
peace process and, ultimately, of its effectiveness.

An intermediary might also be quite outspoken about the normative basis
of his or her involvement in a specific situation and might not accept an
involvement unconditionally. This posture was exemplified by the involvement of Switzerland in facilitating communication between the Ugandan
government and the leaders of the LRA in 2006. As Switzerland's foreign minister, Micheline Calmy-Rey, highlighted, although it may be necessary to talk
with the "bad guys" to give peace a chance, Switzerland had only assumed
its facilitative role and allowed the Swiss expert Julian Hottinger to talk to
Joseph Kony under the "clear condition" that no amnesty would be granted
to the LRA leaders, against whom arrest warrants had already been issued by
the ICC.[742] While it is impossible to know precisely at which point and in
which manner this condition was conveyed to the parties concerned, it can
be concluded that Switzerland recognized and sought to put into practice
the normative principle of not including blanket amnesties for international
crimes into a peace agreement. This recognition certainly had a normative
impact not only on the involvement of Switzerland as a mediator – which
implied not to get involved or to pull out of the process if the grant of amnesties to alleged war criminals were to become part of the discussions – but also
on the negotiations themselves. It might be far-fetched to establish a causal
link between this norm-based approach of Switzerland and the importance
attached to the question of individual accountability in the ensuing negotiations and the conclusion of the Annexure to the Agreement on Accountability
and Reconciliation in 2008; yet it is safe to conclude that Switzerland's position contributed to developing and reinforcing the commitment in the Ugandan
negotiations to providing accountability for the crimes committed by the LRA.

---

[742] "Wer Frieden will, muss auch mit den Bösen reden: Gute Noten für Schweizer
    Konfliktmediation in Afrika" (2008) 11 welt-sichten, online: welt-sichten <http://www
    .welt-sichten.org/artikel/art-11-008/wer-frieden-will-muss-auch-mit-den-boesen-reden.html>.

Switzerland is, of course, not the only actor affirming such conditions with respect to amnesties. The principle that mediators should act in accordance with an increasingly shared consensus among the international legal community as to the inadmissibility of blanket amnesties for grave crimes is recalled explicitly in the UN Guidance for Effective Mediation:

> [Mediators should be] clear that they cannot endorse peace agreements that provide for amnesties for genocide, crimes against humanity, war crimes or gross violations of human rights, including sexual and gender-based violence; amnesties for other crimes and for political offences, such as treason or rebellion, may be considered – and are often encouraged – in situations of non-international armed conflict.[743]

Interestingly, this document also advises mediators not to assume an excessively firm position but to enable a broad-based deliberation on relevant norms: mediators should "balance the need to adhere to international norms without overtly taking on an advocacy role; facilitate access for partners and civil society actors to engage directly with conflict parties and other stakeholders regarding applicable norms".[744]

By focussing on such a process of deliberations rather than on a presumably predetermined outcome, it is possible to appreciate legal obligations as a device and not only perceive them as a constraint. In other words, they illuminate the scope and limits of what will be considered a legitimate process, thus specifying the bargaining range leading to a fair and effective agreement. This solution is unlikely to correspond to externally predetermined and fixed normative standards. In this sense, legal obligations are conceived of as determining the process rather than as demanding a particular outcome. In the words of a conflict resolution specialist recognizing this function of legal obligations, "Law frames the conflict, and structures the analysis of its underlying dynamics".[745] Similar language is employed by the United Nations that affirms that international law guides negotiations by "defining boundaries within which to seek agreement".[746]

With respect to the normative proposition based on international criminal law made to negotiators and mediators, there is definitely value in analysing the legal framework of the ICC and the exact requirements and standards

---

[743] *Strengthening the Role of Mediation, supra* note 328, Annex I, Guidance for Effective Mediation at para 42.

[744] Ibid.

[745] Gallant, *supra* note 387 at 396.

[746] See, for example, Gerard McHugh & Manuel Bessler, "Humanitarian Negotiations with Armed Groups: A Manual for Practitioners" *United Nations* (January 2006), online: OCHA <https:// docs.unocha.org/sites/dms/Documents/HumanitarianNegotiationswArmedGroupsManual. pdf> at 38.

of alternative mechanisms under the complementarity regime. However, the limits of an approach based on an external and universalizing perspective should also be recognized, since it is unconstructive and, in fact, impossible to envisage a preset one-size-fits-all standard or model that could easily be exported from one context to another. In addition to the fact that every mechanism has different features and that every TRC would probably be assessed differently by the ICC, the normative commitment to transitional justice in the context of peace negotiations hence entails, more generally, a nonessentialist approach to transitional justice. As a matter of fact, the legitimacy and effectiveness of transitional justice mechanisms arguably decreases with the perception of external imposition. One of the resulting premises is that external actors should not attempt to prescribe specific responses but rather complement local decisions.[747]

It should be noted that a nonessentialist approach to transitional justice does not imply an absence of cross-influence between different situations and of connections between the relevant actors involved. Experiences and practices linked to transitional justice mechanisms are part of a constant development; the elaboration and functioning of these mechanisms do not surface in a legal vacuum and do not have to be reinvented in every context. An emphasis on the contribution of all actors involved in peace negotiations to creating norms and to respecting and engendering respect for resulting obligations also allows these actors to map out a process that has a higher potential of being considered lawful and legitimate and of being ultimately more effective. The effectiveness of such a legal framework can also be expected to be enhanced for a related reason: when actors contribute to the creation of legal meaning, they will also feel more compelled to respect these legal norms and assume resulting obligations.[748]

An assessment from an outsider's perspective can, therefore, only be one part of the legal-normative picture framing justice and accountability in peace negotiations. For a more accurate picture of the legal obligations assumed by the negotiating parties and mediators, it appears useful to adopt an emic or "insider" perspective, which tries to understand a society the way its members understand it, in order to assess the internalization of legal obligations.

---

[747] For a similar argument, see Louise Mallinder, "Exploring the Practice of States Introducing Amnesties," in Kai Ambos, Judith Large & Marieke Wierda, eds., *Building a Future on Peace and Justice: Studies on Transitional Justice, Peace and Development, the Nuremberg Declaration on Peace and Justice* (Berlin: Springer, 2009), 127, 135.

[748] This draws on Fuller's arguments, e.g. in *The Morality of Law, supra* note 1 at 39–41, 194–195, 222.

5.3. THEORIZING TRANSITIONAL JUSTICE—RELATED
OBLIGATIONS FROM AN INTERACTIONAL PERSPECTIVE

The legal-normative framework of peace negotiations, and more specifically obligations relating to transitional justice, cannot adequately be grasped by an orthodox understanding of international law or by a realist approach put forward in the field of international relations.[749] The driving force for the development of classical public international law and its treaty regime, namely, reciprocity between sovereign states based on their interests, does not affect the dynamics of intrastate peace negotiations to a significant extent. Compared with interstate negotiations, the dynamics are utterly different in the context of the resolution of internal armed conflicts. Moreover, every conflict is distinct, not only regarding the underlying reasons for the conflict, the degree of violence and the issues at stake, but also regarding the legal status of the sometimes numerous warring parties and their willingness to negotiate and to adhere to a peace process. This commitment cannot be properly conceived by conventional international law nor be enforced by existing mechanisms established under international law. It is a commitment towards the peace process and, eventually, towards the peace agreement for its own sake, in other words, a specific normative regime created primarily by the negotiating parties and mediators.

In the field of conflict resolution, law and politics are often viewed as two opposing poles, with law being the *ought* perspective of an outsider with limited grasp on the political realities. The biggest deficiency of law is typically seen to lie in the lack of its enforcement. The frequently lamented "weakness" of the ICC, which must rely on state cooperation and cannot enforce its decisions on its own, is a telling example. This weakness exemplifies the prevalent view that law needs coercive enforcement mechanisms to be considered effective, or even to come into being. Some conflict resolution specialists do, however, frame their understanding of law in a different and more constructive way, which goes beyond opening or closing the law enforcement box. Michelle Gallant, for instance, has framed her understanding of international law and its analysis in a manner similar to the conception of law this book relies on: "compliance without coercion stands as an attribute, not a deficiency, of a legal system. A model of order that relies on consensual observance rather than threat of sanction constitutes a preferred regulatory model".[750]

---

[749] The introduction of the concept of "soft law" is, as argued above in this chapter, not helpful either in attenuating these shortcomings.

[750] Gallant, *supra* note 387 at 400.

The interactional theory of international legal obligations, developed by Jutta Brunnée and Stephen Toope by drawing on Lon Fuller's socio-legal understanding of law,[751] is helpful to analyse the legal-normative framework within which the negotiating parties and mediators interact in a peace process and to grasp more specific obligations relating to transitional justice. This approach emphasizes obligation over form or enforcement and views legal obligations as "internalized commitments".[752] Another advantage of comprehending legal norms governing peace negotiations through the lens of the interactional theory is the inclusiveness of this approach. The role of nonstate actors would indeed be difficult to assess from an orthodox perspective since they appear to be largely beyond the reach of international law. The focus on legal obligations internalized by the relevant actors, however, does not require a differentiation between states and nonstate actors. The formal status of the actors is, in fact, not significant.

Consistent with the argument that "the distinctiveness of law lies not in form or in enforcement but in the creation and effects of legal obligations",[753] legal obligations internalized by the negotiating parties and mediators take effect and form the conduct of the respective actors without following specific rules of recognition. This approach also avoids considering peace processes as primarily shaped by power relations and the conduct of the negotiating parties as being determined by reciprocity and rational choice; it focuses on social interaction and a practice of legality.[754] In this respect, interaction and internalization of legal obligations as crucial steps towards compliance share one of the main features of the theory of transnational legal process. According to Harold H. Koh, the interpretation and internalization of an international norm into the domestic legal system increases compliance and explains why states comply with international legal norms. As Koh argues,

> neither interest nor identity theory fully account for the normativity of transnational legal process .... In part, actors obey international law as a result of repeated interaction with other governmental and

---

[751] See e.g. Fuller, *The Morality of Law*, *supra* note 1.

[752] Brunnée & Toope, *supra* note 79 at 27.

[753] Ibid., 7. Brunnée and Toope also argue that the interactional theory of international legal obligations "provides specific criteria of legality that are essential in creating obligation" (ibid., 16).

[754] See ibid., 7. For an overview of different approaches addressing the effects of a broad definition of law on power relations, see Joost Pauwelyn, "Is It International Law or Not, and Does It Even Matter?," in Joost Pauwelyn, Ramses Wessel & Jan Wouters, eds., *Informal International Lawmaking* (Oxford: Oxford University Press, 2012), 125, 149–150.

nongovernmental actors in the international system.... It is through this repeated process of interaction and internalization that international law acquires its "stickiness".[755]

In other words, although power and force are unquestionably significant in understanding human interaction,[756] analysing peace negotiations solely by taking into account the absolute and relative power, whether military, political or economic, of the different parties misses key elements that shape these processes. They are precisely that: *processes*, which evolve, develop and progress or regress because of human interaction. Such a perspective cannot only build on a socio-legal understanding of law but benefits, once again, from constructivist approaches put forward in the field of international relations, which challenge realist international relations theory and its traditional emphasis on relative power and interests. Similar to Fuller's understanding of law[757] and the view that "shared understandings are inherently interactional, being always at once individual and social",[758] constructivism emphasizes interaction and considers it central in shaping human conduct. Law itself is therefore interactional and is construed as "a set of relationships, processes, and institutions embedded in social context".[759]

The linguistic-anthropological term "emic" is also useful with regard to theorizing the internalization of legal obligations. An emic or "insider" perspective privileges understanding and interpreting members of a society, their concepts and behaviour in terms of their meaning to the members themselves; its counterpart, an etic or "outsider" perspective, is more neutral and aims to

---

[755] Harold H. Koh, "Transnational Legal Process" (1996) 75 *Neb L Rev* 181 at 203–204. See also Harold H. Koh, "Why Do Nations Obey International Law?" (1997) 106 *Yale LJ* 2599. It should be noted that for the *emergence* of legal norms, merely "repeated interaction" must be considered insufficient.

[756] Brunnée & Toope, *supra* note 79 at 30.

[757] See e.g. Fuller, "Human Interaction and the Law," *supra* note 3.

[758] Brunnée & Toope, *supra* note 79 at 64.

[759] Finnemore & Toope, *supra* note 147 at 751. The focus on relationships and human interaction and its benefits are echoed by relational theorists who argue that "simply thinking about relationships or focusing on them generates results". Robert Leckey, *Contextual Subjects: Family, State and Relational Theory* (Toronto: University of Toronto Press, 2008), 14. Relational theorist Jennifer Nedelsky sees "human interactions to be governed ... in terms of the way patterns of relationship can develop and sustain both an enriching collective life and the scope for genuine individual autonomy". Jennifer Nedelsky, "Reconceiving Rights and Constitutionalism" (2008) 7:2 *Journal of Human Rights* 139 at 146. The ambition of many conflict resolution theorists and practitioners to contribute to resolving a conflict and generating lasting peace by improving relationships among the formerly warring parties bears resemblance to the normative commitment of most relational theorists to promoting relational autonomy and constructive relationships. For a discussion on the normative commitment of relational theorists, see Leckey, *supra* note 760 at 17–21.

understand a society in scientific and comparable terms.[760] While the etic perspective could be equated with a universalist assessment of legal obligations from an outsider's perspective, the concept of an emic perspective is valuable as a thinking tool to foster the theorization of the understanding of law and legal obligations through the lens of the framework built by the respective legal actors themselves. It should be noted that the researcher pursuing an emic analysis is not bound by the level of consciousness of the relevant actors; both conscious and unconscious dimensions are relevant, and any normative structures may be abstracted to pursue the analysis.[761]

A peace agreement does not become legal because of its validation by a superior authority or because of its enforceability but because it generates obligations of the negotiating parties vis-à-vis the agreement, in other words, *fidelity*[762] to the specific norms proposed and internalized in the course of the negotiations and the resulting agreement. Similarly, a peace process cannot derive its legitimacy solely from external validation. Rather, it is the development of shared commitments and the fidelity of the parties to the process, as well as the persuasiveness of the normative framework explicitly or – more likely – implicitly agreed on that are relevant.[763] The negotiating parties, mediators as well as other stakeholders, may also use an assessment of compliance with the obligations established to gauge the legitimacy and lawfulness of the conduct of other actors involved in the negotiations. By way of example, if a mediator, be it a state or nonstate actor, attempts to persuade the negotiating parties to adopt a rights-based approach to negotiations, the mediator can be expected, by the other parties involved, to comply with this principle and may be held accountable for his or her own conduct accordingly.[764]

This theoretical approach to peace processes combines the *is* and the *ought* and tries to understand, from an emic viewpoint, the legal obligations as they are perceived by the respective actors themselves. A legal obligation only

---

[760] For the origins of the terms "etic" and "emic" and their use, see Marvin Harris, "History and Significance of the Emic/Etic Distinction" (1976) 5 *Annual Review of Anthropology* 329 at 331–332; for an emic perspective in the study of distributive justice, see Clara Sabbagh & Deborah Golden, "Reflecting upon Etic and Emic Perspectives on Distributive Justice" (2007) 20 *Social Justice Research* 372.

[761] This relies on the point made more generally by Harris with respect to the distinction between emic and etic. Harris, *supra* note 761 at 338.

[762] The term "fidelity" draws on Fuller; see in particular Lon L. Fuller, "Positivism and Fidelity to Law – A Reply to Professor Hart" (1958) 71 *Harv L Rev* 630.

[763] As Brunnée and Toope argue, "When norms are rooted in shared understandings and adhere to the conditions of legality, they generate fidelity" (Brunnée & Toope, *supra* note 79 at 51). It is worth highlighting that contrary to Brunnée and Toope, and also contrary to Fuller, I do not attach much importance to a predetermined, fixed set of criteria of legality.

[764] See similarly Bell, *Law of Peace*, *supra* note 28 at 279.

materializes once it is internalized by the legal actor. The analysis pursued above on transitional-justice related obligations "in action" aimed to describe and understand the facts; the world of the *is*, in other words, the degree to which the negotiating parties evoke, respect or breach their legal obligations in the context of peace negotiations. These obligations are not to be measured according to generalized, "hard" regulatory standards prescribed by external actors, such as a so-called international community. Because the relevant actors engage with normative propositions and have the capacity to decide on their internalization, the normative parameters are rather established by the negotiating parties themselves. In this sense, the legal-normative framework of peace negotiations cannot exist apart from the subjective understanding of peace negotiators and mediators.[765] This will obviously lead to a different legal-normative framework in every conflict or post-conflict situation, and the framework might also evolve in the course of the negotiations.

In addition to describing the obligations as they are perceived by the legal actors, this approach also addresses the *ought* perspective, which enquires what is "right", but viewed primarily through the lens of the respective actors and not through the glasses of a human rights activist or academic. It is not about setting predetermined standards for negotiators and mediators and pre-scribing or even codifying the laws of peace negotiations; key actors assess for themselves which obligations they deem adequate for internalization in order to create truly legal obligations. However, the negotiators and media-tors never float in a legal vacuum. Similar to Sally Falk Moore's notion of the "semi-autonomous social field" that is "set in a larger social matrix, which can, and does, affect and invade it",[766] negotiators and mediators are inevitably influenced by other peace processes and, for instance, the growing significance of legal norms in the field of international human rights law and international criminal law. These developments provoke the internalization of certain obli-gations, although the legal actors may comprehend their obligations in very broad terms, such as what is "right" and what is "wrong", which means that the obligations can hardly be spelled out in prescriptive or positivist-like legal language. These obligations form, nonetheless, the legal-normative frame-work of peace negotiations; symbolize one of the ways negotiators, mediators and stakeholders interact; and describe the legal boundaries within which these actors can manoeuvre. The parties never build their micro-cosmic legal

---

[765] This view draws on Macdonald's approach to legal pluralism. See e.g. Macdonald, "Here, There ... and Everywhere," *supra* note 1 at 406.

[766] Sally F. Moore, "Law and Social Change: The Semi-Autonomous Social Field as an Appropriate Subject of Study" (1973) 7 *Law & Soc'y Rev* 719 at 720.

framework from scratch. The influence of the "macro-world", in other words, key international and national actors, such as the United Nations, influential foreign governments and civil society actors, who all offer obligations to be potentially "selected" for internalization, is substantial.

5.4. CONCLUSION

International law and international legal obligations play a central role in the process of the resolution of internal armed conflicts. Although they may not always determine a particular outcome, they map out the process by clarifying the bargaining range for an agreement that will be recognized as lawful and legitimate. Process-related norms are closely linked to and are highly determinative of substantive outcomes. This correlation manifests itself in the legitimacy of a peace agreement that may be questioned if the issue of accountability for past crimes and other transitional justice concerns are left unaddressed during the negotiations. A peace agreement endorsing impunity may be considered illegal, illegitimate, a rotten compromise disqualifying the whole agreement,[767] or qualified, in simple terms, as "wrong".[768] Similarly, a process that does not even attempt to include a debate about accountability will most likely be considered incomplete and flawed, which entails negative consequences for the effectiveness and durability of a resulting peace agreement.

Taking transitional justice as an example, this chapter has argued that it is necessary and beneficial in conflict and post-conflict situations to turn to legal norms that are formally recognized to a universal or near-universal extent. In addition to relying on such a formal and relatively clear legal framework anchored in international law, it is equally necessary to understand the legal obligations of the negotiating parties and mediators from an emic perspective. Working exclusively with a generalized knowledge structure built by the researcher, which oversimplifies the context and risks ignoring the norm creative capacities of the actors involved in peace negotiations, is unconstructive. To comprehend legal obligations, here related to transitional justice, and to provide a more constructive normative basis for the conduct of peace negotiations and resulting peace agreements, a socio-legal and interactional

---

[767] As Margalit argues, "[A] rotten compromise over an item in an agreement infects an entire, otherwise agreeable agreement" (Margalit, *supra* note 546 at 61). For Margalit, a rotten compromise, which is never justified, is "an agreement to establish or maintain an inhuman regime, a regime of cruelty and humiliation, that is, a regime that does not treat humans as humans" (ibid., 2).

[768] Hayner, "Negotiating Justice," *supra* note 573 at 6.

understanding of law appears more appropriate. Such an approach, in fact, enhances the reach of law on peace negotiations by recognizing and promoting a normative framework that is built on legal obligations internalized by negotiators and mediators.

This increasing internalization of legal obligations with respect to transitional justice reflects a normative trend that bears a significant potential. Indeed, the recognition of transitional justice concerns as an inherent part of a conflict resolution process can be expected to transform the outcome. The emergence of these legal obligations with respect to involving existing or establishing new transitional justice mechanisms in the context of peace negotiations should not be understood as a pre-existing obligation projecting a definite outcome. Rather, this emergence should be imagined as an increasingly internalized obligation towards a more legitimate and comprehensive conflict-resolution process.

6

Conclusion

Peace negotiations are not a normative hole; the negotiating table is not a normative tabula rasa or, in the logic of Carl Schmitt, a state of emergency–like situation that silences law.[769] Law shapes peace negotiations, and peace negotiations generate legal normativity. We – legal scholars, conflict resolution specialists, negotiators and other actors involved in peace negotiations – are simply not always aware of it, and we clearly do not yet seize the full potential that law has in contributing to the peaceful resolution of internal armed conflicts. Neither the legal literature nor the peace and conflict studies literature has been satisfying in this regard so far. In this book, I have offered one way to conceptualize, from a legal perspective, these complex, fairly novel and varyingly normatized processes. Moreover, exploring some of the normative dimensions of peace negotiations has contributed to a better understanding of the creation and role of legal norms, as instantiated by these rich norm generating processes that escape much of the formalism in traditional lawmaking.

An analysis, in Chapter 2, of the texts of peace agreements and of the discourse of peace negotiators, mediators and external actors in the process laid the groundwork, exposed the use of legal norms by these actors and revealed some of the normative trends arising in the context of peace negotiations. Indeed, the discursive practices structure peace negotiations and constitute their legal framework. The subsequent chapters on peace mediation, civil society actors and transitional justice are closely interrelated and revealed several connections, such as the emerging legal obligations of peace mediators relating to the participation of civil society actors and to addressing justice and accountability in the negotiations. However, the conclusions to be drawn regarding the respective normative dimensions are not identical. While the negotiators and external actors are fragmented groups that make use of and

---

[769] For this discussion, see Zumbansen, *supra* note 29 at 5–6 and references in n 17.

are guided by normative considerations in very different ways and to different degrees, peace mediators can be understood as an epistemic community. This community already maps out a more fully shaped normative practice. Because the endeavour of peace mediation has experienced quite a heavy normatization and because of the increasingly assumed normative ambition of mediators, both vis-à-vis the negotiating parties and other peace mediators, the role of legal norms manifests itself quite clearly in this context. In contrast, it seems that the involvement of civil society actors, at this point and as explored in the fourth chapter, still has a thinner and more embryonic normative foundation. This symbolizes the making and remaking of legal norms and associated obligations, in constant interaction among the actors concerned, and promises significant future developments. Although an increasingly shared commitment of negotiators and mediators to involving civil society actors in peace negotiations, with the objective of strengthening the legitimacy of the process and a resulting agreement, can be discerned, many questions remain open. Compared with peace mediators, the legal agency of civil society actors is still in greater need of recognition. The normative parameters regarding which actors should be included in which way and at which stage of the negotiations still appear to be unsettled, and the practice observed does not allow making definite claims. More specifically, while the importance of involving women in peace negotiations is increasingly being recognized, it is not safe to speak of a normative trend suggesting a particular modus operandi. Even the United Nations, despite its declared normative ambition, has not appointed a single woman as special envoy or special representative of the secretary-general to mediate peace negotiations. Far from seeking to draw dogmatic conclusions, I have nevertheless tried to identify areas of current normative consensus. The most evident example, as discussed in Chapter 5, materializes in the context of transitional justice. Mediators, civil society and other external actors, as well as the negotiating parties themselves, increasingly share and internalize a commitment to include issues related to justice and accountability during the negotiations.

The conclusions drawn in each chapter can also be read as reminders of the dangers and downsides of an essentialist approach, be it regarding the conduct and mission of peace mediators, the involvement of civil society actors or ways in which justice and accountability are to be addressed in the negotiations. Indeed, peace negotiations cannot benefit from a one-size-fits-all legalistic approach.[770] Moreover, the still common principled versus pragmatic – or

---

[770] Similarly, the traditional strategy of promoting and protecting human rights, which focuses on the formal reach of human rights instruments and their enforcement, cannot be applied

rights versus power – dichotomy tends to simplify the parties' positions and assumes that their interests are fixed[771] and that they rationally pursue their long-term interests.[772] Especially in the context of long-standing conflicts, such a view artificially entrenches allegedly static standpoints. Both states and nonstate actors never represent perfectly homogenous entities: internal positions, interests and identities are socially constructed and therefore subject to change.[773] For instance, not all Israeli citizens share the official position of their government at the negotiating table with respect to the exclusively Jewish character of the state, which may have significant consequences for the return of Palestinian refugees.[774] Armed opposition groups who have been fighting for decades against the central government, such as the FARC in Colombia or the LRA in Uganda, do not have unchanging objectives and demands. With interests, positions and underlying normative beliefs and obligations being remodelled in continuous interaction with other actors, possible solutions to a conflict also fluctuate.

I have argued that legal norms can and should be used more constructively in the context of the resolution of internal armed conflicts. The success of this endeavour largely depends on our general understanding of the creation and functions of legal norms and associated obligations. My claim is that the actors involved in peace negotiations are and ought to be conceived as legal agents, and that recognizing and promoting this dimension of peace negotiations is particularly relevant in the context of internal armed conflicts. Because of the hybrid nature of intrastate peace agreements, which escape an easy classification along established legal categories,[775] and because of their lack of formal legal status, the creation and effects of legal obligations do not follow the logic of positive law. It is, therefore, even more important for the parties trying to resolve an internal armed conflict to find other means to account for obligations and to establish costs for breaching these obligations. The formal status of the actors involved and the form that a peace agreement may ultimately

---

in exactly the same way in all post-conflict situations. See e.g. Tonya Putnam, "Human Rights and Sustainable Peace," in Stephen John Stedman, Donald Rothchild & Elizabeth M. Cousens, eds., *Ending Civil Wars: The Implementation of Peace Agreements* (Boulder, CO: Lynne Rienner, 2002), 237.

[771] Rempel and Prettitore therefore reject rationalist arguments as the sole explanation for Israel's noncompliance with international law. Rempel & Prettitore, *supra* note 637 at 87.

[772] Jan Egeland, "10 Lessons from 10 Peace Processes," in Susan Allen Nan, Zachariah Cherian Mampilly & Andrea Bartoli, eds., *Peacemaking: From Practice to Theory*, vol. 1 (Santa Barbara, CA: Praeger, 2012), 51, 54.

[773] For this social constructivist argument, see Ruggie, *supra* note 591 at 862–864.

[774] See Rempel & Prettitore, *supra* note 637 at 88.

[775] See Chapter 1, Section 1.2.

take are secondary. What counts is the relevance attached to the process of negotiations and a resulting agreement by the parties: if a process is considered legitimate and an agreement legal, the obligations created will also be taken more seriously.[776] This book, through a pluralistic and socio-legal understanding of law that focuses on human interaction, has emphasized these norm creative capacities of the actors involved in peace negotiations and has thus tried to enhance our understanding of the role that law plays in the context of the resolution of internal armed conflicts. Peace negotiators and mediators, civil society actors and other influential external actors may all contribute to rendering peace negotiations more legitimate and effective; recognizing their respective legal agency is a fundamental, first step, which, consequently, furthers the reach of legal norms on peace negotiations. This normatization should not be understood to be necessarily directed at a specific, measurable outcome but as a way to facilitate a certain form of human interaction and as a source of commitment towards the process itself. In fact, legal normativity itself is a process, an aspirational enterprise and a way to be in relation with one another. Constructed and constantly renegotiated, law is not static. And yet it never becomes an arbitrary list from which to choose norms and obligations: it is only through interaction that the norm creative capacities of the actors involved in peace negotiations can materialize. This relational legal agency allows the development of the very framework that can facilitate the peaceful resolution of internal armed conflicts.

The emphasis on the process also resonates with the idea that peace will always remain "imperfect". Quite in contrast to Kantian-type formulae through which a "perpetual peace" could be achieved,[777] peace itself is a process and not a state that can be accomplished. Francisco A. Muñoz argues persuasively that

> *peace* should not be considered as "total", closed, the endpoint, an almost impossible to achieve "utopian" goal, – except at great expense – unrealistic and, consequently, frustrating, [if not] counterproductive inasmuch as it can be source of violence.... We must make full use of the possibilities offered to us by our present reality in order to project a future in which we are as close to *peace* as possible.[778]

---

[776] As Franck explains this compliance pull generated by legitimacy, "Those addressed [by a rule or a rule-making institution] believe that the rule or institution has come into being and operates in accordance with generally accepted principles of right process". Thomas M. Franck, *The Power of Legitimacy among Nations* (New York: Oxford University Press, 1990), 24 (emphasis omitted).

[777] Immanuel Kant, "Zum ewigen Frieden: Ein philosophischer Entwurf," in Wilhelm Weischedel, ed., *Immanuel Kant's Werke. Band XI* (Frankfurt: Suhrkamp, 1968), 195.

[778] Muñoz, *supra* note 98 at 280–281 (footnotes omitted). As Muñoz points out, this conception goes back to Heraclitus and his insight that "everything flows" (ibid., 259, n 24). Harold Saunders has argued similarly that "peace is never made. It's always in the making". Harold

Some peace researchers have also put forward the idea that we should speak of peace in the plural, since it allows us to better grasp the fact that peace may mean something different, both in time and space. Seeking one uniform type of a presumably perfect peace would be reductionist and even dangerous. As Wolfgang Dietrich and Wolfgang Sützl claim, "This kind of idea of salvation is in itself intellectual violence because it simply lacks respect for otherness and its secrets".[779]

This vision of peace as a continuous process instead of a condition to be perfected confirms one of the main arguments of this book, namely, the necessity of employing a contextual approach to the resolution of armed conflicts and of emphasizing processes over outcomes.

The normative frameworks governing these processes continue to be built. At the time of writing, significant developments are taking place in several contexts. The delegations of the Colombian government and the FARC are meeting in Cuba to negotiate a comprehensive agreement seeking a durable resolution of their conflict. If the parties reach such an agreement, it can be expected to concern not only the disarmament of the FARC but also measures to ensure distributive and reparatory justice, such as a major land reform and a victims' reparation scheme. The so-called Legal Framework for Peace, a controversial law passed in 2012, has, so far, not been able to settle the normative disagreement regarding transitional justice.[780] Initiatives have been made to improve the problematic triadic relationship between the Afghani Taliban, the government in Kabul and the United States with a view to settling the conflict in Afghanistan. However, genuine negotiations are not in sight. The main actors have not been able to move beyond prenegotiations about how and where to communicate; the opening in June 2013, and closure only a few weeks later, of a liaison office of the Taliban in Doha symbolizes this difficulty. The widely held belief that elections may make a vital contribution to the resolution of an internal armed conflict was aptly summarized by a commentator

---

Saunders, "Peacemaking in a Relational Paradigm," in Susan Allen Nan, Zachariah Cherian Mampilly & Andrea Bartoli, eds., *Peacemaking: From Practice to Theory*, vol. 1 (Santa Barbara, CA: Praeger, 2012), 148.

[779] Wolfgang Dietrich & Wolfgang Sützl, "A Call for Many Peaces," in Wolfgang Dietrich, Josefina Echavarría Alvarez & Norbert Koppensteiner, eds., *Schlüsseltexte der Friedensforschung* (Vienna: LIT, 2006), 282, 292. Or, as Belachew Gebrewold has argued, "There cannot be global peace if the global peaces are not given due consideration and respect". Belachew Gebrewold, "T'ùmmu: An East African Perspective," in Wolfgang Dietrich et al., eds., *Peace Studies: A Cultural Perspective* (New York: Palgrave Macmillan, 2011), 428, 440.

[780] The law has been criticized in Colombia, for instance, by the former president Alvaro Uribe, as well as internationally. See e.g. Human Rights Watch, "Colombia: Amend 'Legal Framework for Peace' Bill" (31 May 2012), online: Human Rights Watch <http://www.hrw.org/news/2012/05/31/colombia-amend-legal-framework-peace-bill>.

before the presidential elections in Mali in late July 2013: "Vite, une élection présidentielle pour tourner la page de la crise aiguë au Mali: c'est peut-être la pire des solutions … à l'exception de toutes les autres".[781] The apparently interminable Israeli-Palestinian peace process, which is, once again, faltering, could certainly benefit from a paradigmatic shift. Recognizing the relevance of legal norms, and grounding the negotiations more deeply in a normative framework, would not make the problems and differing interests disappear. Such a recognition could nevertheless contribute to rendering the negotiations more legitimate and effective, thus increasing the prospects of finding a viable solution to the conflict. As for Syria, one of the most acute armed conflicts at the moment, the belligerent parties have not overcome their stalemate. Various external actors, including prominent individuals like Kofi Annan, have not been able so far to create mutually enticing opportunities to ripen the conditions for negotiations. This conflict, which has not only devastated the country but has started to spread across the Syrian borders, highlights the significance of a negotiated resolution of internal armed conflicts. This is not a conflict that is likely to be won on what cannot even be called, in the traditional sense, a "battlefield"; neither can it be "managed" in the long term, the very existence of the shared political space being at stake. In other words, the conflict will have to be resolved through negotiations. As in other situations, such negotiations will be shaped by and also further develop the normative framework, as explored in this book, both regarding the process and the substance of what admittedly appears at the moment as a distant hope for a peace agreement. Who will sit at the table? Who will be considered legitimate representatives of the belligerents and of the population at large? Who mediates, how and on which normative basis? Which items will be put on the agenda? How and to what extent does a sense of legal obligation influence the negotiators and mediators when discussing the involvement of civil society actors, transitional justice and, more specifically, accountability for the undoubtedly numerous and grave crimes committed during the conflict? What kind of peace will be negotiated? It is vital that we continue to ask these normative questions and seek to find answers, even if they may not be perfect and perpetual or apply universally. While the analyses and arguments proposed in this book will not motivate any belligerent party to join the negotiating table, I hope that a better understanding and conceptualization of the normative dynamics of peace negotiations will contribute to making these negotiations more legitimate and more effective.

[781] Thomas Hofnung, "Présidentielle: le Mali poussé aux urnes," *Libération* (26 July 2013), online: Libération <http://www.liberation.fr/monde/2013/07/26/presidentielle-le-mali-pousse-aux-urnes_921140>.

Bibliography

Treaties, Peace Agreements and Legislation

Accord de Linas-Marcoussis, 24 January 2003 (Côte d'Ivoire), online: United States Institute of Peace <http://www.usip.org/files/file/resources/collections/peace_agreements/cote_divoire_01242003en.pdf>.

Accord politique de Ouagadougou, 4 March 2007 (Côte d'Ivoire), online: United Nations Mission in Côte d'Ivoire <http://www.onuci.org/pdf/ouagaaccord.pdf>.

Acuerdo de Santa Fe de Ralito, 15 July 2003, online: Oficina del Alto Comisionado para la Paz <http://www.altocomisionadoparalapaz.gov.co/web/acuerdos/jul_15_03.htm>.

Acuerdo político entre el gobierno nacional, los partidos políticos, el M-19, y la iglesia católica en calidad de tutora moral y espiritual del proceso [Accord between the National Government, the Political Parties, the M-19 and the Catholic Church in the Capacity of a Moral and Spiritual Guide for the Process], 9 March 1990 (Colombia), online: UN Peacemaker <http://peacemaker.un.org/sites/peacemaker.un.org/files/CO_900309_Acuerdo%20Pol%C3%ADtico%20Entre%20El%20Gobierno%20Nacional%20los%20Partidos%20Pol%C3%ADticos%20y%20El%20M-19.pdf>.

Agreement on a Permanent Ceasefire, 23 February 2008 (Uganda), online: UN Peacemaker <http://peacemaker.un.org/sites/peacemaker.un.org/files/UG_080223_Agreement%20on%20a%20Permanent%20Ceasefire.pdf>.

Agreement on the Gaza Strip and the Jericho Area (Cairo Agreement), 4 May 1994, UN Doc. A/49/180.

Annexure to the Agreement on Accountability and Reconciliation, 19 February 2008 (Uganda), online: UN Peacemaker <http://peacemaker.un.org/sites/peacemaker.un.org/files/UG_080219_Annexure%20to%20the%20Agreement%20on%20Accountability%20and%20Reconciliation.pdf>.

Comprehensive Peace Agreement between the Government of the Republic of the Sudan and the Sudan People's Liberation Movement/Sudan People's Liberation Army, 9 January 2005, online: United Nations Mission in Sudan <http://unmis.unmissions.org/Portals/UNMIS/Documents/General/cpa-en.pdf>.

Convention on the Elimination of All Forms of Discrimination against Women, 18 December 1979, 1249 UNTS 13 (entered into force 3 September 1981).

Convention on the Prevention and Punishment of the Crime of Genocide, 9 December 1948, 78 UNTS 277 (entered into force 12 January 1951).

Convention Relating to the Status of Refugees, 28 July 1951, 189 UNTS 137 (entered into force 22 April 1954).

Darfur Peace Agreement, 5 May 2006, online: United Nations Development Programme Sudan <http://www.sd.undp.org/doc/DPA.pdf>.

Declaration of Independence, 4 July 1776 (United States of America), online: National Archives <http://www.archives.gov/exhibits/charters/declaration_transcript.html>.

Framework Agreement for the Resumption of the Negotiating Process between the Government of Guatemala and the UNIDAD Revolucionaria Nacional Guatemalteca, 10 January 1994, UN Doc. A/49/61 and UN Doc. S/1994/53.

Framework Agreement to Resolve the Conflict in Darfur between the Government of Sudan (GoS) and the Justice and Equality Movement Sudan (JEM), 23 February 2010, UN Doc. S/2010/118.

General Framework Agreement for Peace in Bosnia and Herzegovina (Dayton Peace Agreement), 14 December 1995, 35 ILM 75, online: Office of the High Representative and EU Special Representative <http://www.ohr.int/dpa/default.asp?content_id=379>.

General Peace Agreement for Mozambique, 4 October 1992, online: United States Institute of Peace <http://www.usip.org/files/file/resources/collections/peace_agreements/mozambique_1991-92.pdf>.

International Covenant on Civil and Political Rights, 19 December 1966, 999 UNTS 171 (entered into force 23 March 1976).

Israeli-Palestinian Interim Agreement on the West Bank and Gaza Strip (Oslo II), 28 September 1995, UN Doc. A/51/889.

Ley 975 de 2005 [Justice and Peace Law] (Colombia), 25 July 2005.

Lomé Peace Agreement, 7 July 1999 (Sierra Leone), UN Doc. S/1999/777.

Memorando de Entendimento Complementar ao Protocolo de Lusaka para a Cessação das Hostilidades e Resolução das Demais Questões Militares Pendentes nos Termos do Protocolo de Lusaka (Luena Memorandum of Understanding), 4 April 2002 (Angola), UN Doc. S/2002/483.

Protocol Additional to the Geneva Conventions of 12 August 1949, and Relating to the Protection of Victims of Non-International Armed Conflicts (Protocol II), 8 June 1977, 1125 UNTS 609 (entered into force 7 December 1978).

Republic of Côte d'Ivoire, *Declaration Accepting the Jurisdiction of the International Criminal Court,* 18 April 2003, online: International Criminal Court <http://www.icc-cpi.int/NR/rdonlyres/74EEE201-0FED-4481-95D4-C8071087102C/279844/ICDEENG.pdf>.

Rome Statute of the International Criminal Court, 17 July 1998, 2187 UNTS 90, UN Doc. A/CONF.183/9 (entered into force 1 July 2002).

Rules of Procedure and Evidence of the International Criminal Court, 9 September 2002, Assembly of States Parties, 1st sess., ICC-ASP/1/3.

Vienna Convention on the Law of Treaties, 23 May 1969, 1155 UNTS 331 (entered into force 27 January 1980).

United Nations Documents

Commission on Human Rights. *Report of the Representative of the Secretary-General, Mr. Francis Deng, submitted pursuant to Commission resolution 1997/39. Addendum: Guiding Principles on Internal Displacement*, UN Doc. E/CN.4/1998/53/Add.2.

Updated Set of Principles for the Protection and Promotion of Human Rights through Action to Combat Impunity, UN ESCOR, 2005, UN Doc. E/CN.4/2005/102/Add.1.

Division for the Advancement of Women. *Peace Agreements as a Means for Promoting Gender Equality and Ensuring the Participation of Women*. Paper prepared by Christine Chinkin, UN Doc. EGM/PEACE/2003/BP.1 (31 October 2003), online: United Nations <http://www.un.org/womenwatch/daw/egm/peace2003/reports/BPChinkin.PDF>.

Human Rights Committee. *General Comment No. 25: The Right to Participate in Public Affairs, Voting Rights and the Right to Equal Access to Public Services (Art. 25)*, UN Doc. CCPR/C/21/Rev.1/Add.7 (1996).

Legal Empowerment of the Poor and Eradication of Poverty, Report of the Secretary-General, UN Doc. A/64/133 (13 July 2009).

Marshall v. Canada, Communication No. 205/1986, Human Rights Committee, 43d Sess, UN Doc. CCPR/C/43/D/205/1986 (1991).

McHugh, Gerard, & Manuel Bessler. "Humanitarian Negotiations with Armed Groups: A Manual for Practitioners." *United Nations* (January 2006), online: OCHA <https://docs.unocha.org/sites/dms/Documents/Humanitarian NegotiationswArmedGroupsManual.pdf>.

"Press Release: Secretary-General Comments on Guidelines Issued to Envoys," UN Doc. SG/SM/7257 (10 December 1999).

Secretary General's High Level Panel on Threats, Challenges and Change. *A More Secure World: Our Shared Responsibility*, UN Doc. A/59/565 (2004).

Strengthening the Role of Mediation in the Peaceful Settlement of Disputes, Conflict Prevention and Resolution, Report of the Secretary-General, UN Doc. A/66/811 (25 June 2012).

The Nuremberg Declaration on Peace and Justice, UN Doc. A/62/885 (2008).

The Rule of Law and Transitional Justice in Conflict and Post-Conflict Societies, Report of the Secretary-General, UN Doc. S/2004/616 (23 August 2004).

UN SCOR, 55th Year, 4213rd Mtg., UN Doc. S/RES/1325 (2000).

UN SCOR, 64th Year, 6195th Mtg., UN Doc S/RES/1888 (2009).

Jurisprudence

Prosecutor v. Blagoje Simic et al, IT-95-9, Decision on the Prosecution Motion under Rule 73 for a Ruling Concerning the Testimony of a Witness (27 July 1999) (International Criminal Tribunal for the Former Yugoslavia, Trial Chamber).

Prosecutor v. Dusko Tadić, IT-94-1, Decision on the Defence Motion for Interlocutory Appeal on Jurisdiction (2 October 1995) (International Criminal Tribunal for the Former Yugoslavia, Appeals Chamber).

Prosecutor v. Kallon & Kamara, SCSL-2004-15-AR72(E), Decision on Challenge to Jurisdiction: Lomé Accord Amnesty (13 March 2004) (Special Court for Sierra Leone, Appeals Chamber).

Sejdić and Finci v. Bosnia and Herzegovina, nos 27996/06 and 34836/06 (22 December 2009) (European Court of Human Rights, Judgment of the Grand Chamber).

Texaco Overseas Petroleum Co & California Asiatic Oil Co v Government of the Libyan Arab Republic (Merits) (19 Jan 1977), 17 ILM 4.

Secondary Materials: Monographs

Albin, Cecile. *Justice and Fairness in International Negotiation* (Cambridge: Cambridge University Press, 2001).

Allen, Tim. *Trial Justice, The International Criminal Court and The Lord's Resistance Army* (London: International African Institute, 2006).

Arendt, Hannah. *On Revolution* (New York: Viking Press, 1963).

Bell, Christine. *Human Rights and Peace Agreements* (Oxford: Oxford University Press, 2000).

　Peace Agreements and Human Rights (Oxford: Oxford University Press, 2003).

　On the Law of Peace, Peace Agreements and the Lex Pacificatoria (Oxford: Oxford University Press, 2008).

Broomhall, Bruce. *International Justice and the International Criminal Court: Between Sovereignty and the Rule of Law* (Oxford: Oxford University Press, 2003).

Brunnée, Jutta, & Stephen J Toope. *Legitimacy and Legality in International Law: An Interactional Account* (Cambridge: Cambridge University Press, 2010).

Bush, Robert A. Baruch, & Joseph P. Folger. *The Promise of Mediation: Responding to Conflict through Empowerment and Recognition* (San Francisco: Jossey-Brass, 1994).

Campbell, Susanna, David Chandler & Meera Sabaratnam, eds. *A Liberal Peace? The Problems and Practices of Peacebuilding* (London: Zed Books, 2011).

Chandler, David. *Bosnia: Faking Democracy after Dayton*, 2nd ed. (London: Pluto Press, 2000).

Cooley, John W. *The Mediator's Handbook: Advanced Practice Guide for Civil Litigation*, 2nd ed. (Louisville, CO: National Institute for Trial Advocacy, 2006).

Crocker, Chester A., Fen Osler Hampson & Pamela Aall. *Taming Intractable Conflicts: Mediation in the Hardest Cases* (Washington, DC: United States Institute of Peace, 2004).

Derrida, Jacques. *Otobiographies: l'enseignement de Nietzsche et la politique du nom propre* (Paris: Galilée, 1984).

Dietrich, Wolfgang, et al., eds. *Peace Studies: A Cultural Perspective* (New York: Palgrave Macmillan, 2011).

Elster, Jon. *Closing the Books: Transitional Justice in Historical Perspective* (Cambridge: Cambridge University Press, 2004).

Fairclough, Norman. *Critical Discourse Analysis: The Critical Study of Language*, 2nd ed. (Harlow: Longman/Pearson, 2010).

Falola, Toyin, & Hetty ter Haar, eds. *Narrating War and Peace in Africa* (Rochester, NY: Rochester University Press, 2010).

Fisch, Jörg. *Krieg und Frieden im Friedensvertrag. Eine universalgeschichtliche Studie über die Grundlagen und Formelemente des Friedensschlusses* (Stuttgart: Klett-Cotta, 1979).

Franck, Thomas M. *The Power of Legitimacy among Nations* (New York: Oxford University Press, 1990).

Fuller, Lon L. *The Morality of Law*, revised ed. (New Haven, CT: Yale University Press, 1969).

Glenn, H. Patrick. *Legal Traditions of the World*, 3rd ed. (Oxford: Oxford University Press, 2007).

Greenberg, Melanie C., John H. Barton & Margaret E. McGuinness, eds. *Words over War: Mediation and Arbitration to Prevent Deadly Conflict* (Lanham: Rowman & Littlefield, 2000).

Hartzell, Caroline A., & Matthew Hoddie. *Crafting Peace: Power-Sharing Institutions and the Negotiated Settlement of Civil Wars* (University Park: Pennsylvania State University Press, 2007).

Holbrooke, Richard. *To End a War* (New York: Random House, 1998).

International Committee of the Red Cross (Jean-Marie Henckaerts & Louise Doswald-Beck). *Customary International Humanitarian Law, Volume I: Rules* (Cambridge: Cambridge University Press, 2005).

Kastner, Philipp. *International Criminal Justice* in bello? *The ICC between Law and Politics in Darfur and Northern Uganda* (Leiden: Martinus Nijhoff, 2012).

Kennedy, David. *Of War and Law* (Princeton, NJ: Princeton University Press, 2006).

Kirchhoff, Lars. *Constructive Interventions: Paradigms, Process and Practice of International Mediation* (Alphen aan den Rijn: Kluwer Law International, 2008).

Lansing, Robert. *The Peace Negotiations. A Personal Narrative* (Boston: Houghton Mifflin, 1921).

Leckey, Robert. *Contextual Subjects: Family, State and Relational Theory* (Toronto: University of Toronto Press, 2008).

Lederach, John Paul. *The Moral Imagination: The Art and Soul of Building Peace* (New York: Oxford University Press, 2005).

Levitt, Jeremy L. *Illegal Peace in Africa: An Inquiry into the Legality of Power Sharing with Warlords, Rebels, and Junta* (Cambridge: Cambridge University Press, 2012).

Loraux, Nicole. *La cité divisée: L'oubli dans la mémoire d'Athènes* (Paris: Payot et Rivages, 1997).

Luhmann, Niklas. *Das Recht der Gesellschaft* (Frankfurt: Suhrkamp, 1995).

Margalit, Avishai. *On Compromise and Rotten Compromises* (Princeton, NJ: Princeton University Press, 2010).

McCarthy, Dennis J. *Treaty and Covenant: A Study in Form in the Ancient Oriental Documents and in the Old Testament* (Rome: Biblical Institute Press, 1978).

Owen, David. *Balkan Odyssey* (London: Indigo, 1995).

Phelan, James, & Peter J Rabinowitz, eds. *A Companion to Narrative Theory* (Malden, MA: Blackwell, 2005).

Ratner, Steven R. *The New Peacekeeping: Building Peace in Lands of Conflict after the Cold War* (New York: St. Martin's Press, 1995).

Rawls, John. *A Theory of Justice* (Cambridge, MA: Harvard University Press, 1971).

Ross, Carne. *Independent Diplomat: Dispatches from an Unaccountable Elite* (Ithaca, NY: Cornell University Press, 2007).

Sandole, Dennis J. D. *Peace and Security in the Postmodern World: The OSCE and Conflict Resolution* (New York: Routledge, 2007).

Scherrer, Christian P. *Ethnicity, Nationalism and Violence: Conflict Management, Human Rights, and Multilateral Regimes* (Aldershot: Ashgate, 2003).

Schlee, Günther. *How Enemies Are Made. Towards a Theory of Ethnic and Religious Conflicts* (New York: Berghahn, 2008).

Simpson, Gerry. *Law, War and Crimes: War Crimes Trials and the Reinvention of International Law* (Cambridge: Polity Press, 2007).

Sisk, Timothy. *International Mediation in Civil Wars: Bargaining with Bullets* (London: Routledge, 2009).

Solomon, Richard H., & Nigel Quinney. *American Negotiating Behavior: Wheeler-Dealers, Legal Eagles, Bullies, and Preachers* (Washington, DC: United States Institute of Peace, 2010).

Spencer, David, & Michael Brogan. *Mediation Law and Practice* (Cambridge: Cambridge University Press, 2006).

Sriram, Chandra Lekha. *Peace as Governance: Power-Sharing, Armed Groups and Contemporary Peace Negotiations* (New York: Palgrave Macmillan, 2008).

Starkey, Brigid, Mark A. Boyer & Jonathan Wilkenfeld. *Negotiating a Complex World: An Introduction to International Negotiation*, 2nd ed. (Oxford: Rowman & Littlefield, 2005).

Tacsan, Joaquin. *The Dynamics of International Law in Conflict Resolution* (Dordrecht: Martinus Nijhoff, 1992).

Takkenberg, Lex. *The Status of Palestinian Refugees in International Law* (Oxford: Oxford University Press, 1998).

Teitel, Ruti G. *Transitional Justice* (Oxford: Oxford University Press, 2000).

Timm, Uwe. *Am Beispiel meines Bruders* (Cologne: dtv, 2009).

Tolstoy, Leo. *War and Peace*, translated by Louise Maude and Aylmer Maude (New York: Alfred A. Knopf, 1992).

Tully, James. *Strange Multiplicity* (Cambridge: Cambridge University Press, 1995).

Wallensteen, Peter. *Understanding Conflict Resolution*, 3rd ed. (London: Sage, 2012).

Walzer, Michael. *Just and Unjust Wars: A Moral Argument with Historical Illustrations* (New York: Basic Books, 1977).

Watson, Geoffrey R. *The Oslo Accords: International Law and the Israeli-Palestinian Peace Agreements* (Oxford: Oxford University Press, 2000).

Young, Oran. *The Intermediaries: Third Parties in International Crises* (Princeton, NJ: Princeton University Press, 1968).

Zartman, I. William. *Ripe for Resolution: Conflict and Intervention in Africa*, 2nd ed. (New York: Oxford University Press, 1985).

Zegveld, Liesbeth. *Accountability of Armed Opposition Groups in International Law* (Cambridge: Cambridge University Press, 2002).

Secondary Materials: Articles

Abbott, Kenneth W., & Duncan Snidal. "Hard and Soft Law in International Governance" (2000) 54 *International Organization* 421.

Abraham, Arthur. "Dancing with the Chameleon: Sierra Leone and the Elusive Quest for Peace" (2001) 19:2 *Journal of Contemporary African Studies* 205.

Abu-Nimer, Mohammed, & Edward Kaufman. "Bridging Conflict Transformation and Human Rights: Lessons from the Israeli-Palestinian Peace Process." In Julie A. Mertus & Jeffrey W. Helsing, eds., *Human Rights & Conflict: Exploring the Links between Rights, Law, and Peacebuilding* (Washington, DC: United States Institute of Peace, 2006), 277.

Adelman, Howard. "Refugee Repatriation." In Stephen John Stedman, Donald Rothchild & Elizabeth M. Cousens, eds., *Ending Civil Wars: The Implementation of Peace Agreements* (Boulder, CO: Lynne Rienner, 2002), 273.

Adler, Emanuel. "Seizing the Middle Ground: Constructivism in World Politics" (1997) 3:3 *European Journal of International Relations* 319.

Aggestam, Karin. "Mediating Asymmetrical Conflict" (2002) 7:1 *Mediterranean Politics* 69.

Akhavan, Payam. "Are International Criminal Tribunals a Disincentive to Peace? Reconciling Judicial Romanticism with Political Realism" (2009) 31 *Hum Rts Q* 624.

Akram, Susan M., et al. "Introduction." In Susan M. Akram et al., eds., *International Law and the Israel-Palestinian Conflict* (New York: Routledge, 2011), 1.

Albin, Cecilia. "Peace vs. Justice – and Beyond." In Jacob Bercovitch, Victor Kremenyuk & I. William Zartman, eds., *The SAGE Handbook of Conflict Resolution* (London: Sage, 2009), 580.

Ambos, Kai. "The Legal Framework of Transitional Justice." In Kai Ambos, Judith Large & Marieke Wierda, eds., *Building a Future on Peace and Justice: Studies on Transitional Justice, Peace and Development, The Nuremberg Declaration on Peace and Justice* (Berlin: Springer, 2009), 9.

Anderson, Miriam J. "Gender and Peacemaking: Women's Rights in Contemporary Peace Agreements." In Susan Allen Nan, Zachariah Cherian Mampilly & Andrea Bartoli, eds., *Peacemaking: From Practice to Theory*, vol. 1 (Santa Barbara, CA: Praeger, 2012), 344.

Anouilh, Pierre. "Sant'Egidio au Mozambique: de la charité à la fabrique de la paix" (2005) 59 *Revue internationale et stratégique* 9.

Arvelo, José E. "International Law and Conflict Resolution in Colombia: Balancing Peace and Justice in the Paramilitary Demobilization Process" (2005–2006) 37 *Geo J Int'l L* 411.

Astor, Hilary. "Mediator Neutrality: Making Sense of Theory and Practice" (2007) 16:2 *Soc & Leg Stud* 221.

Babbitt, Eileen F. "Conflict Resolution and Human Rights: The State of the Art." In Jacob Bercovitch, Victor Kremenyuk & I. William Zartman, eds., *The SAGE Handbook of Conflict Resolution* (London: Sage, 2009), 613.

Baker, Pauline H. "Conflict Resolution versus Democratic Governance: Divergent Paths to Peace?" In Chester A. Crocker, Fen Osler Hampson & Pamela Aall, eds., *Turbulent Peace* (Washington, DC: United States Institute of Peace, 2001), 753.

Banégas, Richard, & René Otayek. "Le Burkina Faso dans la crise ivoirienne: effets d'aubaine et incertitudes politiques" (2003) 89 *Politique Africaine* 71.

Barton, John H., & Melanie C. Greenberg. "Lessons of the Case Studies." In Melanie C. Greenberg, John H. Barton & Margaret E. McGuinness, eds., *Words over War: Mediation and Arbitration to Prevent Deadly Conflict* (Lanham: Rowman & Littlefield, 2000), 343.

Bass, Gary G. "Jus Post Bellum" (2004) 32:4 *Philosophy & Public Affairs* 384.

Bell, Christine. "Peace Agreements and Human Rights: Implications for the UN." In Nigel D. White & Dirk Klaasen, eds., *The UN, Human Rights and Post-Conflict Situations* (Manchester: Manchester University Press, 2005), 241.

"Human Rights, Peace Agreements and Conflict Resolution: Negotiating Justice in Northern Ireland." In Julie Mertus & Jeffrey W. Helsing, eds., *Human Rights and Conflict: Exploring the Links between Rights, Law and Peacebuilding* (Washington, DC: United States Institute of Peace Press, 2006), 345.

"Peace Agreements: Their Nature and Legal Status" (2006) 100:2 *AJIL* 373.

"The 'New Law' of Transitional Justice." In Kai Ambos, Judith Large & Marieke Wierda, eds., *Building a Future on Peace and Justice: Studies on Transitional Justice, Peace and Development, The Nuremberg Declaration on Peace and Justice* (Berlin: Springer, 2009), 105.

Bell, Christine, Colm Campbell & Fionnula Ni Aolain. "Justice Discourses in Transition" (2004) 13:3 *Soc & Leg Stud* 305.

Bell, Christine, & Catherine O'Rourke. "Does Feminism Need a Theory of Transitional Justice? An Introductory Essay" (2007) 1 *International Journal of Transitional Justice* 23.

"The People's Peace? Peace Agreements, Civil Society, and Participatory Democracy" (2007) 28:3 *International Political Science Review* 293.

"Peace Agreements or Pieces of Paper? The Impact of UNSC Resolution 1325 on Peace Processes and their Agreements" (2010) 59 *ICLQ* 941.

Benjamin, Robert D. "Managing the Natural Energy of Conflict: Mediators, Tricksters, and the Constructive Use of Deception." In Daniel Bowling & David A. Hoffman, eds., *Bringing Peace into the Room: How the Personal Qualities of the Mediator Impact the Process of Conflict Resolution* (San Francisco: Jossey-Bass, 2003), 79.

Bercovitch, Jacob, & S. Ayse Kadayifci-Orellana. "Religion and Mediation: The Role of Faith-Based Actors in International Conflict Resolution" (2009) 14 *International Negotiation* 175.

Berman, Nathaniel. "Privileging Combat? Contemporary Conflict and the Legal Construction of War" (2004) 43:1 *Colum J Transnat'l L* 1.

Bien, William J. "The Oslo Channel." In Melanie C. Greenberg, John H. Barton & Margaret E. McGuinness, eds., *Words over War: Mediation and Arbitration to Prevent Deadly Conflict* (Lanham: Rowman & Littlefield, 2000), 109.

Bowling, Daniel, & David A. Hoffman. "Bringing Peace into the Room: The Personal Qualities of the Mediator and their Impact on the Mediation." In Daniel Bowling & David A. Hoffman, eds., *Bringing Peace into the Room: How the Personal Qualities of the Mediator Impact the Process of Conflict Resolution* (San Francisco: Jossey-Bass, 2003), 13.

Brooks, Peter. "Narrative in and of the Law." In James Phelan & Peter J. Rabinowitz, eds., *A Companion to Narrative Theory* (Malden, MA: Blackwell, 2005), 415.

Brooks, Sean P. "Enforcing a Turning Point and Imposing a Deal: An Analysis of the Darfur Abuja Negotiations of 2006" (2008) 13 *International Negotiation* 413.

Burgerman, Susan D. "Build the Peace by Mandating Reform: United Nations-Mediated Human Rights Agreements in El Salvador and Guatemala" (2000) 27:3 *Latin American Perspectives* 63.

"Voices from the Parallel Table: The Role of Civil Sectors in the Guatemalan Peace Process." In Oliver P. Richmond & Henry F. Carey, eds., *Subcontracting Peace: The Challenges of NGO Peacebuilding* (Aldershot: Ashgate, 2005), 85.

Burgis, Michelle L. "A Discourse of Distinction? Palestinians, International Law, and the Promise of Humanitarianism" (2009) 15 *Palestine Yearbook of International Law* 41.

Cassese, Antonio. "The Special Court and International Law: The Decision Concerning the Lomé Agreement Amnesty" (2004) 2 *Journal of International Criminal Justice* 1130.

Chinkin, Christine. "The Challenge of Soft Law: Development and Change in International Law" (1989) 38:4 *ICLQ* 850.

"Human Rights and Politics of Representation: Is There a Role for International Law?" In Michael Byers, ed., *The Role of Law in International Politics* (Oxford: Oxford University Press, 2000), 131.

Chu Cheow, Eric Teo. "The 'Track 2' Process within ASEAN and Its Application in Resolving the Aceh Conflict in Indonesia." In Jacob Bercovitch, Kwei-Bo Huang & Chung-Chian Teng, eds., *Conflict Management, Security and Intervention in East Asia: Third-Party Mediation in Regional Conflict* (New York: Routledge, 2008), 165.

Clapham, Christopher. "Rwanda: The Perils of Peacemaking" (1998) 35:2 *Journal of Peace Research* 193.

Clements, Kevin. "Towards Conflict Transformation and a Just Peace." In *Berghof Handbook for Conflict Transformation* (Berlin: Berghof Conflict Research, 2001), online: Berghof Conflict Research <http://www.berghof-handbook.net/documents/publications/clements_handbook.pdf>.

Cobb, Sara, & Janet Rifkin. "Practice and Paradox: Deconstructing Neutrality in Mediation" (1991) 16:1 *Law & Soc Inquiry* 35.

Cobb, Sara, & Hussein Yusuf. "Narrative Approach to Peacemaking in Somalia." In Susan Allen Nan, Zachariah Cherian Mampilly & Andrea Bartoli, eds., *Peacemaking: From Practice to Theory*, vol. 1 (Santa Barbara, CA: Praeger, 2012), 328.

Cover, Robert M. "The Supreme Court, 1982 Term – Foreword: *Nomos* and Narrative" (1983) 97:4 *Harv L Rev* 4.

Dajani, Omar M. "Shadow or Shade? The Roles of International Law in Palestinian-Israeli Peace Talks" (2007) 32 *Yale J Int'l L* 61.

"'No Security Without Law': Prospects for Implementing a Rights-Based Approach in Palestinian-Israeli Security Negotiations." In Susan M. Akram et al., eds., *International Law and the Israeli-Palestinian Conflict* (New York: Routledge, 2011), 184.

Darby, John, & Roger Mac Ginty. "Introduction: What Peace? What Process?" In John Darby & Roger Mac Ginty, eds., *Contemporary Peacemaking: Conflict, Violence and Peace Processes* (New York: Palgrave Macmillan, 2003), 1.

Delgado, Richard. "Storytelling for Oppositionists and Others: A Plea for Narrative" (1989) 87 *Mich L Rev* 2411.

Derrida, Jacques. "To Forgive: The Unforgivable and the Imprescriptible." In John D. Caputo, Mark Dooley & Michael J. Scanlon, eds., *Questioning God* (Bloomington: Indiana University Press, 2001), 21.

Díaz, Catalina. "Colombia's Bid for Justice and Peace." In Kai Ambos, Judith Large & Marieke Wierda, eds., *Building a Future on Peace and Justice: Studies on Transitional Justice, Peace and Development, the Nuremberg Declaration on Peace and Justice* (Berlin: Springer, 2009), 469.

Dietrich, Wolfgang, & Wolfgang Sützl. "A Call for Many Peaces." In Wolfgang Dietrich, Josefina Echavarría Alvarez & Norbert Koppensteiner, eds., *Schlüsseltexte der Friedensforschung* (Vienna: LIT, 2006), 282.

Dupont, Christophe, & Guy-Olivier Faure. "The Negotiation Process." In Victor A. Kremenyuk, ed., *International Negotiation: Analysis, Approaches, Issues*, 2nd ed. (San Francisco: Jossey-Bass, 2002), 39.

Dupuy, Pierre-Marie. "Reviewing the Difficulties of Codification: On Ago's Classification of Obligations of Means and Obligations of Result in Relation to State Responsibility" (1999) 10:2 *EJIL* 371.

Durchhardt, Heinz. "Peace Treaties from Westphalia to the Revolutionary Era." In Randall Lesaffer, ed., *Peace Treaties and International Law in European History: From the Middle Ages to World War One* (Cambridge: Cambridge University Press, 2004), 45.

Egeland, Jan. "10 Lessons from 10 Peace Processes." In Susan Allen Nan, Zachariah Cherian Mampilly & Andrea Bartoli, eds., *Peacemaking: From Practice to Theory*, vol. 1 (Santa Barbara, CA: Praeger, 2012), 51.

Elgström, Ole, Jacob Bercovitch & Carl Skau. "Regional Organisations and International Mediation: The Effectiveness of Insider Mediation" (2003) 3:1 *African Journal on Conflict Resolution* 11.

Esquirol, Jorge L. "Can International Law Help? An Analysis of the Colombian Peace Process" (2000–2001) 16 *Conn J Int'l L* 23.

Exon, Susan Nauss. "The Effect that Mediator Styles Impose on Neutrality and Impartiality Requirements of Mediation" (2008) 42 *USF L Rev* 577.

Falk, Richard. "International Law and the Peace Process" (2005) 28:3 *Hasting Int'l & Comp L Rev* 331.

Finnemore, Martha. "Are Legal Norms Distinctive?" (2000) 32 *International Law and Politics* 699.

Finnemore, Martha, & Kathryn Sikkink. "International Norm Dynamics and Political Change" (1998) 52:4 *International Organization* 887.

Finnemore, Martha, & Stephen J. Toope. "Alternatives to 'Legalization': Richer Views of Law and Politics" (2001) 55:3 *International Organization* 743.

Fisher, Ronald J. "Methods of Third Party Intervention." In *Berghof Handbook for Conflict Transformation* (Berlin: Berghof Conflict Research, 2001), online: Berghof Conflict Research <http://www.berghof-handbook.net/documents/publications/fisher_hb.pdf>.

Florini, Ann. "The Evolution of International Norms" (1996) 40:3 *International Studies Quarterly* 363.

Franck, Thomas M. "The Emerging Right to Democratic Governance" (1992) 86:1 *AJIL* 46.

Fuller, Lon L. "Positivism and Fidelity to Law – A Reply to Professor Hart" (1958) 71 *Harv L Rev* 630.

"Human Interaction and the Law" (1969) 14 *Am J Jurisp* 1.

"Mediation – Its Forms and Functions" (1971) 44 *S Cal L Rev* 305.

"Means and Ends." In Kenneth I Winston, ed., *The Principles of Social Order: Selected Essays of Lon L. Fuller* (Durham, NC: Duke University Press, 1981), 61.

Gaeta, Paolo. "The Dayton Agreements and International Law" (1996) 7 *EJIL* 147.

Gallant, Michelle. "Law and Legal Process in Resolving International Conflicts." In Dennis J. D. Sandole et al., eds., *Handbook of Conflict Analysis and Resolution* (New York: Routledge, 2009), 396.

Galtung, Johan. "Violence, Peace, and Peace Research" (1969) 6:3 *Journal of Peace Research* 167.

García Durán, Mauricio, Vera Grabe Loewenherz & Otty Patiño Hormaza. "The M-19's Journey from Armed Struggle to Democratic Politics" (2008) Berghof Transitions Series, online: Berghof Conflict Research <http://www.berghof-conflictresearch.org/documents/publications/transitions_m19.pdf>.

Gebrewold, Belachew. "T'ùmmu: An East African Perspective." In Wolfgang Dietrich et al., eds., *Peace Studies: A Cultural Perspective* (New York: Palgrave Macmillan, 2011), 428.

Giro, Mario. "The Community of Saint Egidio and Its Peace-Making Activities" (1998) 33:3 *The International Spectator* 85.

Glenn, H. Patrick. "La tradition juridique nationale" (2003) 55:2 *RIDC* 263.

Greenberg, Melanie C., John H. Barton & Margaret E. McGuinness. "From Lisbon to Dayton: International Mediation and the Bosnia Crisis." In Melanie C. Greenberg, John H. Barton & Margaret E. McGuinness, eds., *Words over War: Mediation and Arbitration to Prevent Deadly Conflict* (Lanham: Rowman & Littlefield, 2000), 35.

Greenberg, Melanie C., & Margaret E. McGuinness. "Introduction: Background and Analytical Perspectives." In Melanie C. Greenberg, John H. Barton & Margaret E. McGuinness, eds., *Words over War: Mediation and Arbitration to Prevent Deadly Conflict* (Lanham: Rowman & Littlefield, 2000), 1.

Grey, Rosemary, & Laura J. Shepherd. "'Stop Rape Now?': Masculinity, Responsibility, and Conflict-related Sexual Violence" (2012) 16:1 *Men and Masculinities* 115.

Grillo, Trina. "The Mediation Alternative: Process Dangers for Women" (1991) 100 *Yale LJ* 1545.

Haas, Peter M. "Introduction: Epistemic Communities and International Policy Coordination" (1992) 46:2 *International Organization* 1.

Hanieh, Akram. "The Camp David Papers" (2001) 30:2 *Journal of Palestine Studies* 75.

Harbom, Lotta, & Peter Wallensteen. "Armed Conflicts, 1946–2009" (2010) 47:4 *Journal of Peace Research* 501.

Hart, Vivien. "Constitution-Making and the Transformation of Conflict" (2001) 26:2 *Peace & Change* 153.

Harris, Marvin. "History and Significance of the Emic/Etic Distinction" (1976) 5 *Annual Review of Anthropology* 329.

Hassan, Farooq. "The Legal Status of United States Involvement in the Camp David Peace Process" (1983) 16 *Vand J Transnat'l L* 75.

Haug, Hans. "Neutrality as a Fundamental Principle of the Red Cross" (1996) 36:315 *Int'l Rev Red Cross* 627.

Hoffman, David A. "Paradoxes of Mediation." In Daniel Bowling & David A. Hoffman, eds., *Bringing Peace into the Room: How the Personal Qualities of the Mediator Impact the Process of Conflict Resolution* (San Francisco: Jossey-Bass, 2003), 167.

Höglund, Kristine, & Isak Svensson. "'Damned if You Do, and Damned if You Don't': Nordic Involvement and Images of Third-Party Neutrality in Sri Lanka" (2008) 13 *International Negotiation* 341.

Holmes, John T. "The Principle of Complementarity." In Roy S. Lee, ed., *The International Criminal Court: The Making of the Rome Statute – Issues, Negotiations, Results* (Leiden: Martinus Nijhoff, 1999), 41.

Honig, Bonnie. "Declarations of Independence: Arendt and Derrida on the Problem of Founding a Republic" (1991) 85:1 *The American Political Science Review* 97.

Huang, Kwei-Bo. "The Transformation of ASEAN as a Third-Party Mediator in Intra-Regional Disputes of Southeast Asia." In Jacob Bercovitch, Kwei-Bo Huang & Chung-Chian Teng, eds., *Conflict Management, Security and Intervention in East Asia: Third-Party Mediation in Regional Conflict* (New York: Routledge, 2008), 147.

Hyman, Jonathan M. "Swimming in the Deep End: Dealing with Justice in Mediation?" (2004) 6:19 *Cardozo Journal of Conflict Resolution* 19.

Jenatsch, Thomas. "The ICRC as a Humanitarian Mediator in the Colombian Conflict: Possibilities and Limits" (1998) 38:323 *Int'l Rev Red Cross* 303.

Jessop, Maria, Diana Aljets & Betsie Chacko. "The Ripe Moment for Civil Society" (2008) 13 *International Negotiation* 93.

Kalman, Matthew. "The Palestinian Right of Return in International Law – The Israeli Perspective" (2008) 8 *Nexus* 43.

Kant, Immanuel. "Zum ewigen Frieden: Ein philosophischer Entwurf." In Wilhelm Weischedel, ed., *Immanuel Kant's Werke. Band XI* (Frankfurt: Suhrkamp, 1968), 195.

Kasfir, Nelson. "The Conventional Notion of Civil Society: A Critique" (1998) 36:2 *Commonwealth and Comparative Politics* 1.

Kaufman, Edward, & Ibrahim Bisharat. "Introducing Human Rights into Conflict Resolution: The Relevance for the Israeli-Palestinian Peace Process" (2002) 1:1 *Journal of Human Rights* 71.

Keethaponcalan, S. I. "The Indian Factor in the Peace Process and Conflict Resolution in Sri Lanka." In Jonathan Goodhand, Jonathan Spencer & Benedikt Korf, eds., *Conflict and Peacebuilding in Sri Lanka: Caught in the Peace Trap?* (London: Routledge, 2011), 39.

Kelleher, Ann, & James Larry Taulbee. "Building Peace Norwegian Style: Studies in Track 1½ Diplomacy." In Oliver P. Richmond & Henry F. Carey, eds., *Subcontracting Peace: The Challenges of NGO Peacebuilding* (Aldershot: Ashgate, 2005), 69.

Kennedy, David. "Lawfare and Warfare." In James Crawford & Martti Koskenniemi, eds., *The Cambridge Companion to International Law* (Cambridge: Cambridge University Press, 2012), 158.

Klein, Claude, & András Sajó. "Constitution-Making: Process and Substance." In Michael Rosenfeld & András Sajó, eds., *The Oxford Handbook of Comparative Constitutional Law* (Oxford: Oxford University Press, 2012), 419.

Kleinhans, Martha-Marie, & Roderick A Macdonald. "What Is a Critical Legal Pluralism?" (1997) 12 *CJLS* 25.

Koh, Harold H. "Transnational Legal Process" (1996) 75 *Neb L Rev* 181.

"Why Do Nations Obey International Law?" (1997) 106 *Yale LJ* 2599.

Koskenniemi, Martti. "International Law in the World of Ideas." In James Crawford & Martti Koskenniemi, eds., *The Cambridge Companion to International Law* (Cambridge: Cambridge University Press, 2012), 47.

Kovach, Kimberlee K., & Lela P. Love. "'Evaluative' Mediation Is an Oxymoron" (1996) 14:3 *Alternatives to the High Cost of Litigation* 31.

Krapp, Peter. "Amnesty: Between and Ethics of Forgiveness and the Politics of Forgetting" (2005) 6:1 *German Law Journal* 185.

Kratochwil, Friedrich V. "How Do Norms Matter?" In Michael Byers, ed., *The Role of Law in International Politics* (Oxford: Oxford University Press, 2000), 35.

Kress, Claus, & Leena Grover. "International Criminal Law Restraints in Peace Talks to End Armed Conflicts of a Non-International Character." In Morton Bergsmo & Pablo Kalmanovitz, eds., *Law in Peace Negotiations*, 2nd ed. (Oslo: Torkel Opsahl Academic EPublisher, 2010), 41.

Laflin, Maureen E. "Preserving the Integrity of Mediation through the Adoption of Ethical Rules for Lawyer-Mediators" (2000) 14 *Notre Dame JL Ethics & Pub Pol'y* 479.

Lanni, Adriaan. "Transitional Justice in Ancient Athens: A Case Study" (2010) 32:2 *U Pa J Int'l L* 551.

Lavergne, Marc, & Fabrice Weissman. "Sudan, Who Benefits from Humanitarian Aid?" In Fabrice Weissman, ed., *In the Shadow of "Just Wars", Violence Politics and Humanitarian Action* (Ithaca, NY: Cornell University Press, 2004), 137.

Lesaffer, Randall. "Peace Treaties from Lodi to Westphalia." In Randall Lesaffer, ed., *Peace Treaties and International Law in European History: From the Middle Ages to World War One* (Cambridge: Cambridge University Press, 2004), 9.

Lieberfeld, Daniel. "Small Is Credible: Norway's Niche in International Dispute Settlement" (1995) 11:3 *Negotiation Journal* 201.

Macdonald, Roderick A. "The Swiss Army Knife of Governance." In Pearl Eliadis, Margaret M. Hill & Michael Howlett, eds., *Designing Government: From Instruments to Governance* (Montreal: McGill-Queen's University Press, 2005), 203.

"Here, There ... and Everywhere: Theorizing Legal Pluralism; Theorizing Jacques Vanderlinden." In Nicholas Kasirer, ed., *Étudier et enseigner le droit: hier, aujourd'hui et demain – études offertes à Jacques Vanderlinden* (Montreal: Éditions Yvon Blais, 2006), 381.

"Custom Made – For a Non-Chirographic Critical Legal Pluralism" (2011) 26:2 *CJLS* 301.

Macdonald, Roderick A., & David Sandomierski. "Against Nomopolies" (2006) 57 *N Ir Legal Q* 610.

Mallinder, Louise. "Exploring the Practice of States Introducing Amnesties." In Kai Ambos, Judith Large & Marieke Wierda, eds., *Building a Future on Peace and Justice: Studies on Transitional Justice, Peace and Development, the Nuremberg Declaration on Peace and Justice* (Berlin: Springer, 2009), 127.

Markovitz, Irving Leonard. "Uncivil Society, Capitalism and the State in Africa." In Nelson Kasfir, ed., *Civil Society and Democracy in Africa: Critical Perspectives* (London: Frank Cass, 1998), 21.

Massoud, Mark F. "Do Victims of War Need International Law? Human Rights Education Programs in Authoritative Sudan" (2011) 45:1 *Law & Soc'y Rev* 1.

Matlary, Janne Haaland. "The Just Peace: The Public and Classical Diplomacy of the Holy See" (2001) 14:2 *Cambridge Review of International Affairs* 80.

McClintock, Elizabeth A., & Térence Nahimana. "Managing the Tension between Inclusionary and Exclusionary Processes: Building Peace in Burundi" (2008) 13 *International Negotiation* 73.

McCrudden, Christopher, & Brendan O'Leary. "Courts and Consociations, or How Human Rights Courts May De-Stabilize Power-Sharing Settlements" (2013) 24:2 *EJIL* 477.

Mégret, Frédéric. "International Law as Law." In James Crawford & Martti Koskenniemi, eds., *The Cambridge Companion to International Law* (Cambridge: Cambridge University Press, 2012), 64, 78.

Mehler, Andreas. "Not Always in the People's Interest: Power-Sharing Arrangements in African Peace Agreements" (June 2008) BWPI Working Paper 40, online: SSRN <http://ssrn.com/abstract=1200862>.

"Peace and Power-Sharing in Africa: A Not So Obvious Relationship" (2009) 108:432 *African Affairs* 453.

Menkel-Meadow, Carrie. "Peace and Justice: Notes on the Evolution and Purposes of Legal Processes" (2006) 94 *Geo LJ* 553.

Mitchell, Christopher R. "The Motives for Mediation." In Christopher R. Mitchell & Keith Webb, eds., *New Approaches to International Mediation* (New York: Greenwood Press, 1988), 29.

"Asymmetry and Strategies of Regional Conflict Resolution." In I. William Zartman & Victor A. Kremenyuk, eds., *Cooperative Security: Reducing Third World Wars* (Syracuse: Syracuse University Press, 1995), 25.

Moore, Sally F. "Law and Social Change: The Semi-Autonomous Social Field as an Appropriate Subject of Study" (1973) 7 *Law & Soc'y Rev* 719.

Morris, Christine. "The Trusted Mediator: Ethics and Interaction in Mediation." In Julie Macfarlane, ed., *Rethinking Disputes: The Mediation Alternative* (Toronto: Edmond Montgomery Publications, 1997), 301.

Muñoz, Francisco A. "Imperfect Peace." In Wolfgang Dietrich, Josefina Echavarría Alvarez & Norbert Koppensteiner, eds., *Schlüsseltexte der Friedensforschung* (Vienna: LIT, 2006), 241.

Msabaha, Ibrahim. "Negotiating an End to Mozambique's Murderous Rebellion." In I. William Zartman, ed., *Elusive Peace: Negotiating an End to Civil Wars* (Washington, DC: The Brookings Institution, 1995), 204.

Nedelsky, Jennifer. "Reconceiving Rights and Constitutionalism" (2008) 7:2 *Journal of Human Rights* 139.

Ni Aolain, Fionnuala. "The Fractured Soul of the Dayton Peace Agreement: A Legal Analysis" (1998) 19 *Mich J Int'l L* 957.

O'Flaherty, Michael. "Sierra Leone's Peace Process: The Role of the Human Rights Community" (2004) 26:1 *Hum Rts Q* 29.

Orend, Brian. "*Jus Post Bellum*: The Perspective of a Just-War Theorist" (2007) 20 *Leiden J Int'l L* 571.

Orentlicher, Diane. "Settling Accounts: the Duty to Prosecute Human Rights Violations of a Prior Regime" (1990) 100 *Yale LJ* 2537.

Parlevliet, Michelle. "Bridging the Divide – Exploring the Relationship between Human Rights and Conflict Management" (2002) 11:1 *Track Two* 8.

"Rethinking Conflict Transformation from a Human Rights Perspective." In *Berghof Handbook for Conflict Transformation* (Berlin: Berghof Conflict Research, 2009), online: Berghof Conflict Research <http://www.berghof-handbook.net/documents/publications/parlevliet_handbook.pdf>.

Pauwelyn, Joost. "Is It International Law or Not, and Does It Even Matter?" In Joost Pauwelyn, Ramses Wessel & Jan Wouters, eds., *Informal International Lawmaking* (Oxford: Oxford University Press, 2012), 125.

Peceny, Mark, & William Stanley. "Liberal Social Reconstruction and the Resolution of Civil Wars in Central America" (2001) 55:1 *International Organization* 149.

Pfaffenholz, Thania. "Civil Society beyond the Liberal Peace and Its Critique." In Susanna Campbell, David Chandler & Meera Sabaratnam, eds., *A Liberal Peace?* (London: Zed Books, 2011), 138.

Potter, Jonathan, & Margaret Wetherell. "Unfolding Discourse Analysis." In Margaret Wetherell, Stephanie Taylor & Simeon J. Yates, eds., *Discourse Theory and Practice: A Reader* (London: Sage Publications, 2001), 198.

Pressman, Jeremy. "Visions in Collision, What Happened at Camp David and Taba?" (2003) 28:2 *International Security* 5.

Provost, René. "Asymmetrical Reciprocity and Compliance with the Laws of War." In Benjamin Perrin, ed., *Modern Warfare: Armed Groups, Private Militaries, Humanitarian Organizations, and the Law* (Vancouver: UBC Press, 2012), 17.

Putnam, Tonya. "Human Rights and Sustainable Peace." In Stephen John Stedman, Donald Rothchild & Elizabeth M. Cousens, eds., *Ending Civil Wars: The Implementation of Peace Agreements* (Boulder, CO: Lynne Rienner, 2002), 237.

Quigley, John. "The Israel-PLO Interim Agreements: Are They Treaties?" (1997) 30 *Cornell Int'l LJ* 717.

Ratner, Steven R. "Does International Law Matter in Preventing Ethnic Conflict?" (2000) 32 *International Law and Politics* 591.

Reilly, Ben. "Democratic Validation." In John Darby & Roger Mac Ginty, eds., *Contemporary Peacemaking: Conflict, Violence and Peace Processes* (New York: Palgrave Macmillan, 2003), 174.

Reimann, Kim D. "Up to No Good? Recent Critics and Critiques of NGOs." In Oliver P. Richmond & Henry F. Carey, eds., *Subcontracting Peace: The Challenges of NGO Peacebuilding* (Aldershot: Ashgate, 2005), 37.

Rempel, Terry, & Paul Prettitore. "The Palestinian Refugees: Restitution and Compensation." In Susan M. Akram et al., eds., *International Law and the Israeli-Palestinian Conflict* (New York: Routledge, 2011), 69.

Richmond, Oliver P. "The Dilemmas of Subcontracting the Liberal Peace." In Oliver P. Richmond & Henry F. Carey, eds., *Subcontracting Peace: The Challenges of NGO Peacebuilding* (Aldershot: Ashgate, 2005), 19.

Riskin, Leonard L. "Mediator Orientation, Strategies and Techniques" (1994) 12 *Alternatives to the High Cost of Litigation* 111.

Roberts, Adam. "Transformative Military Occupation: Applying the Laws of War and Human Rights" (2006) 100 *AJIL* 580.

Robinson, Darryl. "Serving the Interests of Justice: Amnesties, Truth Commissions and the International Criminal Court" (2003) 14 *EJIL* 481.

Rubin, Jeffrey Z. "Psychological Approach." In Victor A. Kremenyuk, ed., *International Negotiation: Analysis, Approaches, Issues*, 2nd ed. (San Francisco: Jossey-Bass, 2002), 256.

Ruggie, John Gerard. "What Makes the World Hang Together? Neo-Utilitarianism and the Social Constructivist Challenge" (1998) 52:4 *International Organization* 855.

Sabbagh, Clara, & Deborah Golden. "Reflecting Upon Etic and Emic Perspectives on Distributive Justice" (2007) 20 *Social Justice Research* 372.

Sadat, Leila Nadya. "Exile, Amnesty and International Law" (2006) 81 *Notre Dame L Rev* 955.

Samuels, Kirsti. "Post-Conflict Peace-Building and Constitution-Making" (2006) 6:2 *Chicago J Int'l L* 1.

Saunders, Harold. "Peacemaking in a Relational Paradigm." In Susan Allen Nan, Zachariah Cherian Mampilly & Andrea Bartoli, eds., *Peacemaking: From Practice to Theory*, vol. 1 (Santa Barbara, CA: Praeger, 2012), 148.

Schabas, William A. "Gaza, Goldstone, and Lawfare" (2010) 43:1&2 *Case W Res J Int'l L* 307.

Scharf, Michael P. "The Letter of the Law: The Scope of the International Obligation to Prosecute Human Rights Crimes" (1996) 59 *Law & Contemp Probs* 41.

Scharf, Michael P., & Paul R. Williams. "The Functions of Justice and Anti-Justice in the Peace-Building Process" (2003) 35 *Case W Res J Int'l L* 161.

Sguaitamatti, Damiano, & Simon JA Mason. "Vermittler im Vergleich: Bedeutung für die Schweiz als Mediatorin" (2011) 83 *Zürcher Beiträge zur Sicherheitspolitik* 69.

Sheeran, Scott P. "International Law, Peace Agreements and Self-Determination: The Case of the Sudan" (2011) 60:2 *ICLQ* 423.

Simpson, Gerry. "International Law in Diplomatic History." In James Crawford & Martti Koskenniemi, eds., *The Cambridge Companion to International Law* (Cambridge: Cambridge University Press, 2012), 25.

Singer, Joel. "No Palestinian 'Return' to Israel" (2001) 87 *ABA J* 14.

Sivakumaran, Sandesh. "Lost in Translation: UN Responses to Sexual Violence against Men and Boys in Situations of Armed Conflict" (2010) 92:877 *IRRC* 259.

Slaughter, Anne-Marie. "Pushing the Limits of the Liberal Peace: Ethnic Conflict and the 'Ideal Polity.'" In David Wippman, ed., *International Law and Ethnic Conflict* (Ithaca, NY: Cornell University Press, 1998), 128.

Smock, David. "Divine Intervention, Regional Reconciliation through Faith" (2004) 25 *Harvard International Review* 46.

Spears, Ian S. "Understanding Inclusive Peace Agreements in Africa: The Problems of Sharing Power" (2000) 21 *Third World Quarterly* 105.

Stahn, Carsten. "United Nations Peace-Building, Amnesties and Alternative Forms of Justice: A Change in Practice?" (2002) 84:845 *Int'l Rev Red Cross* 191.

"Complementarity, Amnesties and Alternative Forms of Justice: Some Interpretative Guidelines for the International Criminal Court" (2005) 3 *Journal of International Criminal Justice* 695.

"Jus Post Bellum: Mapping the Disciplines." In Carsten Stahn & Jann K Kleffner, eds., *Jus Post Bellum: Toward a Law of Transition from Conflict to Peace* (The Hague: Asser Press, 2008), 93.

Steiger, Heinhard. "Peace Treaties from Paris to Versailles." In Randall Lesaffer, ed., *Peace Treaties and International Law in European History: From the Middle Ages to World War One* (Cambridge: Cambridge University Press, 2004), 59.

Steiner, Henry. "Political Participation as a Human Right" (1988) 1 *Harv Hum Rts YB* 77.

Storholt, Kristine Hauge. "Lessons Learned from the 1990–1997 Peace Process in the North of Mali" (2001) 6 *International Negotiation* 331.

Teitel, Ruti. "Transitional Jurisprudence: The Role of Law in Political Transformation" (1997) 106 *Yale LJ* 2009.

Teng, Chung-Chian. "Introduction: Security, Conflict Management and Resolution in East Asia." In Jacob Bercovitch, Kwei-Bo Huang & Chung-Chian Teng, eds., *Conflict Management, Security and Intervention in East Asia: Third-Party Mediation in Regional Conflict* (New York: Routledge, 2008), 1.

Turk, A. Marco. "The Negotiation Culture of Lengthy Peace Processes: Cyprus as an Example of Spoiling that Prevents a Final Solution" (2009) 3:31 *Loy LA Int'l & Comp L Rev* 327.

Van Es, Robert. "Moral Compromise: Owen and Holbrooke Mediating the Bosnia Conflict" (2002) 7 *International Negotiation* 169.

Vité, Sylvain. "Typology of Armed Conflicts in International Humanitarian Law: Legal Concepts and Actual Situations" (2009) 91:873 *Int'l Rev Red Cross* 69.

Waldman, Ellen A. "Identifying the Role of Social Norms in Mediation: A Multiple Model Approach" (1997) 48 *Hastings LJ* 703.

Walton, Oliver with Paikiasothy Saravanamuttu. "In the Balance? Civil Society and the Peace Process 2002–2008." In Jonathan Goodhand, Jonathan Spencer & Benedikt Korf, eds., *Conflict and Peacebuilding in Sri Lanka: Caught in the Peace Trap?* (London: Routledge, 2011), 183.

Wanis-St. John, Anthony, & Darren Kew. "Civil Society and Peace Negotiations: Confronting Exclusion" (2008) 13 *International Negotiation* 11.

Webb, Keith. "The Morality of Mediation." In Christopher R. Mitchell & Keith Webb, eds., *New Approaches to International Mediation* (New York: Greenwood Press, 1988), 16.

Webber, Jeremy. "Legal Pluralism and Human Agency" (2006) 44 *Osgoode Hall LJ* 167. "Naturalism and Agency in the Living Law." In Marc Hertogh, ed., *Living Law: Reconsidering Eugen Ehrlich* (Oxford: Hart, 2009), 201.

Welchman, Lynn. "The Middle East Peace Process and the Rule of Law: Irreconcilable Objectives?" In Eugene Cotran & Mai Yamani, eds., *The Rule of Law in the Middle East and the Islamic World: Human Rights and the Judicial Processes* (London: I. B. Tauris, 2000), 51.

Weller, Marc. "The Relativity of Humanitarian Neutrality and Impartiality" (1997) 91 *Proceedings of the Annual Meeting of the American Society of International Law* 441.

Werner, Wouter G. "The Curious Career of Lawfare" (2010) 43:1&2 *Case W Res J Int'l L* 61.

Wetherell, Margaret. "Themes in Discourse Research: The Case of Diana." In Margaret Wetherell, Stephanie Taylor & Simeon J Yates, eds., *Discourse Theory and Practice: A Reader* (London: Sage Publications, 2001), 14.

Wetherell, Margaret, Stephanie Taylor & Simeon J. Yates. "Introduction." In Margaret Wetherell, Stephanie Taylor & Simeon J. Yates, eds., *Discourse Theory and Practice: A Reader* (London: Sage Publications, 2001), 1.

Williams, Paul R. "Lawfare: A War Worth Fighting" (2010) 43:1&2 *Case W Res J Int'l L* 145.

Williams, Robert E., & Dan Caldwell. "*Jus Post Bellum*: Just War Theory and the Principles of Just Peace" (2006) 7 *International Studies Perspectives* 309.

Wilson, Richard A. "Reconciliation and Revenge in Post-Apartheid South Africa: Rethinking Legal Pluralism and Human Rights" (2000) 41:1 *Current Anthropology* 75.

Zartman, I. William. "Conflict Resolution and Negotiation." In Jacob Bercovitch, Victor Kremenyuk & I. William Zartman, eds., *The SAGE Handbook of Conflict Resolution* (London: Sage, 2009), 322.

Zartman, I. William, & Jeffrey Z. Rubin. "The Study of Power and the Practice of Mediation." In I. William Zartman & Jeffrey Z. Rubin, eds., *Power and Negotiation* (Ann Arbor: University of Michigan Press, 2000), 3.

Ziegler, Karl-Heinz. "The Influence of Medieval Roman Law on Peace Treaties." In Randall Lesaffer, ed., *Peace Treaties and International Law in European History: From the Middle Ages to World War One* (Cambridge: Cambridge University Press, 2004), 147.

Zumbansen, Peer. "Transitional Justice in a Transnational World: The Ambiguous Role of Law" (2008) 4:8 CELP Research Paper Series, online: SSRN <http://papers.ssrn.com/sol3/papers.cfm?abstract_id=1313725>.

Secondary Materials: Other Sources

"Bashir Calls ICC Arrest Warrant a 'Conspiracy.'" *The Telegraph* (5 March 2009), online: Telegraph <http://www.telegraph.co.uk/news/worldnews/africaandin-dianocean/sudan/4942470/Sudan-President-Omar-al-Bashir-calls-ICC-arrest-warrant-a-conspiracy.html>.

"Blaise Compaoré sur France Ô: «L'Afrique doit assumer ses responsabilités...»" (16 July 2010), online: Congrès pour la Démocratie et le Progrès <http://www.cdp-burkina.org/index.php?option=com_content&view=article&id=454&catid=30>.

"Colombia, FARC Say Peace Talks Advancing." *Reuters* (10 February 2013), online: Reuters <http://www.reuters.com/article/2013/02/10/us-colombia-rebels-talks-idUSBRE9190DM20130210>.

"Colombia's Santos Says FARC Must Be Allowed to Participate in Politics." *CNN* (28 September 2012), online: CNN <http://amanpour.blogs.cnn.com/2012/09/28/colombias-president-on-negotiating-with-farc/?iref=allsearch>.

"FARC Santos Govt Peace Talks, Who and What?" *Colombia Politics* (16 October 2012), online: Colombia Politics <http://www.colombia-politics.com/farc-santos-govt-negotiating-team-and-agenda/>.

"ICC Indictment Could Ruin North–South Sudan Peace – UN." *Sudan Tribune* (6 November 2008) online: Sudan Tribune <http://www.sudantribune.com/spip.php?article29167>.

"JEM Rebels Head to Doha for Talks on Darfur Peace Process." *Sudan Tribune* (12 November 2010), online: Sudan Tribune <http://www.sudantribune.com/spip .php?article36906>.

"Kurdish Militia Signs Ceasefire with Syrian Rebels." *Reuters* (20 February 2013), online: Reuters <http://www.reuters.com/article/2013/02/20/us-syria-crisis-kurds -idUSBRE91J0YE20130220>.

"Oral Histories: The Sudan Experience Project." Online: United States Institute of Peace <http://www.usip.org/publications/oral-histories-the-sudan-experience-project>.

"Uganda's President Hopes Rebels Choose 'Soft Landing.'" *Reuters* (4 June 2007), online: Reuters <http://www.reuters.com/articles/latestCrisis/idUSL04425927>.

"UN Recommends that Colombia Peace-Process Takes into Account Victims of Ongoing Conflict." *United Press International* (13 September 2012), online: United Press International <http://www.upi.com/Top_News/Special/2012/09/13/UN-urges -Colombia-not-to-concede-to-FARC/UPI-47681347565546/>.

"Wer Frieden will, muss auch mit den Bösen reden: Gute Noten für Schweizer Konfliktmediation in Afrika" (2008) 11 welt-sichten, online: welt-sichten <http://www.welt-sichten.org/artikel/art-11-008/wer-frieden-will-muss-auch -mit-den-boesen-reden.html>.

ADR Institute of Canada Inc. *Model Code of Conduct for Mediators of the ADR Institute of Canada,* online: ADR Institute of Canada <http://www.adrcanada.ca/ rules/documents/code_of_conduct2008.pdf>.

Alvarez, Enrique. "The Civil Society Assembly: Shaping Agreement" (2002) 13 *Accord* 48, online: Conciliation Resources <http://www.c-r.org/sites/c-r.org/files/ Accord%2013_9The%20civil%20society%20assembly_2002_ENG_0.pdf>.

Benavides Vanegas, Farid Samir. "Law as a Peace Treaty: The Case of the M-19 and the 1991 Colombian Constitution," online: University of Massachusetts Amherst <http://www.umass.edu/legal/Hilbink/250/Benavides.pdf>.

Buchanan, Cate, et al. "From Clause to Effect: Including Women's Rights and Gender in Peace Agreements" (Centre for Humanitarian Dialogue, 2012), online: HD Centre <http://www.hdcentre.org/uploads/tx_news/24ClausereportwebFINAL.pdf>.

Centre for Security Studies, ETH Zurich. "Dealing with the Past in Peace Mediation" (September 2009), online: Centre for Security Studies (CSS), ETH Zurich <http://www.isn.ethz.ch/isn/Digital-Library/Publications/Detail/?ord538=grp2& size538=10&ots591=eb06339b-2726-928e-0216-1b3f15392dd8&lng=en&id=114851>.

Commission on Legal Empowerment of the Poor. *Making the Law Work for Everyone,* vol. 1 (New York: Commission on Legal Empowerment of the Poor and United Nations Development Programme, 2008).

Commonwealth of Massachusetts. *Supreme Judicial Court Rule 1:18, The Uniform Rules on Dispute Resolution* (June 2005), online: Commonwealth of Massachusetts <http://www.mass.gov/courts/admin/legal/newadrbook.pdf>.

Crisis Management Initiative. "CMI Closely Supports the EU in Peace Mediation" (26 October 2012), online: Crisis Management Initiative <http://www.cmi.fi/ media-2/news/europe/657-cmi-closely-supports-the-eu-in-peace-mediation>.

Doha Declaration, 20 November 2009 (Darfur), English translation available online: Darfur Information Center <http://www.darfurinfo.org/doha-english-rough.pdf>.

Drew, Elizabeth. "Regional Community Peacebuilding and the LRA Conflict: A Conversation with John Baptist Odoma, Archbishop of Gulu, Uganda" (2011) 22

Accord 54, online: Conciliation Resources <http://www.c-r.org/sites/c-r.org/files/ Accord%2022_14Regional%20communiy%20peacebuilding%20and%20the%20 LRA%20conflict_2011_ENG.pdf>.

European Code of Conduct for Mediators, online: European Commission <http:// ec.europa.eu/civiljustice/adr/adr_ec_code_conduct_en.pdf>.

Grono, Nick, & David Mozersky. "Sudan and the ICC: A Question of Accountability" (31 January 2007), online: International Crisis Group <http://www.crisisgroup.org/ en/regions/africa/horn-of-africa/sudan/op-eds/sudan-and-the-icc-a-question-of-accountability.aspx>.

Hayner, Priscilla. "Negotiating Peace in Sierra Leone: Confronting the Justice Challenge." *Centre for Humanitarian Dialogue & International Centre for Transitional Justice* (December 2007), online: International Centre for Transitional Justice <http://www.ictj.org/static/Africa/SierraLeone/HaynerSL1207.eng.pdf>.

"Negotiating Justice: Guidelines for Mediators." *Centre for Humanitarian Dialogue & International Centre for Transitional Justice* (February 2009), online: Centre for Humanitarian Dialogue <http://www.hdcentre.org/files/ negotiating%20justice%20report.pdf>.

Heidelberg Darfur Dialogue Outcome Document (Max Planck Institute for Comparative Public Law and International Law, 2010), online: MPIL <http://www.mpil.de/ shared/data/pdf/hdd_outcome_document.pdf>.

Hofnung, Thomas. "Présidentielle: le Mali poussé aux urnes." *Libération* (26 July 2013), online: Libération <http://www.liberation.fr/monde/2013/07/26/presidentielle-le -mali-pousse-aux-urnes_921140>.

Human Rights Watch. "Colombia: Amend 'Legal Framework for Peace' Bill" (31 May 2012), online: Human Rights Watch <http://www.hrw.org/news/2012/05/31/ colombia-amend-legal-framework-peace-bill>.

Human Security Center. *Human Security Report 2005: War and Peace in the 21st Century* (New York: Oxford University Press, 2005).

Human Security Report Project. *Human Security Report 2009–2010: The Causes of Peace and the Shrinking Costs of War* (New York: Oxford University Press, 2011).

Human Security Report 2012: Sexual Violence, Education and War: Beyond the Mainstream Narrative (Vancouver: Human Security Press, 2012).

International Alert. "Code of Conduct" (1998), online: International Alert <http:// www.international-alert.org/pdf/coc_full.pdf>.

International Commission on Intervention and State Sovereignty. *The Responsibility to Protect* (Ottawa: International Development Research Center, 2001), UN Doc. A/RES/60/1.

International Council on Human Rights Policy. "Negotiating Justice? Human Rights and Peace Agreements" (2006), online: International Council on Human Rights Policy <http://www.ichrp.org/files/reports/22/128_report_en.pdf>.

International Criminal Court. "Press Release: President of Uganda Refers Situation Concerning the Lord's Resistance Army (LRA) to the ICC" (29 January 2004), online: International Criminal Court <http://www.icc-cpi.int/en_menus/icc/ press%20and%20media/press%20releases/2004/Pages/president%20of%20 uganda%20refers%20situation%20concerning%20the%20lord_s%20resistance%20 army%20_lra_%20to%20the%20icc.aspx>.

International Crisis Group. "The War Is Not Yet Over" (28 November 2003), online: International Crisis Group <http://www.crisisgroup.org/~/media/Files/africa/west-africa/cote-divoire/Cote%20dIvoire%20The%20War%20Is%20Not%20Yet%20Over.ashx>.

"Northern Uganda: Seizing the Opportunity for Peace" (26 April 2007), online: International Crisis Group <http://www.crisisgroup.org/home/index.cfm?id=4791>.

"Côte d'Ivoire: faut-il croire à l'accord de Ouagadougou?" (27 June 2007), online: International Crisis Group <http://www.crisisgroup.org/~/media/Files/africa/west-africa/cote-divoire/French%20translations/Cote%20dIvoire%20Can%20the%20Ouagadougou%20Agreement%20Bring%20Peace%20French.ashx>.

"A Strategy for Comprehensive Peace in Sudan" (26 July 2007), online: International Crisis Group <http://www.crisisgroup.org/home/index.cfm?id=4961&l=1>.

Itto, Anne. "Guests at the Table? The Role of Women in Peace Processes" (2006) 18 *Accord* 56, online: Conciliation Resources <http://www.c-r.org/our-work/accord/sudan/women.php>.

Law Society of New South Wales. *The Law Society Guidelines for Those Involved in Mediation* (1993), online: The Law Society of NSW <http://www.lawsociety.com.au/idc/groups/public/documents/internetcontent/026506.pdf>.

Malley, Robert, & Hussein Agha. "Camp David: The Tragedy of Errors." *New York Review of Books* (9 August 2001), online: NYREV <http://www.nybooks.com/articles/archives/2001/aug/09/camp-david-the-tragedy-of-errors/?pagination=false>.

Missire, Gaëlle. *Women's Right to Political Participation in Post-Conflict Transformation* (LLM Thesis, McGill University, Faculty of Law, 2008) [unpublished].

Model Standards of Conduct for Mediators (August 2005), online: American Bar Association <http://www.abanet.org/dispute/news/ModelStandardsofConductfor Mediatorsfinal05.pdf>.

Mukasa, Henry. "Kony to Meet His Peace Team." *New Vision* (21 August 2008), online: New Vision <http://www.newvision.co.ug/PA/8/13/645737>.

Murphy Theodore, & Jérôme Tubiana. "Civil Society in Darfur: The Missing Peace." *Special Report of the United States Institute of Peace* (September 2010), online: United States Institute of Peace http://www.usip.org/files/resources/Civil%20Society%20in%20Darfur%20-%20Sept.%202010.pdf>.

Nathan, Laurie. "Towards a New Era in International Mediation." *Crisis States Research Centre* (May 2010), online: Crisis States <http://www.crisisstates.com/download/Policy%20Directions/Towards%20a%20new%20era%20in%20international%20mediation.pdf>.

Papagianni, Katia. "Partage de pouvoir et gouvernements de transition: le rôle de la médiation." *Centre for Humanitarian Dialogue* (2008), online: Centre for Humanitarian Dialogue <http://www.hdcentre.org/files/Powersharing%20FR%20final.pdf>.

Pfaffenholz, Thania, Darren Kew & Anthony Wanis-St. John. "Civil Society and Peace Negotiations: Why, Whether and How They Could Be Involved" (2006), online: Oslo forum <http://www.osloforum.org/sites/default/files/CivilSocietyand PeaceNegotiations.pdf>.

Potter, Antonia. "Gender Sensitivity: Nicety or Necessity in Peace-Process Management?" (2008), online: Oslo forum <http://www.osloforum.org/sites/default/files/Antonia%20Potter%20Gender%20sensitivity%20WEB.pdf>.

Refugee Law Project. "Behind the Violence: Causes, Consequences and the Search for Solutions to the War in Northern Uganda" (February 2004), online: Refugee Law Project <http://www.refugeelawproject.org/working_papers/RLP.WP11.pdf>.

Ross, Will. "Ugandans Ask ICC to Spare Rebels." *BBC News* (16 March 2005), online: BBC <http://news.bbc.co.uk/2/hi/africa/4352901.stm>.

Slim, Hugo. "Towards Some Ethical Guidelines for Good Practice in Third Party Mediation in Armed Conflict" (2006), online: Oslo forum <http://www.osloforum.org/sites/default/files/TowardssomeEthicalGuidelinesforGoodPracticein3rdPartyMediationinArmedConflict.pdf>.

Tubiana, Jérôme, Victor Tanner & Musa Adam Abdul-Jalil. "Traditional Authorities' Peacemaking Role in Darfur." *Special Report of the United States Institute of Peace* (November 2012), online: United States Institute of Peace <http://www.usip.org/files/resources/PW83.pdf>.

Turay, Thomas Mark. "Civil Society and Peacebuilding: The Role of the Inter-Religious Council of Sierra Leone" (2000) 9 *Accord* 50, online: Conciliation Resources <http://www.c-r.org/sites/c-r.org/files/Accord%2009_10Civil%20society%20and%20peacebuilding_2000_ENG.pdf>.

UNIFEM. "Women's Participation in Peace Negotiations: Connections between Presence and Influence" (August 2010), online: UN Women <http://www.unwomen.org/wp-content/uploads/2012/10/03A-Women-Peace-Neg.pdf>.

United Nations Development Programme. "Issue Brief: The Conflict in Côte d'Ivoire and Its Effect on West African Countries: A Perspective from the Ground" (July 2011), online: UNDP <http://web.undp.org/africa/knowledge/issue-cotedivoire.pdf>.

UN Office for the Coordination of Humanitarian Affairs. "UGANDA: Peace Groups and Government Officials Worried about ICC Probe into LRA" (30 January 2004), online: IRIN <http://www.irinnews.org/Report.aspx?ReportId=48356>.

Uppsala Conflict Data Program (UCDP) & Centre for the Study of Civil Wars, International Peace Research Institute, Oslo (PRIO). *UCDP/PRIO Armed Conflict Database Codebook, version 4-2011*, online: Uppsala University <http://www.pcr.uu.se/digitalAssets/63/63324_Codebook_UCDP_PRIO_Armed_Conflict_Dataset_v4_2011.pdf>.

US Agency for International Development. "Technical Brief: Key Considerations when Supporting Peace Processes" (March 2013), online: USAID <http://www.usaid.gov/sites/default/files/documents/1866/Peace%20Processes%20Technical%20Brief%20FINAL.pdf>.

Vinjamuri, Leslie, & Aaron P. Boesenecker. "Accountability and Peace Agreements: Mapping Trends from 1980 to 2006." *Centre for Humanitarian Dialogue* (September 2007), online: Centre for Humanitarian Dialogue <http://www.hdcentre.org/files/Accountabilityreport.pdf>.

Interview

Interview of Mariama Conteh (17 September 2012).

Internet Sites

Carter Center <http://www.cartercenter.org>.
Centre for Conflict Resolution <http://ccrweb.ccr.uct.ac.za>.
Conciliation Resources <http://www.c-r.org>.
Crisis Management Initiative <http://www.cmi.fi>.
Department of Peace and Conflict Research of the University of Uppsala <http://www.pcr.uu.se/research/ucdp/publications/>.
HD Centre <http://www.hdcentre.org>.
Independent Diplomat <http://www.independentdiplomat.org>.
International Alert <http://www.international-alert.org>.
International Center for Transitional Justice <http://ictj.org>.
International Crisis Group <http://www.crisisgroup.org/en/key-issues/peace-justice.aspx>.
London School of Economics' Centre for Civil Society <http://www.webarchive.org.uk/wayback/archive/20100820110531/http://www.lse.ac.uk/collections/CCS/introduction/what_is_civil_society.htm>.
Mediation Support Network <http://www.mediationsupportnetwork.net>.
Peace Agreements Database, Transitional Justice Institute (University of Ulster) <http://www.peaceagreements.ulster.ac.uk/>.
Public International Law and Policy Group <http://publicinternationallawandpolicygroup.org>.
Stop Rape Now <http://www.stoprapenow.org/about/>.
UN Department of Political Affairs, Mediation Support <http://www.un.org/wcm/content/site/undpa/main/issues/peacemaking/mediation_support>.
UN Peacemaker <http://peacemaker.un.org/>.

Index

CPSIA information can be obtained
at www.ICGtesting.com
Printed in the USA
LVOW10s0908150717

541466LV00019B/425/P